The English Poets
from Chaucer to Edward Thomas

THE ENGLISH POETS
from Chaucer to Edward Thomas

Peter Porter

and

Anthony Thwaite

Secker & Warburg

London

First published in England 1974 by
Martin Secker & Warburg Limited
14 Carlisle Street, London WIV 6NN

SBN: 436 37810 8

Printed in Great Britain by
Western Printing Services Ltd, Bristol

Contents

vi

ACKNOWLEDGMENTS

The editors and publishers gratefully acknowledge permission to reproduce the following copyright material:

Thomas Hardy: 'After a Journey', 'At Castle Boterel' and 'In Church' from *Collected Poems*, Copyright 1925 by Macmillan Publishing Company, Inc. 'The Harbour Bridge' from *Collected Poems*, Copyright 1925 by Macmillan Publishing Company, Inc., renewed 1953 by Lloyds Bank Ltd. Reprinted by permission of the Trustees of the Hardy Estate, Macmillan of London and Basingstoke, the Macmillan Company of Canada and the Macmillan Publishing Company, Inc.

A. E. Housman: 'On Wenlock Edge' from 'A Shropshire Lad' – Authorised Edition – from *Collected Poems*, Copyright 1939, 1940, © 1965 by Holt, Rinehart and Winston, Inc., Copyright © 1967, 1968 by Robert E. Symons. 'In valleys green and still', 'Crossing alone the nighted ferry' and 'Because I liked you better' from *Collected Poems*, Copyright 1922 by Holt, Rinehart and Winston, Inc., Copyright 1950 by Barclays Bank Ltd, Copyright © 1964 by Robert E. Symons. Reprinted by permission of the Society of Authors as the Literary representative of the Estate of A. E. Housman; also Jonathan Cape Ltd and Holt, Rinehart and Winston, Inc.

Rudyard Kipling: 'Danny Deever' from *Barrack Room Ballads* reprinted by permission of Mrs George Bambridge, Methuen & Company Ltd and Doubleday & Company, Inc. 'The Runes on Weland's Sword' from *Puck of Pook's Hill* reprinted by permission of Mrs George Bambridge, Macmillan of London and Basingstoke, the Macmillan Company of Canada and Doubleday & Company, Inc.

W. B. Yeats: 'Among Schoolchildren' from *Collected Poems*, Copyright © 1928 by Macmillan Publishing Co., Inc., renewed 1956 by Georgie Yeats. Reprinted by permission of Mr M. B. Yeats, Macmillan of London and Basingstoke, the Macmillan Company of Canada and the Macmillan Publishing Company, Inc.

The editors and publishers are also grateful to Mrs Myfanwy Thomas, Executrix of the Estate of Edward Thomas, for permission to reproduce 'Old Man' from *Collected Poems* by Edward Thomas.

Introduction

This book is neither a straightforward anthology nor a critical history of English poetry. Yet, as its title shows, it has the same scope as such famous collections as *The Oxford Book of English Verse* and *The Golden Treasury*. Slightly more than a third of the text is prose comment, which serves to set the poems in their time and to relate them to the main course of English literature. We have not attempted criticism in a rigorous academic sense, but we have tried as freshly as possible to evaluate and describe the work of each poet represented. Such a work as Auden's and Pearson's five-volume *Poets of the English Language* stands for one kind of magisterial inclusiveness: the many histories of English poetry on the market attempt another. We believe that this book is something different from either – a conducted tour of the world's richest inheritance of poetry from the beginnings in the fourteenth century up to the First World War. Whether it is read as a continuous story or consulted as an anthology, we shall be equally well pleased.

We have divided the work of five and a half centuries into twenty-six sections. The number twenty-six, with its calendar associations, points to the origin of the book. It was compiled for broadcasting in weekly twenty-minute programmes on BBC Radio Four, where it ran for six months during the autumn and winter of 1971–72. The arbitrary necessity of allotting each poet to one of these twenty-six compartments, far from proving a limitation or an annoyance, spurred us on to examine both our taste in poetry and our critical assumptions. In essence, we have compiled twenty-six short anthologies, each of which is embedded in a running narrative.

While there are no dead periods in English poetry (and only French among Continental literatures has a comparable unbroken succession of poets of the first rank), some centuries and, indeed, some decades are richer than others. Thus each of our twenty-six sections is roughly the same length (having originally to fill the same time on the air), but does not necessarily cover the same span of years. For example, the seventeenth century, the richest of all in poetry, is allotted six sections, yet it is here that we are most conscious of having had to omit much that is first rate. Such a drawback is inherent in any chronological method. Our experience of other anthologies suggests that they are no more free from this disproportion than ours is. A look at the index of poets included should at any rate show every great name in our literature and many who are not as well known as they should be.

A more worrying limitation is the amount of space we have been able to give to each poet. Some important figures are represented by only one poem, and even Shakespeare is allowed only two songs, one sonnet and three speeches from his plays. Cutting down the commentary would render it useless without adding much to the number of pages available for poems. Since we cover the whole range of English poetry, we have sometimes had to be ruthless. Nevertheless, here is the cumulative greatness of the language as expressed in its most concentrated form, and seen against the background of the times in which it was written.

The reader should not approach English poetry looking for development of style or inspired by the notion of perfectibility. Each epoch has its own perfections, and the story of our verse is cumulative, not progressive. This book was written to introduce people to the pleasure of reading poetry, not to add to the weight of studying it. But we have interpreted pleasure more widely than those many anthologists who are biased in favour of the short self-contained lyric. Thus we have included many extracts from long poems, such as *The Canterbury Tales, The Faerie Queen, Paradise Lost, Absalom and Achitophel, The Dunciad, Jubilate Agno, Childe Harold, Don Juan, The Prelude* and *In Memoriam*, as well as several passages from plays. As far as possible, we have detached sections which stand up well in isolation, though dramatic form sometimes precludes this. Some of the greatest poetry ever written in English was intended specifically for the stage. While it is relatively easy to find soliloquies which can be taken out of plays (and which resemble the dramatic monologues of the

2

Victorian era), some equally remarkable verse is written as exchanges between characters. Once or twice (notably in the case of the Jacobean playwright John Ford) we have chosen just such antiphonal verse. We believe the particular dramatic tension survives in its present isolation. At the same time, we have not tried to dethrone the lyric. Somebody once said about music that at its most profound it turns out to be most melodious. By analogy, we have sought out lyricism in English verse – but not just in the short poem. We have tried to track it down in the long poem, the nonsense poem, the play, or wherever else it exists.

Reading through our twenty-six mini-anthologies, we have been struck by one notable aspect of English poetry: a concern for human behaviour. The English have never been a philosophical people, which does not mean that they have been unintelligent or unwitty. Rather, it suggests that they have felt reason as a passion. But they have not been drawn to philosophical or aesthetic rumination; instead, their sense of what constitutes art has been most fully embodied in examinations of the actions of men and women. There is an erroneous view that English poetry is predominantly concerned with Nature; and the revolution in sensibility introduced by Wordworth and Coleridge is felt to be peculiarly English. Yet even with Wordsworth human beings are seen behaving within a natural scene – in a country rather than a town auditorium, but still within society. Pantheism in England has been a sense of society observed out-of-doors, rather than a worshipping of the spirit of Nature.

At the same time, English poets tend to be highly individual, and not given to forming 'groups' or schools, as Continental writers frequently do. Their practice avoids declared beliefs or combative manifestos. Similarly, few English poets are interested in pure aesthetics, and poetry as its own subject is something almost unknown in English until Wallace Stevens in this century. Perhaps Poe (another American) is the only poet of any consequence in our language whose works are musical at the expense of their meaning.

The texts we have used have been those we considered most appropriate to the poet in question and we have, where it seemed necessary, sacrificed consistency to effect. In practice, this has meant that some poems appear in modernised spelling and others in more archaic form, even when they are contemporary.

3

Finally, it is with no sense of chauvinism – and without mere carelessness – that we have included Burns and Yeats (and Vaughan and Edward Thomas) among 'the English poets'. Though a few Scottish, Irish and Welsh listeners to the original programmes objected to our conscription of these poets under such a heading, we believe that English poetry is what is written in English, whether standard or variant, in these islands. A Scot may choose to write in Gaelic, or a Welshman in Welsh; but that is not English poetry.

Each chapter is signed by its compiler, and the allocation of poets and periods was very amicably arrived at. Obviously, each reflects personal taste and temperament, so that anyone sensing a leaning towards religious and reflective verse in Anthony Thwaite and towards realistic and satirical verse in Peter Porter would not be wrong. Yet each found himself on occasion dealing with poetry very unlike his usual preference and being surprised by the excellence of figures he had not previously warmed to.

To sum up, we should like to warn the reader that this is not a prescriptive anthology in any sense. It has no redemptive powers or moral purpose, but is angled wholly towards pleasure. Though it is not so idiosyncratic that it forgets the need to present a balanced picture of a very large subject, it is chiefly the product of the inclinations and enthusiasms of two men who want to communicate their own pleasure to others.

PETER PORTER
ANTHONY THWAITE

Geoffrey Chaucer (c. 1340–1400)   A.T.

When Geoffrey Chaucer died in the year 1400, he was already a famous poet. For almost the whole of his working life he'd been at the centre of affairs, as a courtier, a diplomat and a civil servant. And because he'd been in such a position, he'd been well placed not only to observe a wide range of varied human beings but also to be recognised as a poet: he had a ready-made available audience of sophisticated and sympathetic people. I think it's partly this that gives Chaucer his ease of tone, which we notice even now, more than five and a half centuries after his death. He's speaking directly and without strain to people who'll understand him and accept him – the wide cross-section of life represented in the courts of Edward III, Richard II, John of Gaunt and Henry IV.

There have been times in the past when Chaucer has been misjudged as a crude, naïve poet, as a simple storyteller, or as someone hopelessly old-fashioned and quaint. Even his admirers have helped misjudge him: in the late seventeenth century, for example, John Dryden called Chaucer 'a Rough Diamond' (the first time, incidentally, this metaphorical phrase was so used). A hundred years earlier another poet, Edmund Spenser, wrote of

Dan Chaucer, well of English undefiled

and that picture of him as a sort of pioneer cultural non-Common Marketeer is still fairly widespread. It's true that he's the first great English poet – a fit person with whom to start an anthology of the English poets – but his primary interest and importance isn't as a sort of linguistic fossil. Of course there are difficulties of vocabulary and pronunciation, but I think these have been exaggerated by generations of schoolteachers whose main effort has been to get unwilling children to paraphrase gobbets of *The Canterbury Tales* for examinations. A bit of time spent with

5

a glossary and some reading round the social history of the period clears away most of the difficulty in starting to read Chaucer.

Though Chaucer isn't just a simple storyteller, he doesn't go in for the self-expression, the economical energy, the mysteriousness or the sense of wonder which have become the modern notions of what true poetry should possess. He could use verse to be descriptive, funny, moralising, storytelling, all of them in a *direct* way. But he doesn't seem at all interested in telling you about the problems or tensions or hang-ups of Geoffrey Chaucer. His opinions, experiences, tastes and dislikes come through filtered, not because he lacked strength in his convictions but because, to him and to his age, self-expression wasn't what art was for.

Chaucer's chief and enduring work is, of course, *The Canterbury Tales*, the long and unfinished sequence of stories mostly linked together by introductions and prologues by the characters themselves, who are supposed to be going on pilgrimage to the shrine of Thomas à Becket at Canterbury. He probably wrote most of it during the last fifteen or so years of his life, though some of it was done separately earlier on. Like the *Thousand and One Nights*, the Arabian Nights of Scheherazade, *The Canterbury Tales* are stories within a story; but, unlike them, it's the framework which keeps the whole thing going. In the Prologue to it all, you're given – in the first forty lines – the time of year, the purpose of the visit, the setting at the start, the number of pilgrims, the fact that the poet himself is one of them, and the introduction to the cast list. Here are the first forty-two lines:

Whan that Aprille with his shoures sote
The droghte of Marche hath perced to the rote,
And bathed every veyne in swich licour,
Of which vertu engendered is the flour;
Whan Zephirus eek with his swete breeth
Inspired hath in every holt and heeth
The tendre croppes, and the yonge sonne
Hath in the Ram his halfe cours y-ronne,
And smale fowles maken melodye,
That slepen al the night with open yë,

(So priketh hem nature in hir corages):
Than longen folk to goon on pilgrimages
(And palmers for to seken straunge strondes)
To ferne halwes, couthe in sondry londes;
And specially, from every shires ende
Of Engelond, to Caunterbury they wende,
The holy blisful martir for to seke,
That hem hath holpen, whan that they were seke.
     Bifel that, in that seson on a day,
In Southwerk at the Tabard as I lay
Redy to wenden on my pilgrimage
To Caunterbury with ful devout corage,
At night was come into that hostelrye
Wel nyne and twenty in a companye,
Of sondry folk, by adventure y-falle
In felawshipe, and pilgrims were they alle,
That toward Caunterbury wolden ryde:
The chambres and the stables weren wyde,
And wel we weren esed atte beste.
And shortly, whan the sonne was to reste,
So hadde I spoken with hem everichon,
That I was of hir felawshipe anon,
And made forward erly for to ryse,
To take our wey, there as I yow devyse.
     But natheles, whyl I have tyme and space,
Er that I ferther in this tale pace,
Me thinketh it acordaunt to resoun,
To telle yow al the condicioun
Of ech of hem, so as it semed me,
And whiche they weren, and of what degree;
And eek in what array that they were inne:
And at a knight than wol I first biginne.

There follow descriptions of most of the thirty pilgrims, including their Host at the Tabard Inn, who decides to go with them, and with the significant omission of any description of the poet himself. (Though later on he puts himself in the position of telling one of the most boring and ill-made tales – so boring and ill-made that the Host stops him in mid-career, vigorously maintaining that 'Thy drasty rymyng is nat worth a toord!')

The whole of the General Prologue is not just an extended cast-list but a sort of underpinning for the stories that follow. The Lady Prioress, for example, later on tells a pious, sentimental, religious horror-story, which isn't surprising when one has heard the Prologue's description of the Lady herself:

> Ther was also a Nonne, a PRIORESSE,
> That of hir smyling was ful simple and coy;
> Hir gretteste ooth was but by sëynt Loy;
> And she was cleped madame Eglentyne.
> Ful wel she soong the service divyne,
> Entuned in hir nose ful semely;
> And Frensh she spak ful faire and fetisly,
> After the scole of Stratford atte Bowe,
> For Frensh of Paris was to hir unknowe.
> At mete wel y-taught was she with-alle;
> She leet no morsel from hir lippes falle,
> Ne wette hir fingres in hir sauce depe.
> Wel coude she carie a morsel, and wel kepe,
> That no drope ne fille upon hir brest.
> In curteisye was set ful muche hir lest.
> Hir over lippe wyped she so clene,
> That in hir coppe was no ferthing sene
> Of grece, whan she dronken hadde hir draughte.
> Ful semely after hir mete she raughte,
> And sikerly she was of greet disport,
> And ful plesaunt, and amiable of port,
> And peyned hir to countrefete chere
> Of court, and to been estatlich of manere,
> And to ben holden digne of reverence.
> But, for to speken of hir conscience,
> She was so charitable and so pitous,
> She wolde wepe, if that she sawe a mous
> Caught in a trappe, if it were deed or bledde.
> Of smale houndes had she, that she fedde
> With rosted flesh, or milk and wastel-breed.
> But sore weep she if oon of hem were deed,
> Or if men smoot it with a yerde smerte:
> And al was conscience and tendre herte.
> Ful semely hir wimpel pinched was;

Hir nose tretys; hir eyen greye as glas;
Hir mouth ful smal, and thereto softe and reed;
But sikerly she hadde a fair foreheed;
It was almost a spanne brood, I trowe;
For, hardily, she was nat undergrowe.
Ful fetis was hir cloke, as I was war.
Of smal coral aboute hir arm she bar
A peire of bedes, gauded al with grene;
And theron heng a broche of gold ful shene,
On which there was first write a crowned A,
And after, *Amor vincit omnia*.

In the same way, the description of the Pardoner in the Prologue
and the Pardoner's Tale later on are linked. The Pardoner was a
minor but powerful ecclesiastical officer whose job it was –
put crudely – to sell divine forgiveness for money. Naturally
enough, he was not a popular figure. Here he is in the Prologue:

This pardoner hadde heer as yelow as wex,
But smothe it heng, as dooth a strike of flex;
By ounces henge his lokkes that he hadde.
And therwith he his shuldres overspradde;
But thinne it lay, by colpons oon and oon;
But hood, for jolitee, ne wered he noon,
For it was trussed up in his walet.
Him thoughte, he rood al of the newe jet;
Dischevele, save his cappe, he rood al bare.
Swiche glaringe eyen hadde he as an hare.
A vernicle hadde he sowed in his cappe.
His walet lay biforn him in his lappe,
Bret-ful of pardoun come from Rome al hoot.
A voys he hadde as smal as hath a goot.
No berd hadde he, ne never sholde have,
As smothe it was as it were late y-shave;
I trowe he were a gelding or a mare.
But of his craft, fro Berwik into Ware,
Ne was there swich another pardoner.
For in his male he hadde a pilwe-beer,
Which that, he seyde, was Our Lady veyl;
He seyde, he hadde a gobet of the seyl
That sëynt Peter hadde, whan that he wente

Upon the see, til Jesu Crist him hente.
He hadde a croys of latoun, ful of stones,
And in a glas he hadde pigges bones.
But with thise relikes, whan that he fond
A povre person dwelling upon lond,
Upon a day he gat him more moneye
Than that the person gat in monthes tweye.
And thus, with feyned flaterye and japes,
He made the person and the peple his apes.
But trewely to tellen, atte laste,
He was in chirche a noble ecclesiaste.
Wel coude he rede a lessoun or a storie,
But alderbest he song an offertorie;
For wel he wiste, whan that song was songe,
He moste preche, and wel affyle his tonge,
To winne silver, as he ful wel coude;
Therefore he song so meriely and loude.

Later on, the Pardoner tells one of the most effective tales, about three young gamblers who set out to kill Death and steal his money, but whose greed spells their own ruin. The story is dramatically direct and powerful in its simplicity; the moralising larded in by the Pardoner is entirely in character. This is how the story itself goes, after the Pardoner has laid his hypocritical bait by giving plenty of ghastly moral examples:

Thise ryotoures three, of which I telle,
Longe erst er pryme rong of any belle,
Were set hem in a taverne for to drinke;
And as they satte, they herde a belle clinke
Biforn a cors, was caried to his grave;
That oon of hem gan callen to his knave,
'Go bet,' quod he, 'and axe redily,
What cors is this that passeth heer forby;
And look that thou reporte his name wel,'
    'Sir,' quod this boy, 'it nedeth never-a-del.
It was me told, er ye cam heer, two houres;
He was, pardee, an old felawe of youres;
And sodeynly he was y-slayn to-night,
For-dronke, as he sat on his bench upright;
Ther cam a privee theef, men clepeth Deeth,

That in this contree al the peple sleeth,
And with his spere he smoot his herte a-two,
And wente his wey withouten wordes mo.
He hath a thousand slayn this pestilence:
And, maister, er ye come in his presence,
Me thinketh that it were necessarie
For to be war of swich an adversarie:
Beth redy for to mete him evermore.
Thus taughte me my dame, I sey na-more.'
'By seinte Marie,' seyde this taverner,
'The child seith sooth, for he hath slayn this yeer,
Henne over a myle, within a greet village,
Both man and womman, child and hyne, and page.
I trowe his habitacioun be there;
To been avysed greet wisdom it were
Er that he dide a man a dishonour.'
'Ye, goddes armes,' quod this ryotour.
'Is it swich peril with him for to mete?
I shal him seke by wey and eek by strete,
I make avow to Goddes digne bones!
Herkneth, felawes, we three been al ones;
Lat ech of us holde up his hond til other,
And ech of us bicomen otheres brother,
And we wol sleen this false traytour Deeth;
He shal be slayn, which that so many sleeth,
By Goddes dignitee, er it be night.'
   Togidres han thise three her trouthes plight,
To live and dyen ech of hem for other,
As though he were his owene y-boren brother.
And up they sterte al dronken, in this rage,
And forth they goon towards that village,
Of which the taverner had spoke biforn,
And many a grisly ooth than han they sworn,
And Cristes blessed body they to-rente –
Deeth shal be deed, if that they may him hente.
   Whan they han goon nat fully half a myle,
Right as they wolde han troden over a style,
An old man and a povre with hem mette.
This olde man ful mekely hem grette,
And seyde thus, 'Now, lordes, God yow see!'

The proudest of thise ryotoures three
Answerede agayn, 'What? carl, with sory grace,
Why artow al forwrapped save thy face?
Why livestow so longe in so greet age?'
This olde man gan loke in his visage,
And seyde thus, 'For I ne can nat finde
A man, though that I walked into Inde,
Neither in citee nor in no village,
That wolde chaunge his youthe for myn age;
And therfore moot I han myn age stille,
As longe time as it is Goddes wille.
'Ne Deeth, allas! ne wol nat han my lyf;
Thus walke I, lyk a restelees caityf,
And on the ground, which is my modres gate,
I knokke with my staf, bothe erly and late,
And seye, "Leve moder, leet me in!
Lo, how I vanish, flesh, and blood, and skin!
Allas! whan shul my bones been at reste?
Moder, with yow wolde I chaunge my cheste,
That in my chambre longe tyme hath be,
Ye! for an heyre clout to wrappe me!"
But yet to me she wol nat do that grace,
For which ful pale and welked is my face.
'But, sirs, to yow it is no curteisye
To speken to an old man vileinye,
But he trespasse in worde, or elles in dede.
In holy writ ye may your-self wel rede,
"Agayns an old man, hoor upon his heed,
Ye sholde aryse;" wherfor I yeve yow reed,
Ne dooth unto an old man noon harm now,
Na-more than ye wolde men dide to yow
In age, if that ye so longe abyde;
And God be with yow, wher ye go or ryde.
I moot go thider as I have to go.'
'Nay, olde cherl, by god, thou shalt nat so,'
Seyde this other hasardour anon;
'Thou partest nat so lightly, by seint John!
Thou spak right now of thilke traitour Deeth,
That in this contree alle our frendes sleeth.
Have heer my trouthe, as thou art his aspye,

Tel wher he is, or thou shalt it abye,
By God, and by the holy sacrament!
For soothly thou art oon of his assent,
To sleen us yonge folk, thou false theef!'
    'Now, sirs,' quod he, 'if that yow be so leef
To finde Deeth, turne up this croked wey,
For in that grove I lafte him, by my fey,
Under a tree, and ther he wol abyde;
Nat for your boost he wol him no-thing hyde.
See ye that ook? right ther ye shul him finde.
God save yow, that boghte agayn mankinde,
And yow amende!'—thus seyde this olde man.
And everich of thise ryotoures ran,
Til he cam to that tree, and ther they founde
Of florins fyne of golde y-coyned rounde
Wel ny an eighte busshels, as hem thoughte.
No lenger thanne after Deeth they soughte,
But ech of hem so glad was of that sighte,
For that the florins been so faire and brighte,
That doun they sette hem by this precious hord.
The worste of hem he spake the firste word.
    'Brethren,' quod he, 'tak kepe what I seye;
My wit is greet, though that I bourde and pleye.
This tresor hath fortune unto us yiven,
In mirthe and jolitee our lyf to liven,
And lightly as it comth, so wol we spende.
Ey! Goddes precious dignitee! who wende
To-day, that we sholde han so fair a grace?
But mighte this gold be caried fro this place
Hoom to myn hous, or elles unto youres –
For wel ye woot that al this gold is oures –
Than were we in heigh felicitee.
But trewely, by daye it may nat be;
Men wolde seyn that we were theves stronge,
And for our owene tresor doon us honge.
This tresor moste y-caried be by nighte
As wysly and as slyly as it mighte.
Wherfore I rede that cut among us alle
Be drawe, and lat see wher the cut wol falle;
And he that hath the cut with herte blythe

Shal renne to the toune, and that ful swythe,
And bringe us breed and wyn ful prively.
And two of us shul kepen subtilly
This tresor wel; and, if he wol nat tarie,
Whan it is night, we wol this tresor carie
By oon assent, wher-as us thinketh best,'
That oon of hem the cut broughte in his fest,
And bad hem drawe, and loke wher it wol falle;
And it fil on the youngeste of hem alle;
And forth toward the toun he wente anon.
And al-so sone as that he was gon,
That oon of hem spak thus unto that other,
'Thou knowest wel thou art my sworne brother,
Thy profit wol I telle thee anon.
Thou woost wel that our felawe is agon;
And heer is gold, and that ful greet plentee,
That shal departed been among us three.
But natheles, if I can shape it so
That it departed were among us two,
Hadde I nat doon a freendes torn to thee?'
   That other answerde, 'I noot how that may be;
He woot how that the gold is with us tweye,
What shal we doon, what shal we to him seye?'
   'Shal it be conseil?' seyde the firste shrewe,
'And I shal tellen thee, in wordes fewe,
What we shal doon, and bringe it wel aboute.'
   'I graunte,' quod that other, 'out of doute,
That, by my trouthe, I wol thee nat biwreye.'
   'Now,' quod the firste, 'thou woost wel we be tweye,
And two of us shul strenger be than oon.
Look whan that he is set, and right anoon
Arys, as though thou woldest with him pleye;
And I shal ryve him thurgh the sydes tweye
Whyl that thou strogelest with him as in game,
And with thy dagger look thou do the same;
And than shal al this gold departed be,
My dere freend, bitwixen me and thee;
Than may we bothe our lustes al fulfille,
And pleye at dees right at our owene wille.'
And thus acorded been thise shrewes tweye

To sleen the thridde, as ye han herd me seye.
  This yongest, which that wente unto the toun,
Ful ofte in herte he rolleth up and doun
The beautee of thise florins newe and brighte.
'O Lord!' quod he, 'if so were that I mighte
Have al this tresor to my-self allone,
Ther is no man that liveth under the trone
Of God, that sholde live so mery as I!'
And atte laste the feend, our enemy,
Putte in his thought that he shold poyson beye,
With which he mighte sleen his felawes tweye;
For-why the feend fond him in swich lyvinge,
That he had leve him to sorwe bringe,
For this was outrely his fulle entente
To sleen hem bothe, and never to repente.
And forth he gooth, no lenger wolde he tarie,
Into the toun, unto a pothecarie,
And preyed him, that he him wolde selle
Som poyson, that he mighte his rattes quelle;
And eek ther was a polcat in his hawe,
That, as he seyde, his capouns hadde y-slawe,
And fayn he wolde wreke him, if he mighte,
On vermin, that destroyed him by nighte.
  The pothecarie answerde, 'And thou shalt have
A thing that, al-so god my soule save,
In al this world ther nis no creature,
That ete or dronke hath of this confiture
Noght but the mountance of a corn of whete,
That he ne shal his lyf anon forlete;
Ye, sterve he shal, and that in lasse whyle
Than thou wolt goon a paas nat but a myle;
This poyson is so strong and violent.'
  This cursed man hath in his hond y-hent
This poyson in a box, and sith he ran
Into the nexte strete, unto a man,
And borwed of him large botels three;
And in the two his poyson poured he;
The thridde he kepte clene for his drinke.
For al the night he shoop him for to swinke
In caryinge of the gold out of that place.

And whan this ryotour, with sory grace,
Had filled with wyn his grete botels three,
To his felawes agayn repaireth he.
    What nedeth it to sermone of it more?
For right as they had cast his deeth bifore,
Right so they han him slayn, and that anon.
And whan that this was doon, thus spak that oon,
'Now lat us sitte and drinke, and make us merie,
And afterward we wol his body berie.'
And with that word it happed him, par cas,
To take the botel ther the poyson was,
And drank, and yaf his felawe drinke also,
For which anon they storven bothe two.
    But, certes, I suppose that Avicen
Wroot never in no canon, ne in no fen,
Mo wonder signes of empoisoning
Than hadde thise wrecches two, er hir ending.
Thus ended been thise homicydes two,
And eek the false empoysoner also.

It's impossible in a short space to show the whole range and
richness of *The Canterbury Tales*. Within the frank limits of pro-
viding something which is primarily entertainment, Chaucer
shows a great variety of moods and techniques, and a vivid sense
of human observation and understanding. And I haven't even
mentioned his other poems, such as *Troilus and Criseyde* or *The
Parliament of Fowles* or *The Legend of Good Women*, with its marvel-
lous ballade beginning 'Hyd, Absolon, thy gilte tresses clere; /
Ester, ley thou thy meknesse al adown' – a lyricism, there, which,
with storytelling, was equally a part of medieval English poetry.

Geoffrey Chaucer is the first great 'name' poet in the English language, but so much of the finest poetry of the centuries before 1500 is the work of men whose identities are lost to us. This, a common enough phenomenon in history, is slightly bewildering in literature, an art much preoccupied by the 'cult of personality'. It's worth stressing that the writers of the anonymous lyrics and poems of pre-Renaissance epochs are not less personal and idiosyncratic than the men whose names we celebrate; only that we know them merely by the shadows they cast in their poems. Chaucer is modern in that he worked on a large scale, and like his Italian models, Petrarch and Boccaccio, he imprinted his personality on what he wrote.

Although he left many fine lyrics, part of his greatness lies in his ability to organise long poems which take in many different aspects of the human condition. Chaucer's language isn't completely alien from our own, but many years were to pass before English settled down to the recognisable tongue we speak today. The fourteenth and fifteenth centuries were a time of verbal experiment. The French language was already fully formed, hardly different from what it is today, as the poems of Villon, Machaut and Deschamps show. But if English of the late Middle Ages is a strange language to many of us, the poems written in it already exemplify qualities which we recognise as particularly English, qualities which persist throughout our literature – pungent observation, sardonic wit and great lyrical tenderness. Hundreds of anonymous poems and songs have survived from this formative time – i.e. between Chaucer and the first Tudor kings. Many were intended to be sung, as carols or popular religious songs; others told familiar stories from the Bible, just as the Miracle and Morality Plays did; still others were wholly secular and dealt with the joys and miseries of love and the ever-present threat of death. The poets of these centuries were not unsophisticated – they valued technical skill with words and ideas as much as their descendants in Elizabethan England did, and they relished jokes and games with language. Their poetry has the freshness of a language still young: it's direct and quite without clichés or 'poetical' words, yet it can cope with complex emotions. It's worth keeping in mind that while these poems were being written, the Hundred Years War and the Wars of the Roses were going on. Life was likely to be dangerous and short, but its sweetness and its pleasures were relished the more because of this. However, the predominant tone of the late medieval lyric is grim, such as the brief poem 'How Death Comes', which dates from the end of the thirteenth century. We print it firstly in the original to give some idea of the strange sound and spelling of English at this time. But following the original, there is a translation into modern English.

> Wanne mine eyhnen misten,
> And mine heren sissen,
> And my nose coldet,
> And my tunge foldet,
> And my rude slaket,
> And mine lippes blaken,
> And my muth grennet,
> And my spotel rennet,
> And mine her riset,
> And mine herte griset,
> And mine honden bivien,
> And mine fet stivien –
> Al to late! al to late!
> Wanne the bere is ate gate.
>
> Thanne I schel flutte
> From bedde to flore,
> From flore to here,
> From here to bere,
> From bere to putte,
> And te putt fordut.
> Thanne lyd mienhus uppe mine nose.
> Of al this world ne give I it a pese!

(When my eyes get misty, and my ears are full of hissing, and
my nose gets cold, and my tongue folds, and my face goes
slack, and my lips blacken, and my mouth grins and my spittle
runs, and my hair rises and my heart trembles, and my hands
shake, and my feet stiffen – all too late! when the bier is at
the gate. Then shall I pass from bed to floor, from floor to
shroud, from shroud to bier, from bier to grave, and the grave
will be closed up. Then my house rests on my nose. I don't
care one jot for the whole world.)

Death is the negative end of medieval energy: the same imagina-
tion could rejoice in life, as this short lyric from about half a
century later shows . It's of great simplicity and beauty with many
lines repeated as they would be when sung. It's called 'The
Maiden Lay in the Wilds' and celebrates the Virgin Mary and the
Infant Jesus. It doesn't need translation apart from two words
– the 'primerole' is the primrose, and 'dring' is drink.

> Maiden in the mor lay,
> In the mor lay;
> Sevenight fulle,
> Sevenight fulle,
> Maiden in the mor lay;
> In the mor lay,
> Sevenightes fulle and a day.
>
> Welle was hire mete.
> What was hire mete?
> The primerole and the –
> The primerole and the –
> Welle was hire mete.
> What was hire mete?
> The primerole and the violet.
>
> Well was hire dring.
> What was hire dring?
> The chelde water of the –
> The chelde water of the –
> Welle was hire dring.
> What was hire dring?
> The chelde water of the welle-spring.

Welle was hire bowr.
What was hire bowr?
The red rose and the –
The red rose and the –
Welle was hire bowr.
What was hire bowr?
The red rose and the lilye flour.

Many of the surviving poems of this time are carols. In the Middle Ages carols were sung at almost any time of the year. Some were celebrations of the major feastdays of the Christian year – Advent, Christmas, Easter and Whit Sunday. Some were simple and some were mysterious incantations as difficult to paraphrase as the late poems of W. B. Yeats. They could even be patriotic, like the famous 'Agincourt Song', an early piece of jingoism celebrating Henry V's victory over the French in 1415. The 'Corpus Christi Carol' is one of the glories of English literature: it comes from the early years of the sixteenth century and can be interpreted many ways. Whether you read into it the Eucharist, the Grail and St Joseph of Arimathea, or prefer to think it referred to Anne Boleyn, it remains a riddle we aren't likely to crack at this date. It has a strange beauty unlike any other poem of the time:

Lully, lulley, lully, lulley,
The fawcon hath born my mak away.

He bare him up, he bare him down,
He bare him into an orchard brown.

In that orchard ther was an hall,
That was hangèd with purpill and pall.

And in that hall ther was a bed:
It was hangèd with gold so red.

And in that bed ther lythe a knight,
His woundès bleeding day and night.

By that bedès side ther kneleth a may,
And she wepeth both night and day.

And by that bedès side ther stondeth a ston,
'Corpus Christi' wreten theron.

Another piece intended to be sung provides an interesting link with the most ancient kind of poem still in common use – the nursery rhyme. The early fifteenth-century lyric 'I have a Noble Cock' is both religious and secular. It has a possible *double entendre* and it recalls, in its last line, the nursery rhyme, 'Goosey, goosey, gander . . .' Whatever their origin or purpose, the poems of these centuries had a seemingly effortless lyricism, something which later poets struggled for and invented theories to provide. This was a period in which thought and its expression were immediately linked. Though the language was to progress to greater and more complex triumphs, it never again caught the freshness and transparent beauty of its first poetic fruits. The phrase in the following lyric, 'into the wortewale', means 'up to the root of the spur'.

'I have a Noble Cock'

I have a gentle cock,
Croweth me day:
He doth me risen erly
My matins for to say.

I have a gentle cock,
Comen he is of gret:
His comb is of red coral,
His tail is of jet.

I have a gentle cock,
Comen he is of kinde:
His comb is of red coral,
His tail is of inde.

His legs ben of asor,
So gentle and so smale;
His spores arn of silver whit
Into the wortewale.

His eynen arn of cristal,
Loken all in aumber:
And every night he percheth him
In mine ladye's chaumber.

One of the most famous poems in pre-Shakespearean English is also one of the shortest – the little masterpiece, 'Westron Winde', drenched in the bitterness of lost love. Nobody has ever surpassed this four-line evocation of love's pain – it speaks for all deserted lovers across six centuries:

> Westron winde, when will thou blow,
> The smalle raine downe can raine?
> Christ if my love were in my armes,
> And I in my bed againe.

All the poems quoted so far have been short lyrics. There is one other and much longer kind of poem which was popular in the fifteenth and sixteenth centuries – the ballad. The ballad tells a story, only occasionally a religious story, more usually one based on legend or on some happening in living memory. Ballads were always sung or declaimed and some of the tunes have survived. They are written in rhyming stanzas with strong rhythms and, like songs, often repeat lines and images. Unlike the broadside ballads of the eighteenth and nineteenth centuries and the modern imitations by poets such as Kipling or W. H. Auden, these early ballads are of the same high poetical quality as the lyrics of the period and are neither urban nor sentimental. Most came from the North of England or the Lowlands of Scotland, the best known collection being called *Border Ballads*. Very few survive in their original state and even scholarly texts tend to contain many modernisations. One of the most celebrated is known as 'A Lyke-Wake Dirge'.

It's exactly what the title says, a wake over the dead. Whinny-muir, in the poem, is the gorse-moor where souls are ceaselessly nettled and Brig o'Dread is the narrow bridge to Purgatory from which the wicked topple into hell.

> This ae nighte, this ae nighte,
>   – Every nighte and alle,
> Fire and fleet and candle-lighte,
>   And Christe receive thy saule.
>
> When thou from hence away art past.
>   – Every nighte and alle,
> To Whinny-muir thou com'st at last;
>   And Christe receive thy saule.

If ever thou gavest hosen and shoon,
    – Every nighte and alle,
Sit thee down and put them on;
    And Christe receive thy saule.

If hosen and shoon thou ne'er gav'st nane
    – Every nighte and alle,
The whinnes sall prick thee to the bare bane;
    And Christe receive thy saule.

From Whinny-muir when thou may'st pass,
    – Every nighte and alle,
To Brig o'Dread thou com'st at last;
    And Christe receive thy saule.

From Brig o'Dread when thou may'st pass,
    – Every nighte and alle,
To Purgatory fire thou com'st at last;
    And Christe receive thy saule.

If ever thou gavest meat or drink,
    – Every nighte and alle,
The fire sall never make thee shrink;
    And Christe receive thy saule.

If meat or drink thou ne'er gav'st nane,
    – Every nighte and alle,
The fire will burn thee to the bare bane;
    And Christe receive thy saule.

This ae nighte, this ae nighte,
    – Every nighte and alle,
Fire and fleet and candle-lighte,
    And Christe receive thy saule.

The countryside in which these ballads are set ranges as far north as the coast of Aberdeenshire but the majority are centred in the unquiet Borderlands. 'The Laily Worm, and the Machrel of the Sea' shows the prevalence of witchcraft in the ballad writers' minds. The main department of literature in which England is deficient is the nursery story, the kind of magical folk tale collected by the Brothers Grimm in Germany. The border ballads are our closest approach to this – they are just as fantastic and have the same nightmare atmosphere of riddles, rewards and

violent deaths. 'The Laily Worm' has all the traditional proper-
ties – the wicked stepmother who turns her stepchildren into a
worm and a fish, the chivalrous knight, the king's court and the
final deliverance of the bewitched children back into their
human shape. It has a fine poetic flow as well as great natural
dignity.

'I was but seven year auld
　When my mither she did dee;
My father married the ae warst woman
　The warld did ever see.

'For she has made me the laily worm,
　That lies at the fit o' the tree,
An' my sister Masery she's made
　The machrel of the sea.

'An every Saturday at noon
　The machrel comes to me,
An' she takes my laily head
　An' lays it on her knee,
She kaims it wi' a siller kaim,
　An' washes't in the sea.

'Seven knights hae I slain,
　Sin I lay at the fit of the tree,
An' ye war na my ain father,
　The eighth ane ye should be.' –

'Sing on your song, ye laily worm,
　That ye did sing to me.' –
'I never sung that song but what
　I would sing it to thee.

'I was but seven year auld,
　When my mither she did dee;
My father married the ae warst woman
　The warld did ever see.

'For she changed me to the laily worm,
　That lies at the fit o' the tree,
And my sister Masery
　To the machrel of the sea.

'And every Saturday at noon
    The machrel comes to me,
An' she takes my laily head
    An' lays it on her knee,
An' kames it wi' a siller kame,
    An' washes it i' the sea.

'Seven knights hae I slain
    Sin I lay at the fit o' the tree;
An' ye war na my ain father,
    The eighth ane ye should be.'

He sent for his lady,
    As fast as send could he:
'Whar is my sone that ye sent frae me,
    And my daughter, Lady Masery?' –

'Your son is at our king's court,
    Serving for meat an' fee,
An' your daughter's at our queen's court,
    The queen's maiden to be.' –

'Ye lee, ye lee, ye ill woman,
    Sae loud as I hear ye lee;
My son's the laily worm,
    That lies at the fit o' the tree,
And my daughter, Lady Masery,
    Is the machrel of the sea!'

She has tane a siller wan',
    An' gi'en him strokès three,
And he's started up the bravest knight
    That ever your eyes did see.

She has ta'en a small horn,
    An' loud an' shrill blew she,
An' a' the fish came her untill
    But the machrel of the sea:
'Ye shapiet me ance an unseemly shape,
    'An ye's never mare shape me.'

He has sent to the wood,
    For whins and for hawthorn,

An' he has ta'en that gay lady,
    An' there he did her burn.

One other ballad, 'The Demon Lover', must suffice to represent
the form. It tells of a wife tempted to desert her home and
husband and travel across the sea to the land where the white
lilies grow, the remote country of Italy. It's the Devil himself
who is the tempter and the poem ends in disaster. It has a fair
claim to be considered the finest ballad of them all.

'O where hae ye been, my long, long love,
    These seven long years and more?' –
'O I'm come to seek my former vows,
    That ye promised me before.' –

'Awa' wi' your former vows,' she says,
    'For they will breed but strife;
Awa' wi' your former vows,' she says,
    'For I am become a wife.

'I am married to a ship-carpenter,
    A ship-carpenter he's bound,
I wadna he kenn'd my mind this nichte
    For twice five hundred pound.'

He turn'd him round and round about,
    And the tear blinded his e'e:
'I wad never hae trodden on Irish ground
    If it hadna been for thee.

'I might hae had a noble lady,
    Far, far beyond the sea;
I might hae had a noble lady,
    Were it no for the love o' thee.' –

'If ye might hae had a noble lady,
    Yoursel' ye had to blame;
Ye might hae taken the noble lady,
    For ye kenn'd that I was nane.' –

'O fause are the vows o' womankind,
    But fair is their fause bodie:
I wad never hae trodden on Irish ground,
    Were it no for the love o' thee.' –

'If I was to leave my husband dear,
    And my wee young son alsua,
O what hae ye to tak' me to,
    If with you I should gae?'–

'I hae seven ships upon the sea,
    The eighth brought me to land;
With mariners and merchandise,
    And music on every hand.

'The ship wherein my love sall sail
    Is glorious to behowd;
The sails sall be o' the finest silk,
    And the mast o' beaten gowd.'

She has taken up her wee young son,
    Kiss'd him baith cheek and chin;
'O fare ye weel, my wee young son,
    For I'll never see you again!'

She has put her foot on gude ship-board,
    And on ship-board she has gane,
And the veil that hangit ower her face
    Was a' wi' gowd begane.

She hadna sail'd a league, a league,
    A league but barely twa,
Till she minded on her husband she left
    And her wee young sun alsua.

'O haud your tongue o' weeping,' he says,
    'Let a' your follies a-bee;
I'll show where the white lilies grow
    On the banks o' Italie.'

She hadna sail'd a league, a league,
    A league but barely three,
Till grim, grim grew his countenance
    And gurly grew the sea.

'What hills are yon, yon pleasant hills,
    The sun shines sweetly on?' –
'O yon are the hills o' Heaven,' he said,
    'Where you will never won.' –

'O whaten-a mountain is yon,' she said,
  Sae dreary wi' frost and snae?' –
'O yon is the mountain o' Hell, he said,
  Where you and I will gae,

'But haud your tongue, my dearest dear,
  Let a' your follies a-bee,
I'll show where the white lilies grow,
  In the bottom o' the sea.'

And aye as she turn'd her round about,
  Aye taller he seem'd to be;
Until that the tops o' that gallant ship
  Nae taller were than he.

He strack the top-mast wi' his hand,
  The fore-mast wi' his knee;
And he brake that gallant ship in twain,
  And sank her in the sea.

John Skelton (c. 1460–1529)   A.T.

———◆———

We have to make an effort to understand some poets of the past within the context of their times: perhaps part of the pleasure we get is in that effort, but still, it's their past-ness rather than their present-ness that we grasp first. With John Skelton that doesn't seem so. Though his poems are full of the names and trades and preoccupations of England in the late fifteenth and early sixteenth centuries, the very stuff of the early Tudor age, he strikes us as oddly modern. Poets of our own day such as Robert Graves and Stevie Smith have not only admired Skelton's poems, they've learned from them too, and imitated them. Robert Graves has written of him:

> What could be dafter
> Than John Skelton's laughter?
> What sound more tenderly
> Than his pretty poetry? . . .
> But angrily, wittily,
> Tenderly, prettily,
> Laughingly, learnedly,
> Sadly, madly,
> Helter-skelter John
> Rhymes serenely on,
> As English poets should.
> Old John, you do me good!

That's quite a good imitation of the way in which a number of Skelton's own poems move – short rhyming lines tumbling over each other with exuberance, contempt, humour and sheer cheek. Here is a taste of Skelton himself in his roughest and most realistic mood, describing a real woman, Elinour Rumming, who actually did run a pub near Leatherhead in the early sixteenth century: part of 'The Tunning of Elinour Rumming':

> When she goeth out
> Herself for to shew,
> She driveth down the dew
> With a pair of heeles
> As broad as two wheeles;
> She hobbles as a goose
> With her blanket hose
> Over the fallow;
> Her shoon smeared with tallow,
> Greaséd upon dirt
> That baudeth her skirt.
>
> And this comely dame,
> I understand, her name
> Is Elinour Rumming,
> At home in her wonning;
> And as men say
> She dwelt in Surrey,
> In a certain stead
> Beside Leatherhead.
> She is a tonnish gib,
> The devil and she be sib.
>
> But to make up my tale,
> She breweth nappy ale,
> And maketh thereof pot-sale
> To travellers, to tinkers,
> To sweaters, to swinkers,
> And all good ale-drinkers,
> That will nothing spare
> But drink till they stare
> And bring themselves bare,
> With 'Now away the mare!
> And let us slay care.'
> As wise as an hare!
>
> Come whoso will
> To Elinour on the hill
> With 'Fill the cup, fill!'

And sit there by still,
Early and late.
Thither cometh Kate,
Cisly and Sarah,
With their legs bare,
And also their feet
Hardely full unsweet;
With their heeles daggéd,
Their kirtles all to-jaggéd,
Their smocks all to-ragged,
With titters and tatters,
Bring dishes and platters
With all their might running
To Elinour Rumming
To have of her tunning.
She lendeth them on the same,
And thus beginneth the game.

Some wenches come unlacéd,
Some housewives come unbracéd,
With their naked pappes,
That flippes and flappes,
That wigges and wagges,
Like tawny saffron bagges;
A sort of foul drabbes.
All scurvy with scabbes.
Some be flybitten,
Some skewéd as a kitten;
Some with a shoe-clout
Bind their heades about;
Some have no hair-lace,
Their locks about their face,
Their tresses untrussed
All full of unlust;
Some look strawry,
Some cawry-mawry;
Full untidy tegges,
Like rotten egges.
Such a lewd sort
To Elinour resort

From tide to tide.
Abide, abide!
And to you shall be told
How her ale is sold
To Maud and to Mold.

You mustn't suppose from this that Skelton was nothing but a coarse, straightforward chronicler of the sordid or the everyday. He was a court poet for much of his life, and equally at home at Oxford and Cambridge; in fact he was really the first Poet Laureate, and was even more at the centre of things than Chaucer. Some of his most attractive poems are addressed to the ladies of the young Henry VIII's court. Here is one from a number of them in *The Garland of Laurel*: 'To Mistress Margaret Hussey':

Merry Margaret,
As midsummer flower,
Gentle as falcon
Or hawk of the tower:
With solace and gladness,
Much mirth and no madness,
All good and no badness;
So joyously,
So maidenly,
So womanly
Her demeaning
In every thing,
Far, far passing
That I can indite,
Or suffice to write
Of Merry Margaret
As midsummer flower,
Gentle as falcon
Or hawk of the tower.
As patient and still
And as full of good will
As fair Isaphill,
Coriander,
Sweet pomander,
Good Cassander,

Steadfast of thought,
Well made, well wrought,
Far may be sought
Ere that ye can find
So courteous, so kind
As Merry Margaret,
    This midsummer flower,
Gentle as falcon
Or hawk of the tower.

Skelton's tenderness is also seen in his long poem 'Philip Sparrow' – a poem spoken by a nun whose pet sparrow, called Philip, has been killed by her cat. Here is some of it:

It had a velvet cap,
And would sit upon my lap,
And seek after small wormes,
And sometimes white bread-crumbes;
And many times and oft
Between my breasts soft
It woulde lie and rest;
It was proper and prest.

Sometime he would gasp
When he saw a wasp;
A fly or a gnat,
He would fly at that;
And prettily he would pant
When he saw an ant.
Lord, how he would pry
After the butterfly!
Lord, how he would hop
After the gressop!
And when I said, 'Phip, Phip!'
Then he would leap and skip,
And take me by the lip.
Alas, it will me slo
That Philip is gone me fro! . . .

For it would come and go,
And fly so to and fro;

And on me it woulde leap
When I was asleep,
And his feathers shake,
Wherewith he woulde make
Me often for to wake,
And for to take him in
Upon my naked skin.
God wot, we thought no sin:
What though he crept so low?
It was no hurt, I trow
He did nothing perde,
But sit upon my knee.
Philip, though he were nice,
In him it was no vice.
Philip might be bold
And do what he wold:
Philip would seek and take
All the fleas black
That he could there espy
With his wanton eye . . .

I took my sampler once
Of purpose, for the nonce,
To sew with stitches of silk
My sparrow white as milk,
That be representation
Of his image and fashion
To me it might import
Some pleasure and comfort,
For my solace and sport.
But when I was sewing his beak,
Methought my sparrow did speak,
And opened his pretty bill,
Saying 'Maid, ye are in will
Again me for to kill,
Ye prick me in the head!'
With that my needle waxed red,
Methought, of Philip's blood;
Mine hair right upstood,
I was in such a fray

My speech was taken away.
I cast down that there was,
And said, 'Alas, alas,
How cometh this to pass?'
My fingers, dead and cold,
Could not my sampler hold:
My needle and thread
I threw away for dread.
The best now that I may
Is for his soul to pray . . .

An it were a Jew,
It would make one rue,
To see my sorrow new.
These villainous false cats
Were made for mice and rats,
And not for birdes smale.
Alas, my face waxeth pale,
Telling this piteous tale,
How my bird so fair,
That was wont to repair,
And go in at my spair,
And creep in at my gore
Of my gown before,
Flickering with his wings!
Alas, my heart it stings,
Remembering pretty things!
Alas, mine heart it sleth,
My Philip's doleful death!
When I remember it,
How prettily it would sit,
Many times and oft,
Upon my finger aloft!
I played with him tittle-tattle,
And fed him with my spittle,
With his bill between my lips,
It was my pretty Phips!
Many a pretty kiss
Had I of his sweet muss!
And now the cause is thus,

That he is slain me fro,
To my great pain and woe.

Of fortune this the chance
Standeth on variance:
Oft time after pleasaunce,
Trouble and grievance.
No man can be sure
Alway to have pleasure:
As well perceive ye may
How my disport and play
From me was taken away
By Gib, our cat savage,
That in a furious rage
Caught Philip by the head
And slew him there stark dead!

Between these two extremes of toughness and tenderness, or of rude realism and gently elaborate courtliness, lies a whole area which Skelton commands as a satirist. Remember that this was the court of Henry VIII, and that Skelton spent a good deal of time there while Cardinal Wolsey was the most powerful figure on the scene: fat, arrogant, ambitious, the son of an Ipswich butcher, and a much-feared and much-hated man. But Skelton was in a peculiar position because of his oratory, his learning, his poetry, and – most important – his freedom as a sort of licensed satirist, almost a court jester. Skelton wrote a lot of poems which centred on the court: 'Speak, Parrot', 'Why Come Ye Not To Court?' and, most ambitiously, a sort of early masque play called *Magnificence*, which has characters who are decorated with such splendid names as 'Counterfeit Countenance', 'Crafty Conveyance' and 'Courtly Abusion'. The character called 'Magnificence' is clearly Wolsey, who managed to have Skelton jailed briefly for his persistent criticism. But in the play, Magnificence gets his just deserts in the end. Here are some of the final lines, addressed to the Wolsey-figure, about the capriciousness of Fortune:

Unto this process briefly compiléd,
Comprehending the world casual and transitory,
Who list to consider shall never be beguiléd,

If it be registered well in memory;
A plain example of worldly vain-glory,
How in this world there is no sickerness,
But fallible flattery enmixed with bitterness.

A mirror encircléd is this interlude,
    This life inconstant for to behold and see;
Suddenly advancéd, and suddenly subdued,
    Suddenly riches, and suddenly poverty,
    Suddenly comfort, and suddenly adversity;
Suddenly thus Fortune can both smile and drown,
Suddenly set up, and suddenly cast down.

Suddenly promoted, and suddenly put back,
    Suddenly cherishéd, and suddenly cast aside,
Suddenly commended, and suddenly find a lack,
    Suddenly granted, and suddenly denied,
    Suddenly hid, and suddenly espied;
Suddenly thus Fortune can both smile and frown,
Suddenly set up, and suddenly cast down.

This treatise, deviséd to make you disport,
Sheweth nowadays how the world cumberéd is,
To the pith of the matter who list to resort;
    Today it is well, tomorrow it is all amiss,
    Today in delight, tomorrow bare of bliss,
Today a lord, tomorrow lie in the dust:
Thus in the world there is no earthly trust.

Fortune was one of the great late medieval and Renaissance
themes – we see it again in the poems of Wyatt and Surrey; and
with it went a feeling that the best times were past and that the
present was peculiarly awful – a notion that Skelton pursued
many times in his poems, but perhaps most solidly and surely
in this section from his long poem, 'Speak, Parrot' (concluding
again with an attack on Wolsey):

So many moral matters, and so little uséd;
    So much new making, and so mad time spent;
So much translation into English confuséd;
    So much noble preaching, and so little amendment;
    So much consultation, almost to none intent;

So much provision, and so little wit at need –
Since Deucalion's flood there can no clerkes rede.

So little discretion, and so much reasoning;
   So much hardy dardy, and so little manliness;
So prodigal expense, and so shameful reckoning;
   So gorgeous garments, and so much wretchedness;
   So much portly pride, with purses penniless;
So much spent before, and so much unpaid behind –
Since Deucalion's flood there can no clerkes find.

So much forecasting, and so far an after deal;
   So much politic prating, and so little standeth in stead;
So little secretness, and so much great counsel;
   So many bold barons, their hearts as dull as lead;
   So many noble bodies under a daw's head;
So royal a king as reigneth upon us all –
Since Deucalion's flood was never seen nor shall.

So many complaintes, and so smalle redress;
   So much calling on, and so small taking heed;
So much loss of merchandise, and so remediless;
   So little care for the common weal, and so much need;
   So much doubtful danger, and so little drede;
So much pride of prelates, so cruel and so keen –
Since Deucalion's flood, I trow, was never seen.

So many thieves hangéd, and thieves never the less;
So much 'prisonment for matters not worth an haw;
So much papers wering for right a small excess;
   So much pillory-pageants under colour of good law;
   So much turning on the cuck-stool for every gee-gaw;
So much mockish making of statutes of array –
Since Deucalion's flood was never, I dare say.

So brainless calves' heads, so many sheepes tails;
   So bold a bragging butcher, and flesh sold so dear;
So many plucked partridges, and so fatte quails;
   So mangy a mastiff cur, the great greyhound's peer;
   So big a bulk of brow-antlers cabbaged that year;
So many swannes dead, and so small revel –
Since Deucalion's flood, I trow, no man can tell.

So many truces taken, and so little perfite truth;
　So much belly-joy, and so wasteful banqueting;
So pinching and sparing, and so little profit groweth;
　So many hugy houses building, and so small house-
　　holding;
　Such statutes upon diets, such pilling and polling;
So is all thing wrought wilfully withoute reason and skill –
Since Deucalion's flood the world was never so ill.

So many vagabonds, so many beggars bold;
　So much decay of monasteries and of religious places;
So hot hatred against the church, and charity so cold;
　So much of 'my Lord's Grace,' and in him no graces;
　So many hollow hearts, and so double faces;
So much sanctuary-breaking, and privilege barréd –
Since Deucalion's flood was never seen nor lyerd.

So much ragged right of a rammes horn;
　So rigorous ruling in a prelate specially;
So bold and so bragging, and was so basely born;
　So lordly in his looks and so disdainously;
　So fat a maggot, bred of a fleshe-fly;
Was never such a filthy Gorgon, nor such an epicure,
Since Deucalion's flood, I make thee fast and sure.

So much privy watching in cold winters' nights:
　So much searching of losels, and is himself so lewd;
So much conjurations for elfish mid-day sprites;
　So many bulls of pardon publishéd and shewed;
　So much crossing and blessing, and him all beshrewed;
Such pole-axes and pillars, such mules trapt with gold –
Since Deucalion's flood in no chronicle is told.

This deliberate, serious voice is as characteristic of Skelton as the
'helter-skelter John' whom Robert Graves commemorated. It's
the voice of a man who was very much of the Middle Ages in his
reverence for the Church of which he was an ordained priest,
but who was full of the turbulence and questioning of the
Renaissance too. Without being at all the sort of poet who
founds a school or even 'starts a trend', again and again one is
reminded in reading him of later poets: perhaps, here, last of all,

of both Donne and Hopkins, in Skelton's painful devotional
poem, 'Woefully Arrayed':

> Woefully arrayed,
>   My blood, man,
>   For thee ran,
> It may not be nay'd:
>   My body blo and wan,
>   Woefully arrayed.

Behold me, I pray thee, with all thy whole reason,
And be not so hard-hearted, and for this encheason,
Sith I for thy soul-sake was slain in good season,
Beguiled and betrayed by Judas' false treason:
    Unkindly entreated,
    With sharp cord sore freted,
    The Jewes me threted:
They mowéd, they grinnéd, they scornéd me,
Condemnéd to death, as thou mayest see,
    Woefully arrayed.

Thus naked am I nailéd, O man, for thy sake!
I love thee, then love me; why sleepest thou? awake!
Remember my tender heart-root for thee brake,
With paines my veines constrained to crake:
    Thus tuggéd to and fro,
    Thus wrappéd all in woe,
    Whereas never man was so,
Entreated thus in most cruel wise,
Was like a lamb offered in sacrifice,
    Woefully arrayed.

Of sharp thorn I have worn a crown on my head,
So painéd, so strainéd, so rueful, so red,
Thus bobbéd, thus robbéd, thus for thy love dead,
Unfeignéd I deignéd my blood for to shed:
    My feet and handes sore
    The sturdy nailes bore:
    What might I suffer more
Than I have done, O man, for thee?
Come when thou list, welcome to me,
    Woefully arrayed.

Of record thy good Lord I have been and shall be:
I am thine, thou art mine, my brother I call thee.
Thee love I entirely – see what is befall'n me!
Sore beating, sore threating, to make thee, man, all free:
    Why art thou unkind?
    Why hast not me in mind?
    Come yet and thou shalt find
  Mine endless mercy and grace –
  See how a spear my heart did race,
    Woefully arrayed.

Dear brother, no other thing I of thee desire
But give me thine heart free to reward mine hire:
I wrought thee, I bought thee from eternal fire:
I pray thee array thee toward my high empire
    Above the orient,
    Whereof I am regent,
    Lord God omnipotent,
With me to reign in endless wealth:
Remember, man, thy soules health.

    Woefully arrayed,
      My blood, man,
      For thee ran,
    It may not be nay'd:
      My body blo and wan,
    Woefully arrayed.

Sir Thomas Wyatt (?1503–1542)
Henry Howard, Earl of Surrey (?1517–1547)
Barnaby Googe (1540–1594)   A.T.

––––––––◆––––––––

The poets emphasised in this section are sometimes thought of and written about as if they were a sort of composite animal: Wyattnsurrey. This Wyattnsurrey creature is supposed suddenly to have sprung into life at the time of a blinding revelation called the Renaissance, when everyone stopped being medieval and quaint and plagued with the Black Death and feudalism, and instead started being More Like Us – that is, modern. Wyattnsurrey showed this by reading a lot of Italian poetry and writing poems for the lute, which of course they played just as well as they fenced, rode, spoke foreign languages and, indeed, wrote sonnets. All this happened in order to make everything ready for Shakespeare, who of course is not only the top Renaissance poet but the top poet of all time.

Needless to say, there are some gaps of logic and interpretation and fact in all this. There was no firm break between medieval and Renaissance, as we've already seen in Skelton's poetry. And, though they have some things in common, Sir Thomas Wyatt and Henry Howard, Earl of Surrey, were two separate and distinct poets. But I want to begin with a poem that draws them together: one of two poems Surrey wrote in memory and celebration of Wyatt. Wyatt was a dozen or so years older than Surrey, and predeceased him by five years. They knew one another at the court of Henry VIII, though both were frequently absent from it on foreign missions. Both had periods when they fell out of favour, and both spent spells of imprisonment in the Tower: in fact Surrey was executed there. In this poem – formal, measured, yet also with a personal sense of friendship and loss – Surrey commemorates his fellow poet:

> Wyatt resteth here, that quick could never rest;
> Whose heavenly giftes, encreased by disdayn

And vertue, sank the deper in his brest:
Such profit he by envy could obtain.

A hed, where wisdom misteries did frame;
Whose hammers bet styll in that lively brayn
As on a stithe, where that some work of fame
Was dayly wrought to turne to Britaines gayn.

A visage stern and myld; where bothe did grow
Vice to contemne, in vertue to rejoyce;
Amid great stormes whom grace assured so
To lyve upright and smile at fortunes choyce.

A hand that taught what might be sayd in ryme;
That reft Chaucer the glory of his wit;
A mark the which, unparfited for time,
Some may approche, but never none shall hit.

A toung that served in forein realmes his king;
Whose courteous talke to vertue did enflame
Eche noble hart; a worthy guide to bring
Our English youth by travail unto fame.

An eye, whose judgement none affect could blinde,
Frendes to allure, and foes to reconcile;
Whose persing loke did represent a mynde
With vertue fraught, reposed, voyd of gyle.

A hart, where drede was never so imprest
To hyde the thought that might the trouth avance;
In neyther fortune loft nor yet represt,
To swell in wealth, or yeld unto mischance.

A valiant corps, where force and beawty met;
Happy, alas, too happy, but for foes;
Lived and ran the race that nature set;
Of manhodes shape, where she the molde did lose.

But to the heavens that simple soule is fled,
Which left with such as covet Christ to know
Witnesse of faith that never shall be ded;
Sent for our helth, but not received so.

Thus, for our gilte, this jewel have we lost.
The earth his bones, the heavens possesse his gost.

'A hand that taught what might be sayd in ryme': it's the comment of one practitioner on another, an admiration of technical skill. And this Wyatt certainly had, and was conscious of pursuing, particularly in his reading of the Italian poets. But neither he nor Surrey was slavishly dominated by such poets as Petrarch. A great deal of pure English lyricism, with its roots in the medieval lyric, comes through such a love song as this, by Wyatt; and see how he rings changes on the refrain, plays with it, shifts it to suit his changing purpose:

> Ons in your grace I knowe I was,
> Evyn as well as now ys he;
> Tho fortune so hath tornyd my case,
> That I am doune, and he full hye,
>   Yet ons I was.
>
> Ons I was he that dyd you please
> So well that nothyng dyd I dobte;
> And tho that nowe ye thinke yt ease
> To take him in and throw me out,
>   Yet ons I was.
>
> Ons I was he in tyms past
> That as your owne ye did retayne;
> And tho ye have me nowe out cast,
> Shoyng untruthe in you to raygne,
>   Yet ons I was.
>
> Ons I was he that knyt the knot,
> The whyche ye swore not to unknyt;
> And tho ye fayne yt now forgot,
> In usynge yowr newfangled wyt,
>   Yet ons I was.
>
> Ons I was he to whome ye sayd:
> 'Welcomm, my joy, my hole delight!'
> And tho ye are nowe well apayd
> Of me, your owne, to clame ye quyt,
>   Yet ons I was.

44

Ons I was he to whome ye spake:
'Have here my hart, yt ys thy owne!'
And tho thes wordis ye now forsake,
Sayng thereof my part ys none,
    Yet ons I was.

Ons I was he before reherst,
And nowe am he that nedes must dye;
And tho I dye, yet at the lest,
In your remembrance let yt lye
    That ons I was.

This is lyrical poetry in quite a straightforward literal sense: it's
intimately associated with music, with singing, and much of
Wyatt's output was intended, perhaps primarily, to be sung. 'My
lute, awake!' one of his best-known poems begins, and the lute
almost as much as the voice is the medium of many Wyatt
poems:

My lute awake! perfourme the last
Labour that thou and I shall wast,
    And end that I have now begon;
For when this song is sung and past,
    My lute be still, for I have done.

As to be herd where ere is none,
As lede to grave in marbill stone,
    My song may perse her hert as sone;
Should we then sigh, or syng, or mone?
    No, no, my lute, for I have done.

The Rokkes do not so cruelly
Repulse the waves continuelly
    As she my suyte and affection,
So that I ame past remedy:
    Whereby my lute and I have done.

Proud of the spoyll that thou hast gott
Of simple hertes thorough loves shot,
    By whome, vnkynd, thou hast theim wone,
Thinck not he haith his bow forgot,
    All tho my lute and I have done.

45

Vengeaunce shall fall on thy disdain,
That makest but game on ernest pain;
   Thinck not alone under the sonne
Unquyt to cause thy lovers plain,
   All tho my lute and I have done.

Perchaunce the lye wethered and old,
The wynter nyghtes that are so cold,
   Playnyng in vain unto the mone;
Thy wisshes then dare not be told;
   Care then who lyst, for I have done.

And then may chaunce the to repent
The tyme that thou hast lost and spent
   To cause thy lovers sigh and swoune;
Then shalt thou knowe beaultie but lent,
   And wisshe and want as I have done.

Now cesse, my lute; this is the last
Labour that thou and I shall wast,
   And ended is that we begon;
Now is this song boeth sung and past:
   My lute be still, for I have done.

But Wyatt had other manners too: the steady, stately tread of his sonnets, comparable to the tone of that memorial poem of Surrey's; the plain vigour of his satires; and the sombre disturbance of those poems of his which looked at the dangerous world of court intrigues and the moving wheel of favours and fortune – a theme as much medieval as Renaissance (we saw it in Skelton), and going right on through to the seventeenth century. Here are three Wyatt poems of this sort, the first two very short: this one is addressed to Sir Francis Bryan, a colleague of Wyatt's at court:

Syghes ar my foode, drynke are my teares,
Clynkinge of fetters suche musycke wolde crave,
Stynke and close ayer away my lyf wears:
Innocencie is all the hope I have.
Rayne, wynde, or wether I judge by myne eares.
Mallice assault that rightiousnes should have:
Sure I am, Brian, this wounde shall heale agayne,
But yet, alas, the scarre shall styll remayne.

That was probably a result of a period spent in the Tower, as this next short poem may be too: here we find Wyatt longing for that withdrawal from the hectic and slippery world of ambition and affairs which can be found elsewhere in English poetry, in Cowley, in Pope – in a sense a literary convention, but still the perfectly genuine expression of busy, essentially extrovert men who have found the world too much with them:

> Stond whoso list upon the slipper toppe
> Of courtes estates, and lett me heare rejoyce;
> And use me quyet without lett or stoppe,
> Unknowen in courte, that hath suche brackishe joyes:
> In hidden place, so lett my dayes forthe passe,
> That, when my yeares be done, withouten noyse,
> I may dye aged after the common trace.
> For hym death greep the right hard by the croppe,
> That is moche knowen of other, and of himself, alas,
> Doth dye unknowen, dazed with dreadfull face.

Most heavily and grimly, this troubled note in Wyatt comes through in this next poem, which, it's thought, was inspired by the period he spent in the Tower in 1536, when he saw the execution of Anne Boleyn and her supposed lovers: you feel the shuddering horror of a man who has seen terrible things and who senses, inevitably, that such things may come to him, in the lines:

> The bell tower showed me such a sight
> That in my head sticks day and night;
> There did I learn, out of a grate,
> For all favour, glory or might,
> That yet *circa Regna tonat.*

The refrain is taken from the Roman poet Seneca, and it means: 'It thunders around the throne.' Here is the whole poem:

> Who lyst his welthe and eas retayne,
> Hymselfe let hym unknowne contayne;
> Presse not to fast in at that gatte
> Wher the retorne standes by desdayne:
> For sure, *circa Regna tonat.*
>
> The hye montaynis ar blastyd oft,
> When the lower vaylye ys myld and soft;

Fortune with helthe stondis at debate;
The fall ys grevous frome alofte:
And sure, *circa Regna tonat*.

These blodye dayes have brokyn my hart;
My lust, my youth dyd then departe,
And blynd desyre of astate;
Who hastis to clyme sekes to reverte:
Of truthe, *circa Regna tonat*.

The bell towre showed me suche syght
That in my hed stekys day and nyght;
Ther dyd I lerne, out of a grate,
For all favour, glory or myght,
That yet *circa Regna tonat*.

By profe, I say, ther dyd I lerne,
Wyt helpythe not defence to yerne,
Of innocence to pled or prate;
Ber low, therfor, geve God the sterne,
For sure, *circa Regna tonat*.

But Wyatt's most famous poem, certainly his strangest and most subtle, and I think undoubtedly his best, is a love lyric – one that has an extraordinarily 'modern' ring to it, by which I don't simply mean that its eroticism is more piercing and direct than one finds in most poems of so-called 'courtly love'. This is real feeling, there's no doubt, expressed with passionate realism:

They fle from me that sometyme did me seke
With naked fote stalking in my chambre.
I have sene theim gentill, tame and meke,
That nowe are wyld and do not remembre
That sometyme they put theimself in daunger
To take bred at my hand; and nowe they raunge,
Besely seking with a continuell chaunge.

Thancked be fortune, it hath ben othrewise
Twenty tymes better; but ons in speciall,
In thyn arraye after a pleasaunt gyse,
When her lose gowne from her shoulders did fall,
And she me caught in her armes long and small;

Therewithall swetely did my kysse,
And softly said, 'Dere hert, how like you this?'

It was no dreme: I lay brode waking.
But all is torned thorough my gentilnes
Into a straunge fasshion of forsaking;
And I have leve to goo of her goodeness,
And she also to use newfangilnes.
But syns that I so kyndely ame served,
I would fain knowe what she hath deserved.

Though Surrey's themes are often the same as Wyatt's – frustrated or disdained love, the fickleness of fortune, thoughts of freedom and past happiness during imprisonment – he's an altogether steadier, less verbally surprising poet. But he does have a sharp eye for detail rather than dramatic force, and this comes out well in this sonnet on Spring:

The soote season, that bud and bloom forth brings,
With green hath clad the hill and eke the vale.
The nightingale with feathers new she sings;
The turtle to her make hath told her tale.
Summer is come, for every spray now springs.
The hart hath hung his old head on the pale;
The buck in brake his winter coat he flings;
The fishes float with new repaired scale;
The adder all her slough away she slings;
The swift swallow pursueth the flies small;
The busy bee her honey now she mings;
Winter is worn that was the flowers' bale.
    And thus I see among these pleasant things
    Each care decays; and yet my sorrow springs.

And there's the same fine rhetorical accumulation of detail, this time of a more abstract sort, in this sonnet which links the world of natural decay with that of declining fortune:

Brittle beauty, that Nature made so frail,
Whereof the gift is small, and short the season;
Flowering today, tomorrow apt to fail;
Tickle treasure, abhorred of reason:
Dangerous to deal with, vain, of none avail;

Costly in keeping, past not worth two peason;
Slipper in sliding, as is an eel's tail;
Hard to obtain, once gotten, not geason:
Jewel of jeopardy, that peril doth assail;
False and untrue, enticed oft to treason;
Enemy to youth, that most may I bewail;
Ah! bitter sweet, infecting as the poison,
  Thou farest as fruit that with the frost is taken;
  Today ready ripe, tomorrow all to shaken.

Finally, in a way more crudely and amateurishly, and certainly by a more minor poet, 'Going towards Spain', by Barnaby Googe. Googe was of the generation immediately following that of Wyatt and Surrey, and what I sense here is a breath of that exalted lyrical patriotism which was part of the Elizabethan age – heard much more surely in Shakespeare, of course, but nevertheless poignant and proud in Barnaby Googe. Technically it's old-fashioned; emotionally it's very much part of its time:

Farewell, thou fertyll soyle, that Brutus fyrst out founde,
When he, poore soule, was driven clean from out his
    Countrey ground;
That Northward layst thy lusty sides amyd the ragyng
    Seas;
Whose welthy Land doth foster upp thy people all in ease,
While others scrape and carke abroad, theyr symple foode
    to gett,
And selye Soules toke all for good, that commeth to the
    Net,
Which they with painfull paynes do pynch in barrain,
    burning Realmes,
While we have all without restreint among thy welthy
    streames.
O blest of God, thou Pleasaunt Ile, where welth herself
    doth dwell,
Wherein my tender yeares I past, I byd thee now farewell.
For Fancy dryves me forth abrode, and byds me take
    delyght
In leyving thee and raungyng far, to see some straunger
    syght,

And sayth I was not framed heare to lyve at home with
  eas,
But passynge forth for knowledge sake, to cut the fomyng
  seas.

Sir Philip Sidney (1554–1586)
Edmund Spenser (?1552–1599)

A.T.

———————◆———————

I think it's never necessarily true that the earlier the work of art or the poem, the more likely it is to seem remote to us. For all the difference of their language, their concerns, their world, the poems so far communicate without too much difficulty a present-ness, an immediacy, whether it's in the narrative of Chaucer or a ballad, the hurrying patter or steady scorn of Skelton, or the sombre directness (which, rightly or wrongly, strikes us as *personal* directness) of Wyatt.

Now, as we come to the golden period of Elizabethan court poetry, to Sidney and Spenser, there is inevitably a stronger feeling of remoteness: at least, there is to me. About Spenser in particular I have to make an effort of imagination which I haven't found necessary before. This is partly because of the very fact of his professionalism: Spenser took himself seriously as a professional, and as an innovator, in a way that no English poet so far had done. Though early on he was a junior official in the entourage of the Earl of Leicester, and later became a rather more senior official in the administration of Ireland, he was never an important administrative or ambassadorial figure; instead, he was lucky in his patrons, who made it possible for him to give a great deal of his time to his art. And indeed his output is prodigious: copious, varied, technically adventurous, the product of a man who quite consciously saw himself not just as a literary figure but as a poet who would leave behind a monument. He had more worldly ambitions at one time, was (in his own words) plagued

> Through discontent of his long fruitlesse stay
> In Princes Court, and expectation vaine
> Of idle hopes, which still doe fly away.

But such hopes and discontents were put on one side in the end, so that he could shape himself into the poet he knew he had it in him to be.

I said a moment ago that Spenser was lucky in his patrons; and one of his most generous and sensitive patrons was himself a poet – that great paragon of gentlemanliness to the Elizabethan court, Sir Philip Sidney. When we think of the ideal Renaissance man, it's probably Sidney who comes to mind: soldier, scholar, essayist, horseman and swordsman, incomparably brave and courteous, and a poet. The mixture is almost too good to be true, yet there is plenty of evidence for the accomplishments, and as for the poems, well, they exist all right – not on the scale of Spenser's, for Sidney's life had many other demands and distractions, and indeed his life was shorter: he died campaigning in Holland at the age of 32. But Sidney would in any case be remarkable for being the pioneer in that characteristic high-Elizabethan literary form, the sonnet sequence. Written to 'Stella', Sidney's *Astrophel* sonnets tend to be smooth, mellifluous even, certain of their own subdued rhetoric and balance – technically, perhaps the most perfect poems which had yet been written in English: by which, of course, I don't mean that they were the best. But they *were* superbly ordered in a way that was new, like these two well-known examples, each taking a separate image (the moon, and sleep) and with exquisite surefootedness plotting it through:

> With how sad steps, O Moon, thou climb'st the skies!
>   How silently, and with how wan a face!
> What! may it be that even in heavenly place
> That busy archer his sharp arrows tries?
> Sure, if that long-with-love acquainted eyes
>   Can judge of love, thou feel'st a lover's case;
>   I read it in thy looks; thy languished grace
> To me, that feel the like, thy state descries.
> Then, even of fellowship, O Moon, tell me,
>   Is constant love deemed there but want of wit?
> Are beauties there as proud as here they be?
>   Do they above love to be loved, and yet
>   Those lovers scorn whom that love doth possess?
>   Do they call virtue there ungratefulness?

Come, sleep, O sleep, the certain knot of peace,
 The baiting place of wit, the balm of woe,
The poor man's wealth, the prisoner's release,
 Th'indifferent judge between the high and low;
With shield of proof shield me from out the prease
 Of those fierce darts despair at me doth throw;
O make me in those civil wars to cease;
 I will good tribute pay, if thou do so.
Take thou of me smooth pillows, sweetest bed,
 A chamber deaf to noise and blind to light,
A rosy garland and a weary head;
And if these things, as being thine by right,
 Move not thy heavy grace, thou shalt in me,
 Livelier than elsewhere, Stella's image see.

There is something massive about this work as well as melli-
fluous: the lines, in their structure and their language, have a
solidity. But Sidney could also manage something more purely
lyrical, which seems to anticipate the poets of the Caroline period
thirty or forty years later:

Who hath his fancy pleased
With fruits of happy sight,
Let here his eyes be raised
 On Nature's sweetest light;
A light which doth dissever
 And yet unite the eyes;
A light which, dying never,
 Is cause the looker dies.

She never dies, but lasteth
In life of lover's heart;
He ever dies that wasteth
 In love his chiefest part.
Thus is her life still guarded
 In never-dying faith;
Thus is his death rewarded,
 Since she lives in his death.

Look, then, and die; the pleasure
 Doth answer well the pain;

Small loss of mortal treasure
   Who may immortal gain.
Immortal be her graces,
   Immortal is her mind;
They, fit for heavenly places;
   This, heaven in it doth bind.

But eyes these beauties see not,
   Nor sense that grace descries;
Yet eyes deprived be not
   From sight of her fair eyes;
Which as of inward glory
   They are the outward seal,
So may they live still sorry,
   Which die not in that weal.

But who hath fancies pleased
   With fruits of happy sight,
Let here his eyes be raised
   On Nature's sweetest light!

When we come to Sidney's friend, admirer and protégé, Spenser, it's difficult to select. Like Sidney, Spenser wrote a sequence of sonnets, called *Amoretti*, but they look merely repetitious after those two sonnets of Sidney's. In another sequence of poems, *The Shepherd's Calendar*, Spenser experimented with forms and metres in a way that was quite deliberately new and audacious; but they aren't poems that make a primary appeal to us now. To take only one other example, there's the satire of 'Mother Hubberd's Tale'. But I think justice is best done if one takes one of the two great marriage hymns, 'Epithalamion' or 'Prothalamion', before going on to the impossible job of detaching something from Spenser's masterpiece, *The Faerie Queene*. The 'Epithalamion' is perhaps more perfectly organised than the 'Prothalamion', but it's over 400 lines long and can't be chopped about, I think, without damaging it. The 'Prothalamion' is more manageable: written for the double marriage of the two daughters of the Earl of Worcester, it is a resolutely formal celebratory piece, distinguished for me by the sudden vividness of the eighth stanza (that on London), and by the perfect rightness of its properly famous refrain:

Calme was the day, and through the trembling ayre,
Sweete breathing Zephyrus did softly play
A gentle spirit, that lightly did delay
Hot Titans beames, which then did glyster fayre:
When I whom sullein care,
Through discontent of my long fruitlesse stay
In Princes Court, and expectation vayne
Of idle hopes, which still doe fly away,
Like empty shaddowes, did aflict my brayne,
Walkt forthe to ease my payne
Along the shoare of siluer streaming Themmes,
Whose rutty Bancke, the which his Riuer hemmes,
Was paynted all with variable flowers,
And all the meades adornd with daintie gemmes,
Fit to decke maydens bowres,
And crowne their Paramours,
Against the Brydale day, which is not long:
    Sweete Themmes runne softly, till I end my Song.

There, in a Meadow, by the Riuers side,
A flocke of Nymphes I chaunced to espy,
All louely Daughters of the Flood thereby,
With goodly greenish locks all loose vntyde,
As each had bene a Bryde,
And each one had a little wicker basket,
Made of fine twigs entrayled curiously,
In which they gathered flowers to fill their flasket:
And with fine Fingers, cropt full feateously
The tender stalkes on hye.
Of euery sort, which in that Meadow grew,
They gathered some; the Violet pallid blew,
The little Dazie, that at euening closes,
The virgin Lillie, and the Primrose trew,
With store of vermeil Roses,
To decke their Bridegromes posies,
Against the Brydale day, which was not long:
    Sweete Themmes runne softly, till I end my Song.

With that, I saw two Swannes of goodly hewe,
Come softly swimming downe along the Lee;
Two fairer Birds I yet did neuer see:

The snow which doth the top of Pindus strew,
Did neuer whiter shew,
Nor Ioue himselfe when he a Swan would be
For loue of Leda, whiter did appeare:
Yet Leda was they say as white as he,
Yet not so white as these, nor nothing neare;
So purely white they were,
That euen the gentle streame, the which them bare,
Seem'd foule to them, and bad his billowes spare
To wet their silken feathers, least they might
Soyle thir fayre plumes with water not so fayre,
And marre their beauties bright,
That shone as heauens light,
Against their Brydale day, which was not long:
    Sweete Themmes runne softly, till I end my Song.

Eftsoones the Nymphes, which now had
    Flowers their fill,
Ran all in haste, to see that siluer brood,
As they came floating on the Christal Flood.
Whom when they sawe, they stood amazed still,
Their wondring eyes to fill,
Them seem'd they neuer saw a sight so fayre,
Of Fowles so louely, that they sure did deeme
Them heauenly borne, or to be that same payre
Which through the Skie draw Venus siluer Teeme,
For sure they did not seeme
To be begot of any earthly Seede,
But rather Angels or of Angels breede:
Yet were they bred of Somers-heat they say,
Insweetest Season, when each Flower and weede
The earth did fresh aray,
So fresh they seem'd as day,
Euen as their Brydale day, which was not long:
    Sweete Themmes runne softly, till I end my Song.

Then forth they all out of their baskets drew,
Great store of Flowers, the honour of the field,
That to the sense did fragrant odours yeild,
All which vpon, those goodly Birds they threw,
And all the Waues did strew,

That like old Peneus Waters they did seeme,
When downe along by pleasant Tempes shore
Scattred with Flowers, through Thessaly they streeme,
That they appeare through Lillies plenteous store,
Like a Brydes Chamber flore:
Two of those Nymphes, meane while, two Garlands
    bound,
Of freshest Flowres which in that Mead they found,
The which presenting all in trim Array,
Their snowie Foreheads therewithall they crownd,
Whil'st one did sing this Lay,
Prepar'd against that Day,
Against their Brydale day, which was not long:
   Sweete Themmes runne softly, till I end my Song.

Ye gentle Birdes, the worlds faire ornament,
And heauens glorie, whom this happie hower
Doth leade vnto your louers blisfull bower,
Ioy may you haue and gentle hearts content
Of your loues couplement:
And let faire Venus, that is Queene of loue,
With her heart-quelling Sonne vpon you smile,
Whose smile they say, hath vertue to remoue
All Loues dislike, and friendships faultie guile
For euer to assoile.
Let endlesse Peace your steadfast hearts accord,
And blessed Plentie wait vpon your bord,
And let your bed with pleasures chast abound,
That fruitfull issue may to you afford,
Which may your foes confound,
And make your ioyes redound.
Vpon your Brydale day, which is not long:
   Sweete Themmes run softlie, till I end my Song.

So ended she; and all the rest around
To her redoubled that her vndersong,
Which said, their bridale daye should not be long.
And gentle Eccho from the neighbour ground,
Their accents did resound.
So forth those ioyous Birdes did passe along,
Adowne the Lee, that to them murmured low,

As he would speake, but that he lackt a tong
Yeat did by signes his glad affection show,
Making his streame run slow.
And all the foule which in his flood did dwell
Gan flock about these twaine, that did excell
The rest, so far, as Cynthia doth shend
The lesser starres. So they enranged well,
Did on those two attend,
And their best seruice lend,
Against their wedding day, which was not long:
   Sweete Themmes run softly, till I end my song.

At length they all to mery London came,
To mery London, my most kyndly Nurse,
That to me gaue this Lifes first natiue sourse:
Though from another place I take my name,
An house of auncient fame.
There when they came, whereas those bricky towres,
The which on Themmes brode aged backe doeryde,
Where now the studious Lawyers haue their bowers
There whylome wont the Templer Knights to byde,
Till they decayd through pride:
Next whereunto there standes a stately place,
Where oft I gayned giftes and goodly grace
Of that great Lord, which therein wont to dwell,
Whose want too well now feeles my freendles case:
But Ah here fits not well
Olde woes but ioyes to tell
Against the bridale daye, which is not long:
   Sweete Themmes runne softly, till I end my Song.

Yet therein now doth lodge a noble Peer,
Great Englands glory and the Worlds wide wonder,
Whose dreadfull name, late through all Spaine did
    thunder,
And Hercules two pillors standing neere,
Did make to quake and feare:
Faire branch of Honor, flower of Cheualrie,
That fillest England with thy triumphs fame,
Ioy haue thou of thy noble victorie,
And endlesse happinesse of thine owne name

That promiseth the same:
That through thy prowesse and victorious armes,
Thy country may be freed from forraine harmes:
And great Elisaes florious name may ring
Through al the world, fil'd with thy wide Alarmes,
Which some braue muse may sing
To ages following,
Vpon the Brydale day, which is not long:
   Sweete Themmes runne softly, till I end my Song.

From those high Towers, this noble Lord issuing,
Like radiant Hesper when his golden hayre
In th'Ocean billowes he hath Bathed fayre,
Descended to the Riuers open vewing,
With a great traine ensuing.
Aboue the rest were goodly to bee seene
Two gentle Knights of louely face and feature
Beseeming well the bower of anie Queene,
With gifts of wit and ornaments of nature,
Fit for so goodly stature:
That like the twins of Ioue they seem'd in sight,
Which decke the Bauldricke of the Heauens bright.
They two forth pacing to the Riuers side,
Receiued those two faire Brides, their Loues delight,
Which at th' appointed tyde,
Each one did make his Bryde,
Against their Brydale day, which is not long:
   Sweete Themmes runne softly, till I end my Song.

The Faerie Queene, for all its great length, is an unfinished work.
Spenser intended it to have twelve books, but in fact there are
only seven, and even the seventh is unfinished and detached
from the rest. The whole thing was explained by Spenser himself
as intended to be a 'continued allegory or dark conceit'; and he
also said that its framework was that of 'the twelve moral virtues
as Aristotle hath devised'. What both intentions result in is a
national patriotic vision of Love, Friendship, Beauty and
Courage, as exemplified in the person of the Queen herself,
Elizabeth; but within and beside this run a whole series of
loosely connected or almost entirely unconnected moral ad-
ventures and situations, many of them with quite specific

contemporary references to be read underneath the 'dark conceit'. It is a very literary poem, it's full of conscious archaisms and harkings-back both in language and in plot, and it moves throughout on an exalted level. Though it's been much praised technically, I myself find its steady-paced nine-line stanzas, with their long, trailing, sometimes magnificent, sometimes halting final lines, a bit lacking in thrust and forward movement. But this is to want something that wasn't intended: I suppose one should just sit back and let it all wash over one.

I've chosen two sections from *The Faerie Queene*; each of them can be taken as self-contained without real damage. The first is the description of the Bower of Bliss in Book Two. The central character in this book is Sir Guyon, and the moral virtue is that of Temperance. One of the tempting places that Sir Guyon puts down, with the help of an Elf and a Palmer, is this hedonistic and erotic paradise, where they find a wanton Lady and her lover, whom they tie up:

Eftsoones they heard a most melodious sound,
   Of all that mote delight a daintie eare,
   Such as attonce might not on liuing ground,
   Saue in this Paradise, be heard elsewhere:
   Right hard it was, for wight, which did it heare,
   To read, what manner musicke that mote bee:
   For all that pleasing is to liuing eare,
   Was there consorted in one harmonee,
Birdes, voyces, instruments, windes, waters, all agree.

The ioyous birdes shrouded in chearefull shade,
   Their notes vnto the voyce attempred sweet;
   Th'Angelicall soft trembling voyces made
   To th'instruments diuine respondence meet:
   The siluer sounding instruments did meet
   With the base murmure of the waters fall:
   The waters fall with difference discreet,
   Now soft, now loud, vnto the wind did call:
The gentle warbling wind low answered to all.

There, whence that Musick seemed heard to bee,
   Was the fair Witch her selfe now solacing,
   With a new Louer, whom through sorceree

And witchcraft, she from farre did thither bring:
There she had him now layd a slombering,
In secret shade, after long wanton joyes:
Whilst round about them pleasauntly did sing
Many faire Ladies, and lasciuious boyes,
That euer mixt their song with light licentious toyes.

And all that while, right ouer him she hong,
With her false eyes fast fixed in his sight,
As seeking medicine, whence she was stong,
Or greedily depasturing delight:
And oft inclining downe with kisses light,
For feare of waking him, his lips bedewd,
And through his humid eyes did sucke his spright,
Quite molten into lust and pleasure lewd;
Wherewith she sighed soft, as if his case she rewd.

The whiles some one did chaunt this louely lay;
Ah see, who so faire thing doest faine to see,
In springing flowre the image of thy day;
Ah see the Virgin Rose, how sweetly shee
Doth first peepe forth with bashfull modestee,
That fairer seemes, the lesse ye see her may;
Lo see soone after how more bold and free
Her baréd bosome she doth broad display;
Loe see soone after, how she fades, and falles away.

So passeth, in the passing of a day,
Of mortall life the leafe, the bud, the flowre,
Ne more doth flourish after first decay,
That earst was sought to decke both bed and bowre,
Of many a ladie, and many a Paramowre:
Gather therefore the Rose of loue, whilest yet is prime,
For soone comes age, that will her pride deflowre:
Gather the Rose of loue, whilest yet is time,
Whilst louing thou mayst loued be with equall crime.

He ceast, and then gan all the quire of birdes
Their diuerse notes t'attune vnto his lay,
As in approuance of his pleasing words.
The constant paire heard all, that he did say,
Yet swarued not, but kept their forward way,

Through many couert groues, and thickets close,
 In which they creeping did at last display
 That wanton Ladie, with her louer lose,
Whose sleepie head she in her lap did soft dispose.

Vpon a bed of Roses she was layd,
 As faint through heat, or dight to pleasant sin,
 And was arayd, or rather disarayd,
 All in a vele of silke and siluer thin,
 That hid no whit her alabaster skin,
 But rather shewd more white, if more might bee:
 More subtile web Arachne cannot spin,
 Nor the fine nets, which oft we wouen see
Of scorched deaw, do not in th'aire more lightly flee.

Her snowy brest was bare to readie spoyle
 Of hungry eies, which n'ote therewith be fild,
 And yet through langvour of her late sweet toyle,
 Few drops, more cleare then Nectar, forth distild,
 That like pure Orient perles adowne it trild
 And her fair eyes sweet smyling in delight,
 Moystened their fierie beames, with which she thrild
 Fraile harts, yet quenched not; like starry light
Which sparckling on the silent waues, does seeme more
 bright.

The young man sleeping by her, seemd to bee
 Some goodly swayne of honorable place,
 That certes it great pittie was to see
 Him his nobilitie so foule deface;
 A sweet regard, and amiable grace,
 Mixed with manly sternnesse did appeare
 Yet sleeping, in his well proportiond face,
 And on his tender lips the downy heare
Did now but freshly spring, and silken blossomes beare.

His warlike armes, the idle instruments
 Of sleeping praise, were hong vpon a tree,
 And his braue shield, full of old moniments,
 Was fowly ra'st, that none the signes might see;
 Ne for them, ne for honour cared hee,
 Ne ought, that did to his aduauncement tend,

But in lewd loues, and wastfull luxuree,
  His dayes, his goods, his bodie he did spend:
O horrible enchantment, that him so did blend.

The noble Elfe, and careful Palmer drew
  So nigh them, minding nought, but lustfull game,
  That sudden forth they on them rusht, and threw
  A subtile net, which onely for the same
  The skilfull Palmer formally did frame.
  So held them vnder fast, the whiles the rest
  Fled all away for feare of fowler shame.
  The faire Enchauntresse, so vnwares opprest,
Tryde all her arts, and all her sleights, thence out to wrest.

And eke her louer stroue: but all in vaine;
  For that same net so cunningly was wound,
  That neither guile, nor force might it distraine.
  They tooke them both, and both them strongly bound
  In captiue bandes, which there they readie found:
  But her in chaines of adamant he tyde;
  For nothing else might keepe her safe and sound;
  But Verdant (so he hight) he soone vntyde,
And counsell sage insteed thereof to him applyde.

But all those pleasant bowres and Pallace braue,
  Guyon broke downe, with rigour pittilesse;
  Ne ought their goodly workmanship might saue
  Them from the tempest of his wrathfulnesse,
  But that their blisse he turn'd to balefulnesse:
  Their groues he feld, their gardins did deface,
  Their arbers spoyle, their Cabinets suppresse,
  Their banket houses burne, their buildings race,
And of the fairest late, now made the fowlest place.

The second extract from *The Faerie Queene* has much less connection with the whole work than the Bower of Bliss: it comes from the final, unfinished book, and is a description of the Seasons, the Months, the Hours, Life and Death, as they parade as symbols of change, of mutability. The whole performance is like a court masque, such as might have been enacted before Elizabeth; but here the characters are the very fabric of life itself:

64

So, forth issew'd the Seasons of the yeare;
  First, lusty Spring, all dight in leaues of flowres
  That freshly budded and new bloomes did beare
  (In which a thousand birds had built their Bowres
  That sweetly sung, to call forth Paramours):
  And in his hand a iauelin he did beare,
  And on his head (as fit for warlike stoures)
  A guilt engrauen morion he did weare;
That as some did him loue, so others did him feare.

Then came the iolly Sommer, being dight
  In a thin silken cassock coloured greene,
  That was vnlyned all, to be more light:
  And on his head a girlond well beseene
  He wore, from which as he had chauffed been
  The sweat did drop; and in his hand he bore
  A boawe and shaftes, as he in forrest greene
  Had hunted late the Libbard or the Bore,
And now would bathe his limbes, with labor heated sore.

Then came the Autumne all in yellow clad,
  As though he ioyed in his plentious store,
  Laden with fruits that made him laugh, full glad
  That he had banisht hunger, which to-fore
  Had by the belly oft him pinched sore.
  Vpon his head a wreath that was enrold
  With eares of corne, of euery sort he bore:
  And in his hand a sickle he did holde,
To reape the ripened fruits the which the earth had yold.

Lastly, came Winter cloathed all in frize,
  Chattering his teeth for cold that did him chill,
  Whil'st on his hoary beard his breath did freese;
  And the dull drops that from his purpled bill
  As from a limbeck did adown distil.
  In his right hand a tipped staffe he held,
  With which his feeble steps he stayed still:
  For, he was faint with cold, and weak with eld;
That scarse his loosed limbes he hable was to weld.

These, marching softly, thus in order went,
  And after them, the Monthes all riding came;

First, sturdy March with brows full sternly bent,
And armed strongly, rode vpon a Ram,
The same which ouer Hellespontus swam:
Yet in his hand a spade he also hent,
And in a bag all sorts of seeds ysame,
Which on the earth he strowed as he went,
And fild her womb with fruitful hope of nourishment.

Next came fresh April full of lustyhed,
And wanton as a Kid whose horne new buds:
Vpon a Bull he rode, the same which led
Europa floting through th'Argolick fluds:
His hornes were gilden all with golden studs
And garnished with garlonds goodly dight
Of all the fairest flowres and freshest buds
Which th'earth brings forth, and wet he seem'd in sight
With waues, through which he waded for his loues delight.

Then came faire May, the fayrest mayd on ground,
Deckt all with dainties of her seasons pryde,
And throwing flowres out of her lap around:
Vpon two brethrens shoulders she did ride,
The twinnes of Leda; which on eyther side
Supported her like to their soueraine Queene.
Lord! how all creatures laught, when her they spide,
And leapt and daunc't as they had rauisht beene!
And Cupid selfe about her fluttred all in greene.

And after her, came iolly Iune, arrayed
All in green leaues, as he a Player were;
Yet in his time, he wrought as well as playd,
That by his plough-yrons mote right well a peare:
Vpon a Crab he rode, that him did beare
With crooked crawling steps an vncouth pase,
And backward yode, as Bargemen wont to fare
Bending their force contrary to their face,
Like that vngracious crew which faines demurest grace.

Then came hot Iuly boyling like to fire,
That all his garments he had cast away:
Vpon a Lyon raging yet with ire
He boldy rode and made him to obay:

66

It was the beast that whylome did forray
The Nemaean forrest, till th'Amphytrionide
Him slew, and with his hide did him array;
Behinde his back a sithe, and by his side
Vnder his belt he bore a sickle circling wide.

The sixt was August, being rich arrayd
In garment all of gold downe to the ground
Yet rode he not, but led a louely Mayd
Forth by the lilly hand, the which was cround
With eares of corne, and full her hand was found;
That was the righteous Virgin, which of old
Liv'd here on earth, and plenty made abound;
But, after Wrong was lov'd and Iustice solde,
She left th'vnrighteous world and was to heauen extold

Next him, September marched eeke on foote;
Yet was he heauy laden with the spoyle
Of haruests riches, which he made his boot,
And him enricht with bounty of the soyle:
In his one hand, as fit for haruests toyle,
He held a knife-hook; and in th'other hand
A pair of waights, with which he did assoyle
Both more and lesse, where it in doubt did stand,
And equall gaue to each as Iustice duly scann'd.

Then came October full of merry glee:
For, yet his noule was totty of the must,
Which he was treading in the wine-fats see,
And of the ioyous oyle, whose gentle gust
Made him so frollick and so full of lust:
Vpon a dreadfull Scorpion he did ride,
The same which by Dianaes doom vniust
Slew great Orion: and eeke by his side
He had his ploughing share, and coulter ready tyde.

Next was Nouember, he full grosse and fat,
As fed with lard, and that right well might seeme;
For, he had been a fatting hogs of late,
That yet his browes with sweat, did reek and steem,
And yet the season was full sharp and breem;
In planting eeke he took so small delight:

Whereon he rode, not easie was to deeme;
For it a dreadfull Centaure was in sight,
The seed of Saturne, and faire Nais, Chiron hight.

And after him, came next the chill December:
Yet he through merry feasting which he made,
And great bonfires, did not the cold remember;
His Sauiours birth his mind so much did glad:
Vpon a shaggy-bearded Goat he rode,
The same wherewith Dan Ioue in tender yeares,
They say, was nourisht by th'Idaean mayd;
And in his hand a broad deepe boawle he beares;
Of which, he freely drinks an health to all his peeres.

Then came old Ianuary, wrapped well
In many weeds to keep the cold away;
Yet did he quake and quiuer like to quell,
And blowe his nayles to warme them if he may:
For, they were numbd with holding all the day
An hatchet keene, with which he felled wood,
And from the trees did lop the needlesse spray:
Vpon an huge great Earth-pot steane he stood;
From whose wide mouth, there flowed forth the Romane
      floud.

And lastly, came cold February, sitting
In an old wagon, for he could not ride;
Drawne of two fishes for the season fitting,
Which through the flood before did softly slyde
And swim away: yet had he by his side
His plough and harnesse fit to till the ground,
And tooles to prune the trees, before the pride
Of hasting Prime did make them burgein round:
So past the twelue Months forth, and their dew places
      found.

And after these, there came the Day, and Night,
Riding together both with equall pase,
Th'one on a Palfrey blacke, the other white;
But Night had couered her vncomely face
With a blacke veile, and held in hand a mace,
On top whereof the moon and stars were pight,

And sleep and darknesse round about did trace:
  But Day did beare, vpon his scepters hight,
The goodly Sun, encompast all with beames bright.

Then came the Howres, faire daughters of high Ioue,
  And timely Night, the which were all endewed
  With wondrous beauty fit to kindle loue;
  But they were Virgins all, and loue eschewed,
  That might forslack the charge to them foreshewed
  By mighty Ioue; who did them Porters make
  Of heauens gate (whence all the gods issued)
  Which they did dayly watch, and nightly wake
By euen turnes, ne euer did their charge forsake.

And after all came Life, and lastly Death;
  Death with most grim and griesly visage seene,
  Yet is he nought but parting of the breath;
  Ne ought to see, but like a shade to weene,
  Vnbodied, vnsoul'd, vnheard, vnseene.
  But Life was like a faire young lusty boy,
  Such as they faine Dan Cupid to haue beene,
  Full of delightfull health and liuely ioy,
Deckt all with flowres, and wings of gold fit to employ.

Christopher Marlowe (1564–1593)
Thomas Nashe (1567–1601)
William Shakespeare (1564–1616)   P.P.

———————◆————————

As Swinburne pointed out, English poetry is unique in European literature in that its greatest achievements were written for the stage and not the library. Nothing is more remarkable than the perfecting of blank verse in a matter of 70 years, from 1570 to 1640, producing in that time a multitude of masterpieces of which Shakespeare's plays are only the peak, and which contain enough superb poetry to content another language for a millennium. It's become customary to say that, with the exception of Ben Jonson, the Elizabethan and Jacobean playwrights were mere sensationalists beside Shakespeare. This is a ridiculous concept. Hardly one of their hundreds of plays is negligible – they nearly all act well, and the language, though sometimes excessive, is amazingly plastic and richly wrought. Blank verse was the ideal form for the restless minds who worked in the Elizabethan theatre. Edmund Spenser may be considered the apotheosis of the old convention in English poetry – the long poem in stanzas imitated from foreign romances, such as those of Ariosto and Tasso in Italian. But the playwrights who flocked to the theatres at the end of Elizabeth's reign needed something much more immediate, and blank verse, with its changes of pace, lack of rhymes and infinite flexibility, suited them perfectly. They were able to develop their most characteristic device – the poetical metaphor, a necessity on stages devoid of scenery. All that blank verse insists upon is the observance of five metrical feet to the line and a general iambic beat. Beyond that, lines can be shared between characters, other stresses introduced, lines run over into very long sentences and punctuation of any sort used. This gives maximum freedom while still preserving the sound and density of poetry. It's an essentially practical kind of poetry, unlike French alexandrines or couplets.

From the early Elizabethan plays, barnstorming works such as *Gorboduc* and *The Spanish Tragedy*, it's only a few years to the naturalisation of the new dramatic form at the hands of Christopher Marlowe. Marlowe can be stiff and metronomic when contrasted with Shakespeare, but in his short life he established beyond doubt the 'mighty line' of English dramatic verse. His examples were followed immediately by a score of masterpieces for the theatre including Shakespeare's, and three of his plays remain among the most successful in the history of the English stage – *Doctor Faustus*, *Tamburlaine the Great* and *Edward II*. *Faustus* starts finely, has a knockabout middle section, but recovers to end in a scene of great power. In this excerpt, the scholar Faust, having sold his soul to Mephistophiles, the Devil, waits in his cell for the hour of reckoning. It's the first great soliloquy in the English theatre.

Ah Faustus,
Now hast thou but one bare hour to live,
And then thou must be dammed perpetually.
Stand still, you ever-moving spheres of heaven,
That time may cease and midnight never come.
Fair nature's eye, rise rise again, and make
Perpetual day. Or let this hour be but
A year, a month, a week, a natural day,
That Faustus may repent and save his soul.
O lente, lente, currite noctis equi.
The stars move still, time runs, the clock will strike.
The devil will come, and Faustus must be damned.
Oh, I'll leap up to my God: who pulls me down?
See, see, where Christ's blood streams in the firmament.
One drop would save my soul, half a drop. Ah, my Christ!
Ah, rend not my heart for naming of my Christ!
Yet will I call on him. Oh, spare me, Lucifer!
Where is it now? 'Tis gone: And see where God
Stretcheth out his arm, and bends his ireful brows.
Mountains and hills, come, come, and fall on me,
And hide me from the heavy wrath of God.
No, no.
Then will I headlong run into the earth.
Earth, gape! Oh no, it will not harbour me.

You stars that reigned at my nativity,
Whose influence hath allotted death and hell,
Now draw up Faustus like a foggy mist
Into the entrails of yon labouring cloud,
That when you vomit forth into the air
My limbs may issue from your smoky mouths,
So that my soul may but ascend to heaven.
    (*The watch strikes.*)
Ah! half the hour is past,
'Twill all be past anon.
Oh God, if thou wilt not have mercy on my soul,
Yet, for Christ's sake whose blood hath ransomed me,
Impose some end to my incessant pain.
Let Faustus live in hell a thousand years,
A hundred thousand, and at last be saved.
Oh, no end is limited to damned souls.
Why wert thou not a creature wanting soul?
Or why is this immortal that thou hast?
Ah, Pythagoras' metempsychosis, were that true
This soul should fly from me, and I be changed
Unto some brutish beast. All beasts are happy,
For when they die,
Their souls are soon dissolved in elements,
But mine must live still to be plagued in hell.
Cursed be the parents that engendered me!
No, Faustus, curse thyself, curse Lucifer,
That hath deprived thee of the joys of heaven.
    (*The clock strikes twelve.*)
Oh, it strikes, it strikes! Now body turn to air,
Or Lucifer will bear thee quick to hell.
    (*Thunder and lightning.*)
Oh soul, be changed into little water drops
And fall into the ocean, ne'er be found.
    (*Thunder. Enter the* DEVILS.)
My God, my god, look not so fierce on me.
Adders and serpents, let me breathe awhile.
Ugly hell, gape not, come not, Lucifer!
I'll burn my books. Ah, Mephostophilis!
    (*Exeunt with him.*)

EPILOGUE
(Enter the CHORUS)

Cut is the branch that might have grown full straight,
And burned is Apollo's laurel bough,
That sometime grew within this learned man.
Faustus is gone. Regard his hellish fall,
Whose fiendful fortune may exhort the wise
Only to wonder at unlawful things,
Whose deepness doth entice such forward wits,
To practise more than heavenly power permits.
(Terminat hora diem, Terminat Author opus. . . .)

The Elizabethan stage was in every way a commercial theatre
and attracted ambitious and hungry young men of talent – some
were university-trained like Marlowe, Greene, Peele and
Marston and some had 'little Latin and less Greek' like Shake-
speare and Dekker. There is very little difference in outlook
between the several schools of drama, Shakespeare's plays being
just as full of classical allusions as those of his university rivals.
Each playwright had to be able to keep the box-office running
and that meant entertaining the groundlings as well as the
gentlemen connoisseurs. Such classical requirements as the
Unities of Time, Place and Action, which the French theatre
took over from Aristotle, went by the board in England. If the
play moved well, was tragic or funny enough and had plenty of
excitement in it, then it could take any shape the author pleased.
The division into five acts, which is usual, bore no relation to the
actual running of the play, since there was no curtain and no set
climax to work for. Every scene was given its own shape and
some of the plays were extremely complex, with several plots
running at the same time. The spectacle-play was highly popular
too. This often took the form of a masque or a tableau. One of
this order was Thomas Nashe's *Summer's Last Will and Testament*,
written in plague time, which includes the following famous
lament. Nash calls it a song.

Adieu, farewell earth's bliss
This world uncertain is.
Fond are life's lustful joys,
Death proves them all but toys.
None from his darts can fly:

73

I am sick, I must die.
    Lord have mercy on us!

Rich men, trust not in wealth;
Gold cannot buy you health.
Physic himself must fade:
All things to end are made.
The plague full swift goes by.
I am sick, I must die.
    Lord have mercy on us!

Beauty is but a flower,
Which wrinkles will devour:
Brightness falls from the air;
Queens have died young and fair.
Dust hath closed Helen's eye.
I am sick, I must die.
    Lord have mercy on us!

Strength stoops unto the grave:
Worms feed on Hector brave.
Swords may not fight with fate:
Earth still holds ope her gate.
Come, come the bells do cry.
I am sick, I must die.
    Lord have mercy on us!

Wit with his wantonness,
Tasteth death's bitterness.
Hell's executioner
Hath no ears for to hear
What vain art can reply.
I am sick, I must die.
    Lord have mercy on us!

Haste therefore each degree
To welcome destiny:
Heaven is our heritage,
Earth but a player's stage.
Mount we unto the sky.
I am sick, I must die.
    Lord have mercy on us!

Songs and music played a great part in the Elizabethan theatre, especially in Shakespeare. Our habit of detaching Shakespeare's songs from his plays gives them a rather unreal, flimsy appearance. They were all designed to be heard dramatically, often ironically. Studies of the use of music in Shakespeare reveal his highly sophisticated approach to the character-delineating power of music, and its considerable effect in establishing a mood or creating an ambiguous tone. One example must suffice. In *Antony and Cleopatra*, there is a stage direction, '*Music of hautboys under the stage.*' One of Antony's soldiers says: ' 'Tis the god Hercules, whom Antony lov'd/Now leaves him.' The mood of bitter premonition is both presaged by the music and given its chance to attain expression thereafter in words. Plays such as *The Tempest* and *Pericles* would be unimaginable without music, as would the majority of Shakespeare's comedies. The very fluidity of Shakespeare's imagination makes him a very difficult poet to quote from without serious dislocation. Here are two songs from his plays, both well known and each possessing that unrivalled aphoristic truthfulness which he mixed in with his lyricism so beautifully. The first is the song which ends *Twelfth Night*.

When that I was and a little tiny boy,
   With hey, ho, the wind and the rain;
A foolish thing was but a toy,
   For the rain it raineth every day.

But when I came to man's estate,
   With hey, ho, the wind and the rain;
'Gainst knaves and thieves men shut their gates,
   For the rain it raineth every day.

But when I came, alas! to wive,
   With hey, ho, the wind and the rain;
By swaggering could I never thrive,
   For the rain it raineth every day.

But when I came unto my beds,
   With hey, ho, the wind and the rain;
With toss-pots still had drunken heads,
   For the rain it raineth every day.

A great while ago the world begun,
   With hey, ho, the wind and the rain;

But that's all one, our play is done,
　　And we'll strive to please you every day.

The second is the 'Dirge' from *Cymbeline*.

Fear no more the heat o' the sun,
　　Nor the furious winter's rages;
Thou thy worldly task hast done,
　　Home art gone, and ta'en thy wages;
Golden lads and girls all must,
　　As chimney-sweepers, come to dust.

Fear no more the frown o' the great,
　　Thou are past the tyrant's stroke:
Care no more to clothe and eat;
　　To thee the reed is as the oak;
The sceptre, learning, physic must
　　All follow this, and come to dust.

Fear no more the lightning-flash,
　　Nor the all-dreaded thunder-stone;
Fear not slander, censure rash;
　　Thou hast finished joy and moan:
All lovers young, all lovers must
　　Consign to thee, and come to dust.

No exorciser harm thee!
　　Nor no witchcraft charm thee!
Ghost unlaid forbear thee!
　　Nothing ill come near thee!
Quiet consummation have;
　　And renowned be thy grave!

Since Shakespeare is the greatest poet England and probably the world has ever known, any treatment of him here must be cursory. It's worth stressing, however, that he was of his own age as well as for all time and that he shares many qualities with his contemporaries, however far he surpasses them. His immediate influence was enormous and all the playwrights who came after him reflect his style. From the beginning, he did far better what Marlowe and the others were doing.

　　Early plays like *Love's Labours Lost* and *A Midsummer Night's Dream* are mines of original and jewelled language. His range is

76

from the sweet and sensuous to the harsh and gritty – he can be extraordinarily simple and almost incomprehensibly elaborate. The next extract is from his high noon – the date is 1599, the play *King Henry V*. This is blank verse used orthodoxly but with a richness never equalled by anyone else. It's the chorus which introduces the Fourth Act and is a description of the English and French Armies encamped the night before the Battle of Agincourt.

> Now entertain conjecture of a time
> When creeping murmur and the poring dark
> Fills the wide vessel of the universe.
> From camp to camp, through the foul womb of night,
> The hum of either army stilly sounds,
> That the fix'd sentinels almost receive
> The secret whispers of each other's watch:
> Fire answers fire, and through their paly flames
> Each battle sees the other's umber'd face:
> Steed threatens steed, in high and boastful neighs
> Piercing the night's dull ear; and from the tents
> The armourers, accomplishing the knights,
> With busy hammers closing rivets up,
> Give dreadful note of preparation.
> The country cocks do crow, the clocks do toll,
> And the third hour of drowsy morning name.
> Proud of their numbers, and secure in soul,
> The confident and over-lusty French
> Do the low-rated English play at dice;
> And chide the cripple tardy-gaited night
> Who, like a foul and ugly witch, doth limp
> So tediously away. The poor condemned English,
> Like sacrifices, by their watchful fires
> Sit patiently, and inly ruminate
> The morning's danger, and their gesture sad
> Investing lank-lean cheeks and war-worn coats
> Presenteth them unto the gazing moon
> So many horrid ghosts. O! now, who will behold
> The royal captain of this ruin'd band
> Walking from watch to watch, from tent to tent,
> Let him cry 'Praise and glory on his head!'

For forth he goes and visits all his host,
Bids them good morrow with a modest smile,
And calls them brothers, friends, and countrymen.
Upon his royal face there is no note
How dread an army hath enrounded him;
Nor doth he dedicate one jot of colour
Unto the weary and all-watched night:
But freshly looks and overbears attaint
With cheerful semblance and sweet majesty;
That every wretch, pining and pale before,
Beholding him, plucks comfort from his looks.
A largess universal, like the sun
His liberal eye doth give to every one,
Thawing cold fear. Then mean and gentle all,
Behold, as may unworthiness define,
A little touch of Harry in the night.

As he grew older, Shakespeare's imagination became more sombre. His great tragedies, *Macbeth, King Lear* and *Hamlet*, are more oppressive than Greek tragedies, since they are higher-pitched and are less concerned with divine justice. Also, his later comedies, though they have happy endings, pass through many sour and despairing phases in the course of their action. One such is *Measure For Measure*, which deals with two of his chief preoccupations – sexual desire and false friendship. Running through this and many of its neighbouring plays is Shakespeare's obsession with death. In this passage the Duke of Vienna tells the offending Claudio to prepare for his forthcoming execution.

Be absolute for death; either death or life
Shall thereby be the sweeter. Reason thus with life:
If I do lose thee, I do lose a thing
That none but fools would keep: a breath thou art,
Servile to all the skyey influences,
That dost this habitation, where thou keep'st,
Hourly afflict. Merely, thou art death's fool;
For him thou labour'st by thy flight to shun,
And yet run'st toward him still. Thou art not noble:
For all th'accommodations that thou bear'st
Are nurs'd by baseness. Thou art by no means valiant;
For thou dost fear the soft and tender fork

Of a poor worm. Thy best of rest is sleep,
And that thou oft provok'st; yet grossly fear'st
Thy death, which is no more. Thou art not thyself;
For thou exist'st on many a thousand grains
That issue out of dust. Happy thou art not;
For what thou has not, still thou striv'st to get,
And what thou hast, forget'st. Thou art not certain;
For thy complexion shifts to strange effects,
After the moon. If thou art rich, thou'rt poor;
For, like an ass whose back with ingots bows,
Thou bear'st thy heavy riches but a journey,
And death unloads thee. Friend hast thou none;
For thine own bowels, which do call thee sire,
The mere effusion of thy proper loins,
Do curse the gout, serpigo, and the rheum,
For ending thee no sooner. Thou hast nor youth nor age;
But, as it were, an after-dinner's sleep,
Dreaming on both; for all thy blessed youth
Becomes as agèd, and doth beg the alms
Of palsied eld; and when thou art old and rich,
Thou hast neither heat, affection, limb, nor beauty,
To make thy riches pleasant. What's yet in this
That bears the name of life? Yet in this life
Lie hid moe thousand deaths: yet death we fear,
That makes these odds all even.

Space must be found for one of his sonnets. In these he gave full rein to his taste for the proverbial. The control of the writing is absolute, the motion of the verse supremely smooth. The peak of his achievement in non-dramatic poetry is Sonnet No. 94, a difficult and profound poem which ruminates on man's mixed nature in a way which anticipates the psychological insights of William Blake.

They that have the power to hurt and will do none,
That do not do the thing they most do show,
Who, moving others, are themselves as stone,
Unmoved, cold, and to temptation slow;
They rightly do inherit heaven's graces,
And husband nature's riches from expense;
They are the lords and owners of their faces,

Others but stewards of their excellence.
The summer's flower is to the summer sweet,
Though to itself it only live and die,
But if that flower with base infection meet,
The basest weed outbraves his dignity:
For sweetest things turn sourest by their deeds;
Lilies that fester smell far worse than weeds.

Shakespeare made his own farewell to his art in *The Tempest*, his last play, where Prospero, the humane master of all magic, renounces his powers and his craft. After this, the poet himself returned to his home at Stratford, where he quietly died. His greatness was fully recognised in his lifetime and his reputation has grown even surer. But this fame shouldn't distance us from his work – no poetry is as approachable as Shakespeare's and none keeps its power so well despite over-familiarity. The following lines of Prospero are among the best-known passages in English verse. It's impossible to imagine them ever losing their force.

Ye elves of hills, brooks, standing lakes and groves;
And ye, that on the sands with printless foot
Do chase the ebbing Neptune and do fly him
When he comes back; you demi-puppets, that
By moonshine do the green sour ringlets make
Whereof the ewe not bites; and you, whose pastime
Is to make midnight mushrooms; that rejoice
To hear the solemn curfew; by whose aid, –
Weak masters though ye be – I have bedimm'd
The noontide sun, call'd forth the mutinous winds,
And 'twixt the green sea and the azur'd vault
Set roaring war: to the dread-rattling thunder
Have I given fire and rifted Jove's stout oak
With his own bolt: the strong-bas'd promontory
Have I made shake; and by the spurs pluck'd up
The pine and cedar: graves at my command
Have wak'd their sleepers, op'd, and let them forth
By my so potent art. But this rough magic
I here abjure; and, when I have requir'd
Some heavenly music, – which even now I do,-
To work mine end upon their senses that

This airy charm is for, I'll break my staff,
Bury it certain fathoms in the earth,
And, deeper than did ever plummet sound,
I'll drown my book.

Ben Jonson (?1573–1637)
John Webster (?1580–1638)
Cyril Tourneur (?1575–1626)
Thomas Middleton (?1570–1627)
John Ford (?1586–1639)   P.P.

Shakespeare retired from the theatre in 1610, the year of Ben
Jonson's greatest play, *The Alchemist*. We know very little about
Shakespeare's life, which is a boon to contentious scholars and
fanciful biographers, but we do know that he was friendly with
Ben Jonson and that each had considerable respect for the other.
Shakespeare acted in Jonson's *Every Man in his Humour*, and
Jonson wrote the famous poem in Shakespeare's memory which
introduces the Folio Collection of Shakespeare's Plays of 1623.
Nevertheless, they are at opposite poles of temperament and
talent, and Jonson is the only writer who shows almost no
influence of Shakespeare. The vogue for masques which came
in with James I suited Jonson very well and he wrote many,
which were lavishly mounted by the great designer/architect
Inigo Jones. Jonson was much more the poet in the theatre than
the dramatist proper, though *Volpone* and *The Alchemist* are
admirably constructed plays. He was happier drawing types or
humours (classified by the Greek writer Theophrastus under
some fifty satirical headings), and his wit is pungent, realistic and
unforgiving. Jonson can rise to great heights when he gives one
of his characters a self-revealing monologue, but he has little of
Shakespeare's sweetness and harmony of language. He is
England's closest approach to the Latin poets of Rome's Silver
Age. He translated Martial, though he resembles Juvenal more.
In tragedy he is completely dominated by the frigid Senecan
models, and plays like *Catiline* and *Sejanus* are failures. He comes
into his own in satirical farce – he did not hate people, as Shake-
speare in his black moods did, but he excoriated their follies
82

unmercifully. *Volpone* and *The Alchemist* are both studies of men's greed and credulity: each of the characters in these plays exhibits one predominant trait, be it lust, avarice, self-love, quackery or ignorance. Ironically, Jonson's reputation as a great classical scholar has done him harm – people warm to the unlettered more than the educated – but his greatest works are not dependent on classical references or modelled on classical examples. When he is developing a vein of inspired lunacy in a character (and the 'gull' or victim is seldom innocent in Jonson; he's usually motivated by greed or snobbery and deserves to be taken in), then Jonson can inflate his rhetoric to a higher pitch than almost any other English poet. He is thoroughly at ease in the consumer society of his time, and loves to catalogue the brand names and status symbols which dominated the lives of King James's subjects as much as they do our own.

The Alchemist of the play, whose name is Subtle (Jonson's names are character-guides, but not yet complete giveaways as names became in the Restoration theatre), is gulling a foolish knight, Sir Epicure Mammon, into subsidising his pursuit of the philosopher's stone, that devoutly-to-be-wished formula for turning base metal into gold. Sir Epicure is not just a greedy man, he has visions of incomparable social grandeur, he is carried away by the figure he will cut when he possesses the secret of limitless wealth. Here Jonson reaches the pinnacle of his poetical invention – the language is extraordinarily rich and yet wildly satirical. This excerpt featuring Sir Epicure Mammon is from Act Two of the play, talking to Subtle's creature, Face.

MAMMON: I will have all my beds blown up, not stuffed;
   Down is too hard. And then, mine oval room
   Filled with such pictures as Tiberius took
   From Elephantis, and dull Aretine
   But coldly imitated. Then my glasses,
   Cut in more subtle angles, to disperse
   And multiply the figures as I walk
   Naked between my succubae. My mists
   I'll have of perfume, vapoured 'bout the room,
   To lose ourselves in; and my baths like pits
   To fall into, from whence we will come forth
   And roll us dry in gossamer and roses.

(Is it arrived at ruby?) – Where I spy
A wealthy citizen or rich lawyer
Have a sublimed pure wife, unto that fellow
I'll send a thousand pound, to be my cuckold.
FACE: And I shall carry it?
MAMMON: No. I'll ha' no bawds,
    But fathers and mothers. They will do it best,
    Best of all others. And my flatterers
    Shall be the pure and gravest of divines,
    That I can get for money. My mere fools
    Eloquent burgesses, and then my poets,
    The same that writ so subtly of the fart,
    Whom I will entertain still for that subject.
    The few that would give out themselves to be
    Court and town stallions and each-where belie
    Ladies who are known most innocent for them:
    Those will I beg to make me eunuchs of,
    And they shall fan me with ten estrich tails
    A-piece, made in a plume, to gather wind.
    We will be brave, Puff, now we ha' the medicine.
    My meat shall all come in in Indian shells,
    Dishes of agate, set in gold, and studded
    With emeralds, sapphires, hyacinths and rubies.
    The tongues of carps, dormice, and camels' heels
    Boiled i' the spirit of Sol, and dissolved pearl
    (Apicius's diet 'gainst the epilepsy).
    And I will eat these broths with spoons of amber,
    Headed with diamond and carbuncle.
    My foot-boy shall eat pheasants, calvered salmons,
    Knots, godwits, lampreys. I myself will have
    The beards of barbels served instead of salads,
    Oiled mushrooms, and the swelling unctuous paps
    Of a fat pregnant sow, newly cut off,
    Dressed with an exquisite and poignant sauce.
    For which I'll say unto my cook 'There's gold:
    Go forth and be a knight.'

While Shakespeare could be a very morbid writer, this tendency
in his work is balanced by an equal emphasis on pleasure and
natural beauty. His successors among the poets who wrote for

the theatres of James I and Charles I were much more drawn to his misanthropic vein than to his happier moods. It's hard to account for this: life was no more brutal than before or death and disease more prevalent. If King James appointed secret police to sniff out conspiracies, Queen Elizabeth and her ministers, Burghley and Walsingham, had done so even more thoroughly. Perhaps the sombre atmosphere of the Counter Reformation on the Continent influenced thinking in England, and the artists of the age, acting as early warning systems, were already pointing to the horrors of the Thirty Years War and the English Civil War. Whatever the reason, the plays of John Webster, Cyril Tourneur, Thomas Middleton and John Ford are bloodthirsty, cruel and conspiratorial to a degree that seems exaggerated to us. They delighted in recounting ingenious ways of killing people – kissing the poisoned lips of a picture, a poisoned skull or a poisoned bible, having your back broken on a vaulting horse, the floor opening up on a supper party to impale the guests on concealed spikes: these playwrights were the Hammer Film men of their day. But with one significant difference – the violence and extravagance of their action enabled them to indulge their talent for highly-coloured emotional poetry. Often enough, what happened was Grand Guignol or Sweeney Todd – what was said, however, transcended the situation and produced magnificent poetry. And they had more than a little justification in their predilection for the grotesque. The courts of Renaissance Italy, after the French and Spanish invasions of the sixteenth century which led to the collapse of the Florentine Republic, degenerated into just such vile and treacherous places as are portrayed on the Jacobean stage. Webster based his play, *The White Devil*, on a series of events connected with the Medicean Grand Duchy of Tuscany and the story of the famous courtesan Vittoria Accoromboni, and several of Middleton's plays follow Italian plots closely. Of course, the detail of the treacheries was taken from the horrors closer to home – familiar terrors at the Court of St James. Webster is a unique artist – there is nobody quite like him. He can make the most extravagant scenes of torture lyrical and somehow uplifting. Shakespeare had already developed the mad scene from its early prototype in *The Spanish Tragedy*. Ophelia in *Hamlet* is the best-known example. Webster served it up in a

85

full dish in *The White Devil* and *The Duchess of Malfi*, his two masterpieces. The following extract is from *The White Devil*. The plot is complicated. Flamineo, who is the real hero, or perhaps villain of the play, is the brother of the courtesan Vittoria. To test the truthfulness of his sister he has pretended to shoot himself, after having obtained from her a promise that she will commit suicide immediately following his death. Thinking him dying, she no longer conceals that she has no intention of keeping her part of the contract. He then reveals that the bullets were blanks and having uncovered her deceit is about to kill her. At this point, the Duke of Florence's men come in and proceed to execute them both by protracted torture.

VITTORIA: What, are you drop't.
FLAMINEO: I am mixt with Earth already: As you are Noble
             Performe your vowes, and bravely follow mee.
VITTORIA: Whither, to hell?
ZANCHE: To most assured damnation.
VITTORIA: O thou most cursed devill.
ZANCHE: Thou art caught.
VITTORIA: In thine owne Engine, I tread the fire out
             That would have bene my ruine.
FLAMINEO: Will you be perjur'd? what a religious oath was
             Styx that the Gods never durst sweare by and violate?
                 O that wee had such an oath to minister, and to
                 be so well kept in our Courts of Justice.
VITTORIA: Thinke whither thou art going.
ZANCHE: And remember
             What villanies thou hast acted.
VITTORIA: This thy death,
             Shall make me like a blazing ominous starre,
             Looke up and tremble.
FLAMINEO: O I am caught with a springe!
VITTORIA: You see the Fox comes many times short home,
             'Tis here prov'd true.
FLAMINEO: Kild with a couple of braches.
VITTORIA: No fitter offring for the infernall furies
             Then one in whom they raign'd while hee was living.
FLAMINEO: O the waies darke and horrid! I cannot see,
             Shall I have no company?

86

VITTORIA: O Yes thy sinnes,
Do runne before thee to fetch fire from hell,
To light thee thither.

FLAMINEO: O I smell soote, most stinking soote, the chimnie
is a fire,
My livers purboil'd like scotch holly-bread;
There's a plumber, laying pipes in my guts, it
scalds;
Will thou out-live mee?

ZANCHE: Yes, and drive a stake
Through thy body; for we'le give it out,
Thou didst this violence upon thy selfe.

(Flamineo riseth.)

FLAMINEO: O cunning Devils! now I have tri'd your love,
And doubled all your reaches. I am not wounded:
The pistols held no bullets: 'twas a plot
To prove your kindnesse to mee: and I live
To punish your ingratitude, I knew
One time or other you would finde a way
To give me a strong potion, O Men
That lye upon your death-beds, and are haunted
With howling wives, neere trust them, they'le re
marry
Ere the worme pierce your winding sheete: ere the
Spider
Make a thinne curtaine for your Epitaphes.
How cunning you were to discharge? Do you
practise at the Artillery yard? Trust a woman;
never, never; Brachiano bee my President: we lay
our soules to pawne to the Devill for a little
pleasure and a woman makes the bill of sale. That
ever man should marry! For one Hypermnestra
that sav'd her Lord and husband, forty nine of
her sisters cut their husbands throates all in one
night. There was a shole of vertuous horse-
leeches.

(The next passage does not follow immediately. In the omitted
lines, the Duke of Florence's executioners have arrived.)

VITTORIA: My soule, like to a ship in a blacke storme,
Is driven I know not whither.
FLAMINEO: Then cast ancor.
Prosperity doth bewitch men seeming cleere,
But seas doe laugh, shew white, when Rocks are neere.
Wee cease to greive, cease to be fortunes slaves,
Nay cease to dye by dying. Art thou gonne
And thou so neare the bottome: falce reporte
Which saies that woemen vie with the nine Muses
For nine tough durable lives: I doe not looke
Who went before, nor who shall follow mee;
Noe, at my selfe I will begin and end:
While we looke up to heaven wee confound
Knowledge with knowledge. O I am in a mist.
VITTORIA: O happy they that never saw the Court,
Nor ever knew great Men but by report.

(Vittoria dyes.)

FLAMINEO: I recover like a spent taper, for a flash
And instantly go out.
Let all that belong to Great men remember th'
ould wives tradition, to be like the Lyons i'th
Tower on Candlemas day to mourne if the
Sunne shine, for feare of the pittiful remainder
of winter to come.
'Tis well yet there's some goodnesse in my death,
My life was a blacke charnell: I have caught
An everlasting could. I have lost my voice
Most irrecoverably: Farewell glorious villaines,
This busie trade of life appeares most vaine,
Since rest breeds rest, where all seeke paine by paine.
Let no harsh flattering Bels resound my knell,
Strike thunder, and strike lowde to my farewell.

(Flamineo dies.)

Cyril Tourneur is less episodic in his construction than Webster and brings a terrible logic to his storytelling. He adds misogyny to Webster's misanthropy but he also has a sprightliness and lack of self-pity which distinguishes him from Webster and Shakespeare. His play, *The Revenger's Tragedy*, is like a theorem drawn in blood.

In this passage, Vendice is soliloquising over the skull of his dead beloved – not at all an unlikely circumstance in Tourneur's world. His business is to avenge her murder, but here briefly he draws a general picture of the vanity and eclipse of man's mortal life.

VENDICE: And now methinks I could e'en chide myself
  For doting on her beauty, though her death
  Shall be reveng'd after no common action.
  Does the silk-worm expend her yellow labours
  For thee? for thee does she undo herself?
  Are lordships sold to maintain ladyships
  For the poor benefit of a bewildering minute?
  Why does yon fellow falsify high-ways,
  And put his life between the judge's lips,
  To refine such a thing? Keeps horse and men
  To beat their valours for her?
  Surely we are all mad people, and they
  Whom we think are, are not; we mistake those:
  'Tis we are mad in sense, they but in clothes.
HIPPOLITO: Faith, and in clothes too we, give us our due.
VENDICE: Does every proud and self-affecting dame
  Camphor her face for this? and grieve her maker
  In sinful baths of milk, when many an infant starves
  For her superfluous outside – all for this?
  Who now bids twenty pound a night, prepares
  Music, perfumes and sweetmeats? All are hush'd;
  Thou may'st lie chaste now. It were fine, methinks,
  To have thee seen at revels, forgetful feasts,
  And unclean brothels; sure, 'twould fright the sinner,
  And make him a good coward, put a reveller
  Out of his antic amble,
  And cloy an epicure with empty dishes.
  Here might a scornful and ambitious woman
  Look through and through herself; – see, ladies, with false forms
  You deceive men, but cannot deceive worms.

Thomas Middleton has many qualities which duplicate those of

Webster and Tourneur. His greatest plays, *The Changeling* and *Women Beware Women*, are firmly drawn pictures of depravity, stronger perhaps in character and plot than in poetry. Indeed, the conspirator, De Flores, in *The Changeling* is generally considered the most rounded-out figure in Jacobean drama outside Shakespeare. Middleton is a shadowy man – he did not cut a figure in the literary world as Jonson did, nor loom as a mysterious creative force like Shakespeare. Born today, he'd be a TV playwright refusing interviews in Portugal – a sort of B. Traven, since the cast of his mind is sceptical and rebellious. One of his plays, *A Game at Chess*, cost him a spell in prison. The most remarkable aspects of his work are his down-to-earth descriptions, which foreshadow the realism of the prose dramatists of the Restoration, especially Wycherly and Vanbrugh. He uses blank verse, but so conversationally the heroic beat has almost disappeared. Here is a speech from his comedy of London manners, entitled *A Chaste Maid in Cheapside*. This soliloquy is by the complaisant Allwit, a Shavian character who earns his living by letting another man maintain his household and even relieve him of the duty of sleeping with his wife.

ALLWIT: The founder's come to town: I'm like a man
    Finding a table furnished to his hand,
    As mine is still to me, prays for the founder, –
    Bless the right worshipful the good founder's life!
    I thank him, has maintained my house this ten years;
    Not only keeps my wife, but 'a keeps me
    And all my family; I'm at his table:
    He gets me all my children, and pays the nurse
    Monthly or weekly; puts me to nothing, rent,
    Nor church duties, not so much as the scavenger:
    The happiest state that ever man was born to!
    I walk out in a morning; come to breakfast,
    Find excellent cheer; a good fire in winter;
    Look in my coal-house about midsummer eve,
    That's full, five or six chaldron new laid up;
    Look in my back-yard, I shall find a steeple
    Made up with Kentish faggots, which o'erlooks
    The water-house and the windmills: I say nothing,
    But smile and pin the door. When she lies in,

As now she's even upon the point of grunting,
A lady lies not in like her; there's her embossings,
Embroiderings, spanglings, and I know not what,
As if she lay with all the gaudy-shops
In Gresham's Burse about her; then her restoratives,
Able to set up a young 'pothecary,
And richly stock the foreman of a drug-shop;
Her sugar by whole loaves, her wines by rundlets.
I see these things, but, like a happy man,
I pay for none at all; yet fools think's mine;
I have the name, and in his gold I shine:
And where some merchants would in soul kiss hell
To buy a paradise for their wives, and dye
Their conscience in the bloods of prodigal heirs
To deck their night-piece, yet all this being done,
Eaten with jealousy to the inmost bone, –
As what affliction nature more constrains,
Than feed the wife plump for another's veins? –
These torments stand I freed of; I'm as clear
From jealousy of a wife as from the charge:
O, two miraculous blessings! 'tis the knight
Hath took that labour all out of my hands:
I may sit still and play; he's jealous for me,
Watches her steps, sets spies; I live at ease,
He has both the cost and torment: when the string
Of his heart frets, I feed, laugh, or sing.

The last great dramatist of this incomparably rich age is John
Ford. The title of his most famous play, *'Tis Pity She's a Whore*,
has misled generations of readers. Ford is one of the least
prurient of playwrights. His work is darkened by a great
melancholy: his concern is with love, not sex. His tone is gentler
than his predecessors and more resigned. All his best plays were
published as late as the middle of the 1630s, well into the reign
of Charles I. His play *The Broken Heart* is one of the most moving
in the language. Set in ancient Sparta, its classical names, each
embodying a passion, have encouraged some of our shallower
dramatic critics to poke fun at Ford. But in performance *The
Broken Heart* is the one English play which reproduces the tragic
inevitability of ancient Greek drama. In this extract, Penthea, the

woman dying of a broken heart, is talking with three men – her brother Ithocles (his name is Greek for 'honour of loveliness'), Bassanes (Greek for 'vexation') and Orgilus (Greek for 'anger'). Penthea's marriage to Bassanes was mere rape, but it makes her love for Orgilus impossible. Penthea's own name means 'lamenting' and it's interesting to note the much quieter way Ford portrays her madness than either Webster or Shakespeare would have done.

PENTHEA: Sure, if we were all Sirens, we should sing
   pitifully;
   And 'twere a comely music, when in parts
   One sung another's knell. The turtle sighs
   When he hath lost his mate; and yet some say
   'A must be dead first. 'Tis a fine deceit
   To pass away in a dream; indeed, I've slept
   With mine eyes open a great while. No falsehood
   Equals a broken faith; there's not a hair
   Sticks on my head but like a leaden plummet
   It sinks me to the grave. I must creep thither;
   The journey is not long.

ITHOCLES: But thou, Penthea,
   Hast many years, I hope, to number yet,
   Ere thou canst travel that way.

BASSANES: Let the sun first
   Be wrapped up in an everlasting darkness,
   Before the light of nature, chiefly formed
   For the whole world's delight, feel an eclipse
   So universal.

ORGILUS: Wisdom, look'ee, begins
   To rave. – Art thou mad, too, antiquity?

PENTHEA: Since I was first a wife,
   I might have been Mother to many pretty prattling
   babes.
   They would have smiled when I smiled, and for
   certain
   I should have cried when they cried: – truly,
   brother,
   My father would have picked me out a husband,
   And then my little ones had been no bastards.

But 'tis too late for me to marry now,
I am past child-bearing; 'tis not my fault.

BASSANES: Fall on me, if there be a burning Etna,
And bury me in flames. Sweats hot as sulphur
Boil through my pores. Affliction hath in store
No torture like to this.

ORGILUS: Behold a patience!
Lay by thy whining grey dissimulation,
Do something worth a chronicle; show justice
Upon the author of this mischief; dig out
The jealousies that hatched this thraldom first
With thine own poniard. Every antic rapture
Can roar as thine does.

ITHOCLES: Orgilus, forbear.

BASSANES: Disturb him not; it is a talking motion
Provided for my torment. What a fool am I
To bandy passion! Ere I'll speak a word,
I will look on and burst.

PENTHEA (*to* ORGILUS):   I loved you once.

ORGILUS: Thou didst, wronged creature, in despite of
    malice;
For it I love thee ever.

PENTHEA: Spare your hand;
Believe me, I'll not hurt it.

ORGILUS: Pain my heart too!

PENTHEA: Complain not though I wring it hard. I'll kiss it;
Oh, 'tis a fine soft palm! Hark, in thine ear:
Like whom do I look, prithee? Nay, no whispering.
Goodness! we had been happy; too much happiness
Will make folk proud, they say – but that is he –
                    (*points at* ITHOCLES)
And yet he paid for 't home; alas, his heart
Is crept into the cabinet of the princess;
We shall have points and bride-laces. Remember,
When we last gathered roses in the garden,
I found my wits; but truly you lost yours.
That's he, and still 'tis he.
                    (*points at* ITHOCLES *again*)

ITHOCLES: Poor soul, how idly
Her fancies guide her tongue.

BASSANES: Keep in, vexation,
And break not into clamour.
ORGILUS: She has tutored me;
Some powerful inspiration checks my laziness. –
Now let me kiss your hand, grieved beauty.
PENTHEA: Kiss it. –
Alack, alack, his lips be wondrous cold;
Dear soul, h'as lost his colour: have 'ee seen
A straying heart? All crannies! every drop
Of blood is turned to an amethyst,
Which married bachelors hang in their ears.
ORGILUS: Peace usher her into Elysium.
If this be madness, madness is an oracle.

Thomas Campion (1567–1620)
Sir Walter Raleigh (?1552–1618)
Fulke Greville, Lord Brooke (1554–1628)
John Donne (1572–1631)   P.P.

———————◆———————

There's a strange law of human vitality which ensures that a brilliant epoch will spread its achievements in almost every direction; so that while England in Elizabeth's and James's reigns was less powerful politically than her Continental neighbours, she was experiencing great success in all areas that were new. The foundations of her overseas Empire were being laid (Sir Walter Raleigh established the colony of Virginia not long after the defeat of the Spanish Armada), and at home the first and greatest flowering of English literature was taking place. Also, composers such as Byrd, Morley, Weelkes, Wilbye, Dowland and Gibbons were bringing English music to a height never reached before. The same Sir Walter Raleigh to whom we owe potatoes and tobacco was one of the finest writers of lyrics of the age, and almost all his fellow-courtiers were accomplished in poetry and music. The great stage-plays, in which our most virile poetry lies, were by no means the only achievements of the poets of the time. Translation flourished, imitations of the classics were published and lyrical poetry enjoyed a rare popularity. The arts complemented each other, and one reason for their high standard was the quality of the audience. Readers of poetry were also able to write it, and Queen Elizabeth's skill at the keyboard encouraged her subjects to play as well as to listen to music. Some of the English madrigalist composers, notably Thomas Weelkes, John Wilbye, John Ward and Orlando Gibbons, had very good taste in poetry and selected the poems they set with care. The madrigal, like so many Elizabethan forms, was an Italian invention and was already old-fashioned on the Continent when it was taken up in England. But the English

95

genius has always been able to find the new inside the old, and in the hands of the composers of Elizabeth's last years the madrigal was a much more original and audacious composition than it had been in Italy. Weelkes, whose music has many bizarre twists of melody and harmony, liked to use equally original and *outré* poems. Here are two of them, both anonymous and each reflecting Weelkes's sardonic humour. The first, 'Thule, The Period of Cosmography', sets sailors' tales from the northern and southern oceans as small wonders beside the extremities of love. The music is sombre and brilliant by turns, with remarkable harmonic progressions. The second is a light-hearted but satirical *scherzo*; the sort of thing Ben Jonson might have written if he'd been a musician.

Thule, the period of cosmography,
    Doth vaunt of Hecla, whose sulphureous fire
Doth melt the frozen clime and thaw the sky;
    Trinacrian Etna's flames ascend not higher;
These things seem wondrous, yet more wondrous I,
Whose heart with fear doth freeze, with love doth fry.

The Andalusian merchant, that returns
    Laden with cochineal and china dishes,
Reports in Spain how strangely Fogo burns
    Amidst an ocean full of flying fishes:
These things seem wondrous, yet more wondrous I,
Whose heart with fear doth freeze, with love doth fry.

        Ha ha! ha ha! This world doth pass
        Most merrily, I'le bee sworne,
        For many an honest Indian Asse
        Goes for a unicorne,

          Farra diddle diddle dyno
          This is idle fyno.

        Tee hee! tee hee! O sweet delight,
        He tickles this age that can
        Call Tullia's Ape a Marmasyte,
        And Leda's goose a swan.

          Farra diddle diddle dyno,
          This is idle fyno.

So so! so so! fine English dayes,
For false play is no reproach,
For he that doth the Coachman prayse,
May safely use the Coach.

Farra diddle diddle dyno,
This is idle fyno.

The solo song, usually accompanied by a lute, was almost as
popular as the concerted madrigal. The unchallenged master of
the form was John Dowland, the one English musician with a
widespread Continental reputation. Dowland was renowned for
his richly decorated melancholy tunes – he even took as his
motto, *Semper Dowland, semper dolens* (Dowland is always doleful).
We don't know who wrote most of the poems he set; perhaps he
himself had a hand in them.

One uncharacteristically cheerful piece by him, 'Fine knacks for
ladies', is not only an excellent lyric but also impersonates just
such a sententious vagabond as Shakespeare created in the person
of Autolycus in *The Winter's Tale*.

Fine knacks for ladies, cheap, choice, brave and new!
    Good pennyworths – but money cannot move:
I keep a fair but for the Fair to view –
    A beggar may be liberal of love.
Though all my wares be trash, the heart is true,
                    The heart is true.

Great gifts are guiles and look for gifts again;
    My trifles come as treasures from my mind:
It is a precious jewel to be plain;
    Sometimes in shell the orient'st pearls we find.
Of others take a sheaf, of me a grain!
                    Of me a grain!

Within this pack pins, points, laces, and gloves,
    And divers toys fitting a country fair;
But in my heart, where duty serves and loves,
    Turtles and twins, court's brood, a heavenly pair –
Happy the heart that thinks of no removes!
                    Of no removes!

The most singular of the lutanist composers was Thomas

Campion, who wrote all his own lyrics and many more for his composer friend, Philip Rosseter. Campion was a fine poet with an excellent knowledge of Greek and Latin prosody. He was also a physician and a deviser of masques for the stage. While Campion's music is less adventurous than Dowland's, his poems are among the most perfect lyrics in English. They are all short, as he usually wrote in slow time, taking great care in the setting that each word should be heard. Two brief and exquisite poems are 'Thrice toss these oaken ashes in the air' and 'Never weather-beaten saile' – the one a ritual to invoke love, and the other a prayer to God.

Thrice toss these oaken ashes in the air;
Thrice sit thou mute in this enchanted chair;
Then thrice three times tie up this true love's knot,
And murmur soft: 'She will, or she will not.'
Go burn these poisonous weeds in yon blue fire,
These screech-owl's feathers and this prickling briar,
This cypress gathered at a dead man's grave,
That all thy fears and cares an end may have.
Then come, you fairies, dance with me a round;
Melt her hard heart with your melodious sound.
In vain are all the charms I can devise;
She hath an art to break them with her eyes.

Never weather-beaten Saile more willing bent to shore,
Never tyred Pilgrims limbs affected slumber more,
Than my wearied spright now longs to flye out of my
    troubled brest.
O come quickly, sweetest Lord, and take my soule to rest,

Ever-blooming are the joys of Heav'ns high paradice,
Cold age deafes not there our eares, nor vapour dims our
    eyes:
Glory there the Sun outshines, whose beames the blessed
    onely see;
O come quickly, glorious Lord, and raise my spright to thee.

Though Orlando Gibbons set one of Sir Walter Raleigh's poems as a madrigal, that tough courtier was generally too sardonic and disillusioned to attract musicians. Raleigh was soldier, courtier, privateer, explorer and patron of the arts and sciences, as well as poet. Those of his poems which have survived combine directness with a sharp and fanciful imagination. The realities of power at close quarters (and Raleigh spent his whole life at court) made him a sceptic of all the outward trappings of magnificence, as his poem 'The Lie' reveals. His judgment on courts and courtiers had a grim justice, since he was himself executed in old age for disappointing the expectations of King James I.

Goe soule the bodies guest
   upon a thanklesse arrant,
Feare not to touch the best,
   the truth shall be thy warrant:
Goe since I needs must die,
   and give the world the lie.

Say to the Court it glowes,
   and shines like rotten wood,
Say to the Church it showes
   what's good, and doth no good.
If Church and Court reply,
   then give them both the lie.

Tell Potentates they live
   acting by others action,
Not loved unlesse they give,
   not strong but by affection.
If Potentates reply,
   give Potentates the lie.

Tell men of high condition,
   that mannage the estate,
Their purpose is ambition,
   their practise onely hate:
And if they once reply,
   then give them all the lie.

Tell them that brave it most,
   they beg for more by sepending,
Who in their greatest cost
   seek nothing but commending.

And if they make replie,
  then give them all the lie.

Tell zeale it wants devotion
  tell love it is but lust
Tell time it meets but motion,
  tell flesh it is but dust.
And wish them not replie
  for thou must give the lie.

Tell age it daily wasteth,
  tell honour how it alters.
Tell beauty how she blasteth
  tell favour how it alters
And as they shall reply,
  give every one the lie.

Tell wit how much it wrangles
  in tickle points of nycenesse,
Tell wisedome she entangles
  her selfe in over wisenesse.
And when they doe reply
  straight give them both the lie.

Tell Phisicke of her boldness,
  tell skill it is prevention:
Tell charity of coldness,
  tell law it is contention,
And as they doe reply
  so give them still the lie.

Tell fortune of her blindnesse,
  tell nature of decay,
Tell friendship of unkindnesse,
  tell justice of delay.
And if they will reply,
  then give them all the lie.

Tell arts they have no soundnesse,
  but vary by esteeming,
Tell schooles they want profoundnes
  and stand too much on seeming.

If arts and schooles reply,
　giue arts and schooles the lie.

Tell faith it's fled the Citie,
　tell how the country erreth,
Tell manhood shakes off pitie,
　tell vertue least preferreth
And if they doe reply,
　spare not to give the lie.

So when thou hast as I,
　commanded thee, done blabbing,
Because to give the lie,
　deserves no lesse then stabbing,
Stab at thee he that will,
　no stab thy soule can kill.

A courtier of less volatile disposition, who was also a great poet, was Fulke Greville, Lord Brooke. Greville has been overlooked in the standard histories of English literature, since his philosophical temperament makes him unsympathetic to admirers of the simpler forms of Elizabethan lyricism. Greville had more in common with Continental writers, such as Pascal, than with his English colleagues. He handles rhymed verse with great skill, but does not concern himself with brilliance or virtuosity. The ordered security of his language and the excellence of his reasoning make him one of our most intellectual poets. His cast of mind was pessimistic and he was without Raleigh's impetuosity or his friend Sir Philip Sidney's hedonism. Greville stands alone in his own time and there have been few like him since. His poetry had a special flavour, neither bitter nor reconciled, but reflective and aphoristic. One of his best-known poems is the 'Chorus Sacerdotum' from his closet-drama *Mustapha*. It's not the finest thing he wrote, but its gloomy authority is entirely characteristic and shows Greville's considerable talent for generalising.

Oh, wearisome condition of humanity,
Born under one law, to another bound;
Vainly begot, and yet forbidden vanity,
Created sick, commanded to be sound.
What meaneth nature by these diverse laws?

Passion and reason self-division cause.
It is the mark and majesty of power
To make offences that it may forgive.
Nature herself doth her own self deflower.
To hate those errors she herself doth give.
For how should man think that he may not do,
If nature did not fail and punish too?
Tyrant to others, to herself unjust,
Only commands things difficult and hard,
Forbids us all things which it knows is lust,
Makes easy pains, unpossible reward.
If nature did not take delight in blood,
She would have made more easy ways to good.
We that are bound by vows and by promotion,
With pomp of holy sacrifice and rites,
To teach belief in God and still devotion,
To preach of heaven's wonders and delights –
Yet, when each of us in his own heart looks,
He finds the God there far unlike his books.

Except for Shakespeare the greatest poet of the age was John
Donne. Donne, for all his intellectual power, was an amateur,
attracted neither to the formal world of letters presided over by
Ben Jonson, nor to the theatre, where so many famous names
prospered. Donne's passionate nature and split personality
make him very modern. His invention of a style of wit-writing,
which sprang from a fashionable interest in science and philo-
sophy, plus the townsman's need for up-to-date metaphors,
and which has been mis-named 'metaphysical', changed the
entire course of English poetry. Donne was precocious, ambitious
and wayward, but he had the ability to make himself loved. He
pursued God in his later years with the same extravagant
declarations he devoted to women in his youth. Indeed, if there
is one consistent attitude throughout his writings, it is his
casting of himself in the role of a wooer. Whether or not he
expected the women he wooed to yield, he bombarded them
with audacious poems. His wooing of God has the same mixture
of rhetorical bullying and proud humility. He is never moderate,
but always at extremes. In a late devotional poem, he apologises
to God for all his profane mistresses, yet the terms of his devotion

to the Almighty are equally jealous. As a young man at Lincoln's Inn, he was described by a friend as 'very neat, a great visitor of ladies', and if his ladies had any taste for verse, they must have found it hard to resist so passionate a pleader. Donne never saw any incompatibility between cleverness and sincerity. His sexual sieges were in earnest, but his poems remained playful and exaggerated. The word 'conceit', used to describe his far-fetched comparisons, is only a corruption of the word 'concept'. Donne was a great conceptualiser – many of his poems are burlesques which say 'what if?' or 'suppose' or 'since that is so, then why not this?' Getting between the sheets with a girl was often his first purpose but the poem itself was an even greater challenge. Here we must follow the course of Donne's career – from sexual matters to sacred – in just three poems. Though the object and purpose change, the manner remains the same. First, an early poem entitled 'The Flea'. In the first stanza the blood of poet and girl has already mixed in the flea which has bitten each of them. Donne suggests that like the flea their sexual joy will grow by feeding on the bodies of them both. In the second stanza, she has threatened to kill the flea – i.e. to destroy their love. He points out that if she does so, she also kills part of himself and herself, and he blasphemously draws a parallel with the Trinity. In the third stanza, she has done it – purpled her nail with the flea's blood. The flea is now her honour and not their love. She has killed the thing she thought danger-ous – their love – but his wit has turned it back into something he wishes her to be rid of – her own honour. The poem has come full circle and the girl has now no good reason to refuse him.

It's entirely typical of Donne that he should argue from so unaphrodisiac an object as a body flea. Yet the intensity of his regard for physical love cannot be doubted.

> Marke but this flea, and marke in this,
> How little that which thou deny'st me is;
> It suck'd me first, and now sucks thee,
> And in this flea, our two bloods mingled bee;
> Thou know'st that this cannot be said
> A sinne, nor shame, nor losse of maidenhead,
>   Yet this enjoyes before it wooe,

And pamper'd swells with one blood made of two,
And this, alas, is more than wee would doe.

Oh stay, three lives in one flea spare,
Where wee almost, yea more than maryed are.
This flea is you and I, and this
Our mariage bed, and mariage temple is;
Though parents grudge, and you, w'are met,
And cloysterd in these living walls of Jet.
　　Though use make you apt to kill mee,
　　Let not to that, selfe murder added bee,
　　And sacrilege, three sinnes in killing three.

Cruell and sodaine, hast thou since
Purpled thy naile, in blood of innocence?
Wherein could this flea guilty bee,
Except in that drop which it suckt from thee?
Yet thou triumph'st, and saist that thou
Find'st not thy selfe, nor mee the weaker now;
　　'Tis true, then learne how false feares bee;
　　Just so much honor, when thou yeeld'st to mee,
　　Will wast, as this flea's death tooke life from thee.

The second poem is, on the face of it, more circumstantial. It abounds in the sort of practical detail of love affairs which the novelist Laclos put into his *Les Liaisons dangereuses*. But the fantastic element is not absent. The scene is a girl's house – she and the poet have been making love and although he has covered his tracks perfectly, he is betrayed to her family by the perfume she was wearing, which now hangs about him. The situation is not entirely serious – it may never have taken place but been culled from the hundreds of stories of love and deception which abound in European literature, such as those in the *Decameron* of Boccaccio.

But Donne plants it superbly before our eyes in verse of concrete detail. It is his Fourth Elegy, entitled 'The Perfume', and is written in the form Alexander Pope was later to bring to perfect proportions – the heroic couplet, rhymed iambic pentameter. Donne is not very strict with metre or rhyme; everything is subordinated to dramatic effect.

104

Once, and but once found in thy company,
All thy suppos'd escapes are laid on mee;
And as a thiefe at barre, is question'd there
By all the men, that have beene rob'd that yeare,
So am I, (by this traiterous meanes surpriz'd)
By thy Hydroptique father catechiz'd.
Though he had wont to search with glazed eyes,
As though he came to kill a Cockatrice,
Though hee hath oft sworne, that hee would remove
Thy beauties beautie, and food of our love,
Hope of his goods, if I with thee were seene,
Yet close and secret, as our soules, we'have beene.
Though thy immortall mother which doth lye
Still buried in her bed, yet will not dye,
Takes this advantage to sleepe out day-light,
And watch thy entries, and returnes all night,
And, when she takes thy hand, and would seeme kind,
Doth search what rings, and armelets she can finde,
And kissing notes the colour of thy face,
And fearing least thou'art swolne, doth thee embrace;
To trie if thou long, doth name strange meates,
And notes thy palenesse, blushing, sighs, and sweats;
And politiquely will to thee confesse
The sinnes of her owne youths ranke lustinesse;
Yet love these Sorceries did remove, and move
Thee to gull thine owne mother for my love.
Thy little brethren, which like Faiery Sprights
Oft skipt into our chamber, those sweet nights,
And kist, and ingled on thy fathers knee,
Were brib'd next day, to tell what they did see:
The grim eight-foot-high iron-bound serving-man,
That oft names God in oathes, and onely then,
He that to barre the first gate, doth as wide
As the great Rhodian Colossus stride,
Which, if in hell no other paines there were,
Makes mee feare hell, because he must be there:
Though by thy father he were hir'd to this,
Could never witnesse any touch or kisse.
But Oh, too common ill, I brought with mee
That, which betray'd mee to my enemie:

A loud perfume, which at my entrance cryed
Even at thy fathers nose, so were wee spied.
When, like a tyran King, that in his bed
Smelt gunpowder, the pale wretch shivered.
Had it beene some bad smell, he would have thought
That his owne feet, or breath, that smell had wrought.
But as wee in our Ile emprisoned,
Where cattell onely, and diverse dogs are bred,
The pretious Unicornes, strange monsters call,
So thought he good, strange, that had none at all.
I taught my silkes, their whistling to forbeare,
Even my opprest shoes, dumbe and speechlesse were,
Onely, thou bitter sweet, whom I had laid
Next mee, mee traiterously hast betraid,
And unsuspected hast invisibly
At once fled unto him, and staid with mee.
Base excrement of earth, which dost confound
Sense, from distinguishing the sicke from sound;
By thee the seely Amorous sucks his death
By drawing in a leprous harlots breath;
By thee, the greatest staine to mans estate
Falls on use, to be call'd effeminate;
Though you be much lov'd in the Princes hall,
There, things that seeme, exceed substantiall.
Gods, when yee fum'd on altars, were pleas'd well,
Because you'were burnt, not that they lik'd your smell;
You'are loathsome all, being taken simply alone,
Shall wee love ill things joyn'd, and hate each one?
If you were good, your good doth soone decay;
And you are rare, that takes the good away.
All my perfumes, I give most willingly
To'embalme thy fathers corse; What? will hee die?

Donne married Ann More against her family's wishes when
he was twenty-nine. He loved her greatly but the marriage nearly
ruined him and set his career back by many years. She bore him
eleven children and his struggle to support them and the gradual
darkening of his mind led him back to the Church. His marriage
had ruled out a court appointment, so his best chance of prefer-
ment lay in taking orders. Eventually, he became Dean of St

Paul's Cathedral and attracted large congregations to listen to his elaborate and frightening sermons. His later poems are all religious, though just as impassioned as his early love lyrics. England was not unaffected by the Counter-Reformation and Donne's baroque poems are full of the hysteria which accompanied the return to faith on the Continent. It was well in character for him to pose for a painting in his shroud only a month or so before his death. Perhaps the most remarkable of his religious poems are the Holy Sonnets. One of these is the third Donne poem to be quoted. It's No. 17, and takes his grief at his wife's death as the occasion to bring himself closer to God. It's less famous than some of the others, being quieter in tone and more euphonious in language. But it shows very well how, even in his devotional mood, Donne felt love (including physical love) to be the mainspring of human life and of poetical creation.

Since she whom I lov'd hath payd her last debt
To Nature, and to hers, and my good is dead,
And her Soule early into heaven ravished,
Wholly on heavenly things my mind is sett.
Here the admyring her my mind did whett
To seeke thee God; so streames do shew the head;
But though I have found thee, and thou my thirst hast fed,
A holy thirsty dropsy melts mee yett.
But why should I begg more Love, when as thou
Dost wooe my soule for hers; offring all thine:
And dost not only feare least I allow
My Love to Saints and Angels things divine,
But in thy tender jealousy dost doubt
Least the World, Fleshe, yea Devill putt thee out.

George Herbert (1593–1633) A.T.

With George Herbert, the mistake is to suppose that he was a simple soul. He valued simplicity, and his poems aren't difficult if one has a reasonable familiarity with the Bible; but Herbert himself was a complex, sophisticated man, born into an aristocratic family, brought up to value intellectual attainments, apt and practised in rhetorical and linguistic nimbleness, and for much of his life ambitious for worldly success. Like Spenser, he arrived at a point in his career when he realised that these ambitions were likely to come to nothing; but, unlike Spenser, he used that realisation not to withdraw into his own creative life and concentrate solely on his poetry, but to take the unusual step – for a man of such background and attainments – of becoming a country parson. His final years were spent in the happy self-abnegation of looking after his parishioners, not with resigned or bitter austerity but apparently with joy. The whole exercise was one of reconciliation, and Herbert's poetry is a poetry of reconciliation.

The world of privileged scholarship, of the court and courtliness, and of sexual passion – the world he renounced – is seen persuasively yet steadily in his poem 'The Pearl': this is the 'pearl of great price' which, paradoxically, he gained through making his priestly decision:

> I know the wayes of Learning; both the head
> And pipes that feed the presse, and make it runne;
> What Reason hath from Nature borrowèd,
> Or of itself, like a good huswife, spunne
> In laws and policie; what the starres conspire,
> What willing Nature speaks, what forc'd by fire;
> Both th'old discoveries and the newfound seas,
> The stock and surplus, cause and historie, –

All these stand open, or I have the keyes:
                    Yet I love Thee.

I know the wayes of Honour, what maintains
The quick returns of courtesie and wit;
In vies of favours whether partie gains;
When glorie swells the heart, and moldeth it
To all expressions both of hand and eye;
Which on the world a true-love knot may tie,
And bear the bundle, wheresoe're it goes;
How many drammes of spirit there must be
To sell my life unto my friends or foes:
                    Yet I love Thee.

I know the ways of Pleasure, the sweet strains,
The lullings and the relishes of it;
The propositions of hot bloud and brains;
What mirth and musick mean; what Love and Wit
Have done these twentie hundred years and more;
I know the projects of unbridled store:
My stuffe is flesh, not brasse; my senses live,
And grumble oft that they have more in me
Then He that curbs them, being but one to five:
                    Yet I love Thee.

I know all these, and have them in my hand:
Therefore not seelèd, but with open eyes
I fly to Thee, and fully understand
Both the main sale and the commodities;
And at what rate and price I have Thy Love,
With all the circumstances that may move:
Yet through these labyrinths, not my groveling wit,
But thy silk-twist let down from heav'n to me,
Did both conduct and teach me how by it
                    To climb to Thee.

'Therefore not seelèd, but with open eyes . . .': Herbert knew
what he was doing, and accepted the cost. But it couldn't be
done without some strain, and it's that sense of strain, of
rebelliousness against discipline, that he handles so dramatically

and with such an inevitable rhythm of movement towards peace in his poem 'The Collar'. It opens with the thrust and colloquial rapidity of Donne, whose poems Herbert had almost certainly read in manuscript, for his mother, Magdalen Herbert, was a friend and patron of Donne's:

I struck the board, and cry'd, No more;
I will abroad.
What, shall I ever sigh and pine?
My lines and life are free; free as the road,
Loose as the winde, as large as store.
Shall I be still in suit?
Have I no harvest but a thorn
To let me bloud, and not restore
What I have lost with cordiall fruit?
Sure there was wine
Before my sighs did drie it; there was corn
Before my tears did drown it;
Is the year onely lost to me?
Have I no bayes to crown it,
No flowers, no garlands gay? all blasted,
All wasted?
Not so, my heart; but there is fruit,
And thou hast hands.
Recover all thy sigh-blown age
On double pleasures; leave thy cold dispute
Of what is fit and not, forsake thy cage,
Thy rope of sands
Which pettie thoughts have made, and made to thee
Good cable, to enforce and draw,
And be thy law,
While thou didst wink and wouldst not see.
Away! take heed;
I will abroad.
Call in thy death's-head there, tie up thy fears;
He that forebears
To suit and serve his need
Deserves his load.
But as I rav'd and grew more fierce and wilde
At every word,

> Methought I heard one calling, 'Childe';
> And I reply'd, 'My Lord.'

Already, in those two poems, you'll perhaps have noticed one of the characteristics of Herbert: his technical variety. Though there's a common tone of voice, as it were, in Herbert – they couldn't have been written by anyone else, unless it might be Henry Vaughan imitating him – he used an astonishing range of metrical forms and of kinds of stanza. Though the total body of his English verse consists of fewer than 200 poems, which might lead one to expect a consistency of forms, in fact he hardly ever uses the same form twice: there's a handful of sonnets, but the rest are adventurously *ad hoc*, as if he saw each new poem as a fresh formal challenge, something to be worked out in its own terms. Let's see him at his simplest, with a sonnet that's a direct piece of narrative parable. This sonnet is called 'Redemption':

> Having been tenant long to a rich Lord,
>   Not thriving, I resolvèd to be bold,
> And make a suit unto Him, to afford
>   A new small-rented lease, and cancell th' old.
>
> In heaven at His manour I Him sought:
>   They told me there, that He was lately gone
> About some land, which he had deerly bought
>   Long since on Earth, to take possession.
>
> I straight return'd, and knowing His great birth,
>   Sought Him accordingly in great resorts –
>   In cities, theatres, gardens, parks and courts:
> At length I heard a raggèd noise and mirth
>   Of theeves and murderers; there I Him espied,
>   Who straight, 'Your suit is granted' said, and died.

The simplicity and directness of that is concentratedly channelled towards its final line – 'Who straight, "Your suit is granted" said, and died'. In such simplicity and directness I think we hear the country preacher Herbert was, not condescending to his simple parishioners but not talking above their heads either. Contrast with that the stranger, much more fragmented, much more exotic display we find in another sonnet, handled so differently that one can hardly believe, until one counts the lines and rhymes, that both are written in the same form. Here, in Herbert's sonnet

'Prayer', all the energy goes into a proliferation of metaphors, all circling and wheeling round the central subject:

> Prayer, the Churche's banquet, Angels' age,
>   God's breath in man returning to his birth,
> The soul in paraphrase, heart in pilgrimage,
>   The Christian plummet sounding heav'n and earth;
>
> Engine against th' Almightie, sinner's towre,
>   Reversèd thunder, Christ-side-piercing spear,
> The six-daies-world transposing in an houre,
>   A kinde of tune which all things heare and fear;
>
> Softnesse, and peace, and joy, and love, and blisse,
>   Exalted manna, gladnesse of the best,
> Heaven in ordinarie, man well drest,
>   The milkie way, the bird of Paradise,
>
> Church-bels beyond the stars heard, the soul's bloud,
> The land of spices, something understood.

None of Herbert's mature poems, written in the last few years of his quite short life (he died at 39), has other than a religious subject: and Herbert is, at the very least, the chief ornament of the Anglican Church. But just as there is great variety formally, so there is spiritually. There are poems of self-doubt, of self-disgust, of exaltation and celebration, of patient didacticism, of playful ingenuity. Above all, there is stress on unity and order, on the divine harmony of things – capable of surviving disaster and misery, and exemplified in Herbert's poem 'Man', where man is seen as the 'little world made cunningly' which reflects both the harmony of the greater world in which he is set and the harmony of his creator:

> My God, I heard this day
> That none doth build a stately habitation
>   But he that means to dwell therein.
>   What house more stately hath there been,
> Or can be, than is Man? to whose creation
>   All things are in decay.
>
> For Man is ev'ry thing,
> And more: he is a tree, yet bears more fruit;

A beast, yet is, or should be, more:
  Reason and speech we onely bring;
Parrats may thank us, if they are not mute,
    They go upon the score.

    Man is all symmetrie,
Full of proportions, one limbe to another,
  And all to all the world besides;
    Each part may call the farthest brother,
For head with foot hath private amitie,
    And both with moons and tides.

    Nothing hath got so farre
But Man hath caught and kept it as his prey;
  His eyes dismount the highest starre;
  He is in little all the sphere;
Herbs gladly cure our flesh, because that they
    Finde their acquaintance there.

    For us the windes do blow,
The earth resteth, heav'n moveth, fountains flow;
  Nothing we see but means our good,
    As our delight or as our treasure;
The whole is either our cupboard of food
    Or Cabinet of pleasure.

    The starres have us to bed,
Night draws the curtain, which the sunne withdraws;
  Musick and light attend our head.
  All things unto our flesh are kinde
In their descent and being; to our minde
    In their ascent and cause.

    Each thing is full of dutie:
Waters united are our navigation;
  Distinguishèd, our habitation;
  Below, our drink; above, our meat;
Both are our cleanlinesse. Hath one such beautie?
    Then how are all things neat!

    More servants wait on Man
Than he'l take notice of: in ev'ry path
  He treads down that which doth befriend him

When sicknesse makes him pale and wan.
Oh mightie love! Man is one world, and hath
   Another to attend him.

   Since then, my God, Thou hast
So brave a palace built, O dwell in it,
   That it may dwell with Thee at last!
   Till then afford us so much wit,
That, as the world serves us, we may serve Thee,
   And both Thy servants be.

That is a poem standing at a distance as it plots out its course: it
has a steady objectivity. We've already seen a more personal
expression in Herbert, in 'The Pearl' and 'The Collar'. This comes
out rather differently in a couple of poems he wrote about the
very business of writing a poem – usually a subject best avoided,
perhaps, because it can lead to dreadful self-consciousness; but
here it's done with that characteristic Herbert mixture of
genuine warmth and assured coolness. This is the second of the
two poems called 'Jordan':

When first my lines of heav'nly joyes made mention,
Such was their lustre, they did so excell,
That I sought out quaint words and trim invention;
My thoughts began to burnish, sprout, and swell
Curling with metaphors a plain intention,
Decking the sense as if it were to sell.

Thousands of notions in my brain did runne,
Offring their service, if I were not sped:
I often blotted what I had begunne –
This was not quick enough, and that was dead;
Nothing could seem too rich to clothe the sunne,
Much lesse those joyes which trample on his head.

As flames do work and winde when they ascend,
So did I weave myselfe into the sense;
But while I bustled I might hear a friend
Whisper, 'How wide is all this long pretence!
There is in love a sweetnesse ready penn'd;
Copie out onely that, and save expense.'

Another poem in which Herbert looks at himself as a poet,

though only glancingly, is 'The Flower'; but here the scope is much wider, for when he sees with delight his creative gift returning to him after a period of barrenness, this is caught up in a larger view of renewal and, indeed, of resurrection:

How fresh, O Lord, how sweet and clean
Are Thy returns! ev'n as the flow'rs in Spring,
  To which, besides their own demean,
The late-past frosts tributes of pleasure bring;
        Grief melts away
      · Like snow in May,
  As if there were no such cold thing.

Who would have thought my shrivel'd heart
Could have recover'd greennesse? It was gone
  Quite under ground; as flow'rs depart
To see their mother-root, when they have blown,
        Where they together
        All the hard weather,
  Dead to the world, keep house unknown.

These are Thy wonders, Lord of power,
Killing and quickning, bringing down to Hell
  And up to Heaven in an houre;
Making a chiming of a passing-bell.
        We say amisse
        This or that is;
  Thy word is all, if we could spell.

O that I once past changing were,
Fast in Thy Paradise, where no flower can wither;
  Many a Spring I shoot up fair,
Offring at Heav'n, growing and groning thither;
        Nor doth my flower
        Want a Spring-showre,
  My sinnes and I joyning together.

But while I grow in a straight line,
Still upwards bent, as if Heav'n were mine own,
  Thy anger comes, and I decline:
What frost to that? what pole is not the zone
        Where all things burn,

When Thou dost turn,
And the least frown of Thine is shown?

And now in age I bud again,
After so many deaths I live and write;
I once more smell the dew and rain,
And relish versing: O, my onely Light,
It cannot be
That I am he
On whom Thy tempests fell all night.

These are Thy wonders, Lord of love,
To make us see we are but flow'rs that glide;
Which when we once can find and prove,
Thou hast a garden for us where to bide;
Who would be more,
Swelling through store,
Forfeit their Paradise by their pride.

Then, before leaving Herbert to turn to an anonymous poem which has much of the feel of Herbert about it, here is probably his best-known poem – though I wish I could have found room for his longest and one of his finest, 'The Sacrifice'. In this poem, 'Love', the dramatic simplicity of Herbert, his plain domestic strength, his rhythmical subtlety, delicacy and suppleness, all combine:

Love bade me welcome; yet my soul drew back,
Guilty of dust and sin.
But quick-ey'd Love, observing me grow slack
From my first entrance in,
Drew nearer to me, sweetly questioning
If I lack'd any thing.

'A guest,' I answer'd, 'worthy to be here':
Love said, 'You shall be he.'
'I, the unkind, ungrateful? Ah, my dear,
I cannot look on Thee.'
Love took my hand, and smiling did reply,
'Who made the eyes but I?'

'Truth, Lord; but I have marr'd them; let my shame
Go where it doth deserve.'
'And know you not,' says Love, 'Who bore the blame?'

'My dear, then I will serve.'
'You must sit down,' says Love, 'and taste My meat,'
So I did sit and eat.

Finally, the anonymous poem I mentioned, which comes from a manuscript at Christ Church, Oxford. It's good enough, I think, in its cadences and its orderliness to stand alongside Herbert; and it reminds us that this first half of the seventeenth century was a period – whatever one's beliefs or lack of them – of our finest religious poetry. This poem is called 'The Guest':

Yet if his majesty, our Soveraign lord,
Should of his owne accord
Friendly himselfe invite,
And say I'll be your guest tomorrowe night,
How should we stir ourselves, call and command
All hands to worke! 'Let no man idle stand.
Set me fine Spanish tables in the hall,
See they be fitted all;
Let there be roome to eate,
And order taken that there want no meate.
See every sconce and candlestick made bright,
That without tapers they may give a light.
Look to the presence: are the carpets spred,
The dazie o'er the head,
The cushions in the chayre,
And all the candles lighted on the staire?
Perfume the chambers, and in any case
Let each man give attendance in his place.'
Thus if the king were coming would we do;
And 'twere good reason too;
For 'tis a duteous thing
To show all honor to an earthly king;
And, after all our travayle and our cost,
So he be pleas'd, to think no labour lost.
But at the coming of the King of heaven
All's set at six and seven:
We wallow in our sin;
Christ cannot finde a chamber in the inn.
We entertain him alwayes like a stranger,
And, as at first, still lodge him in the manger.

Henry Vaughan (1621–1695)
Richard Crashaw (?1612–1649)
Thomas Traherne (1638–1674)

A.T.

The poets in this section were all not only aware of George Herbert's poetry, they were quite happily indebted to it too. Vaughan said he owed his conversion to reading Herbert; Crashaw gave to one of his books the title *Steps to the Temple*, thereby consciously drawing attention to Herbert's title 'The Temple'; and Traherne's poems have many echoes of Herbert's forms and phrases. As far as religious poetry goes, indeed, Herbert was the most influential poet of the seventeenth century. Donne's painful religious meditations in the Holy Sonnets, Milton's massive theological argument in *Paradise Lost*, really had much less effect on actual practitioners than did Herbert.

Yet Vaughan and Crashaw and Traherne each have their special gifts and excellences: they were not just imitators. What they share, and what makes them quite distinct from Herbert, is a visionary or mystical sense. Herbert's message is the lessons of the scriptures seen in the life we live, and in particular in the worshipping life of the Church on earth. Vaughan, Crashaw and Traherne shoot beyond that to supernatural experiences, which are sometimes more brilliant in flashes but also sometimes cloudier in execution; and their poems are most successful when they manage to find images for their experiences which are as exact as Herbert's.

First, Henry Vaughan. He was a Welshman, very conscious of that and proud of it, who lived for almost his whole life on his small family estate between the Brecon Beacons and the Black Mountains. He practised as a country doctor, but you get little sense of his everyday life from his poems, though his early ones attempt to follow the witty, over-ingenious, gossipy, rather metropolitan tone of the day, and indeed aren't religious at all.

The breakthrough – following his reading of Herbert – came in 1646, and lasted for about ten years. To these years belong his best and best-known poems.

To begin with, here is Vaughan at his closest to Herbert, yet clearly doing something different. You'll remember that poem by Herbert called 'Man' – a poem about the orderliness of man, the neat way he fits into God's system. Here is Vaughan's poem called 'Man', which plots out the *contrast* between the orderliness of the rest of the universe and the 'irregularity' of man. It's only one step from this to the dissatisfaction with all earthly things which tends to be a mark of the mystic, to whom the only true experiences are un-earthly ones:

> Weighing the stedfastness and state
> Of some mean things which here below reside,
> Where birds like watchful Clocks the noiseless date
>   And Intercourse of times divide,
> Where Bees at night get home and hive, and flowrs
>   Early, as wel as late,
> Rise with the Sun, and set in the same bowrs;
>
> I would (said I) my God would give
> The staidness of these things to man! for these
> To his divine appointments ever cleave,
>   And no new business breaks their peace;
> The birds nor sow, nor reap, yet sup and dine,
>   The flowres without clothes live,
> Yet *Solomon* was never drest so fine.
>
> Man hath stil either toyes, or Care,
> He hath no root, nor to one place is ty'd,
> But ever restless and Irregular
>   About this Earth doth run and ride,
> He knows he hath a home, but scarce knows where,
>   He sayes it is so far
> That he hath quite forgot how to go there.
>
> He knocks at all doors, strays and roams,
> Nay hath not so much wit as some stones have
> Which in the darkest nights point to their homes,
>   By some hid sense their Maker gave;

Man is the shuttle, to whose winding quest
　　And passage through these looms
God order'd motion, but ordain'd no rest.

Vaughan's whole spiritual and poetic effort is away from the earthly and towards the transcendental, the heavenly. Thinking of his friends who have died, he sees death not as darkness but as light, and in this poem catches wonderfully a sense of yearning and exaltation:

They are all gone into the world of light!
　　And I alone sit lingring here;
Their very memory is fair and bright,
　　And my sad thoughts doth clear.

It glows and glitters in my cloudy brest
　　Like stars upon some gloomy grove,
Or those faint beams in which this hill is drest,
　　After the Sun's remove.

I see them walking in an Air of glory,
　　Whose light doth trample on my days:
My days, which are at best but dull and hoary,
　　Meer glimmering and decays.

O holy hope! and high humility,
　　High as the Heavens above!
These are your walks, and you have shew'd them me
　　To kindle my cold love.

Dear, beauteous death! the Jewel of the Just,
　　Shining nowhere, but in the dark;
What mysteries do lie beyond thy dust;
　　Could man outlook that mark!

He that hath found some fledg'd birds nest, may know
　　At first sight, if the bird be flown;
But what fair Well, or Grove he sings in now,
　　That is to him unknown.

And yet, as Angels in some brighter dreams
　　Call to the soul, when man doth sleep:
So some strange thoughts transcend our wonted theams,
　　And into glory peep.

If a star were confin'd into a Tomb
    Her captive flames must needs burn there;
But when the hand that lockt her up, gives room,
    She'l shine through all the sphaere.

O Father of eternal life, and all
    Created glories under thee!
Resume thy spirit from this world of thrall
    Into true liberty.

Either disperse these mists, which blot and fill
    My perspective (still) as they pass,
Or else remove me hence unto that hill,
    Where I shall need no glass.

Again, in his poem 'The World' Vaughan contrasts the worldly
activities of the lover, the statesman, the miser and the epicure
(all of them in their various ways preferring 'dark night') with
the world of light which is eternity. Images of light persist and
glow in Vaughan's work:

I saw Eternity the other night
Like a great *Ring* of pure and endless light,
    All calm, as it was bright,
And round beneath it, Time in hours, days, years
    Driv'n by the spheres
Like a vast shadow mov'd, in which the world
    And all her train were hurl'd;
The doting Lover in his queintest strain
    Did their Complain,
Neer him, his Lute, his fancy, and his flights,
    Wits sour delights,
With gloves, and knots the silly snares of pleasure
    Yet his dear Treasure
All scatter'd lay, while he his eyes did pour
    Upon a flowr.

The darksome States-man hung with weights and woe
Like a thick midnight-fog mov'd there so slow
    He did nor stay, nor go;
Condemning thoughts (like sad Ecclipses) scowl
    Upon his soul,

And Clouds of crying witnesses without
   Pursued him with one shout.
Yet dig'd the Mole, and lest his ways be found
   Workt under ground,
Where he did clutch his prey, but one did see
   That policie,
Churches and altars fed him, Perjuries
   Were gnats and flies,
It rain'd about him bloud and tears, but he
   Drank them as free.

The fearfull miser on a heap of rust
Sate pining all his life there, did scarce trust
   His own hands with the dust,
Yet would not place one peece above, but lives
   In feare of theeves.
Thousands there were as frantick as himself
   And hug'd each one his pelf,
The down-right Epicure plac'd heav'n in sense
   And scorn'd pretence
While others slipt into a wide Excesse
   Said little lesse;
The weaker sort slight, triviall wares Inslave
   Who think them brave,
And poor, despised truth sate Counting by
   Their Victory.

Yet some, who all this while did weep and sing,
And sing, and weep, soar'd up into the *Ring*,
   But most would use no wing.
O fools (said I,) thus to prefer dark night
   Before true light,
To live in grots, and caves, and hate the day
   Because it shews the way,
The way which from this dead and dark abode
   Leads up to God,
A way where you might tread the Sun, and be
   More bright than he.
But as I did their madnes so discusse
   One whisper'd thus,

> *This Ring the Bride-groome did for none provide*
> *But for his bride.*

There's light again in his poem 'The Retreat', here seen as the natural accompaniment to the child – the child interpreted as being closest to God when he is born, gradually growing away from him with the years, and then declining towards the light again as he dies: an image which Wordsworth, years later, caught from Vaughan, and used in his 'Ode on the Intimations of Immortality':

> Happy those early dayes! when I
> Shin'd in my Angell-infancy.
> Before I understood this place
> Appointed for my second race,
> Or taught my soul to fancy ought
> But a white, Celestiall thought,
> When yet I had not walkt above
> A mile, or two, from my first love,
> And looking back (at that short space,)
> Could see a glimpse of his bright-face;
> When on some *gilded cloud*, or *flowre*
> My gazing soul would dwell an houre,
> And in those weaker glories spy
> Some shadows of eternity;
> Before I taught my tongue to wound
> My conscience with a sinfull sound,
> Or had the black art to dispence
> A sev'rall sinne to ev'ry sence,
> But felt through all this fleshly dresse
> Bright shootes of everlastingnesse.
>   O how I long to travell back
> And tread again that ancient track!
> That I might once more reach that plaine,
> Where first I left my glorious traine,
> From whence th' Inlightend spirit sees
> That shady City of Palme trees;
> But (ah!) my soul with too much stay
> Is drunk, and staggers in the way.
> Some men a forward motion love,
> But I by backward steps would move,

And when this dust falls to the urn
In that state I came return.

Finally from Vaughan, his splendid image of heaven itself,
showing him at his most intense and least cloudy. Incidentally,
the words of this poem may be most familiar through the set-
ting Vaughan Williams gave them in a frequently sung hymn:

My Soul, there is a Countrie
    Far beyond the stars,
Where stands a wingéd Centrie
    All skilfull in the wars,
There above noise, and danger
    Sweet peace sits crown'd with smiles,
And one born in a Manger
    Commands the Beauteous files,
He is thy gracious friend,
    And (O my Soul awake!)
Did in pure love descend
    To die here for thy sake,
If thou canst get but thither,
    There growes the flowre of peace,
The Rose that cannot wither,
    Thy fortresse, and thy ease;
Leave then thy foolish ranges;
    For none can thee secure,
But one, who never changes,
    Thy God, thy life, thy Cure.

Richard Crashaw is a more difficult case than Vaughan: there's
intensity all right, but of such a highly-coloured and hotly
emotional sort that he's been called England's only baroque poet.
And indeed much of the experience and work that influenced
him was foreign; he became a convert to Roman Catholicism
during the Civil War, lived in exile for much of his life in France
and Italy, and though he acknowledged his debt to Herbert and
was very friendly with (and much admired by) Abraham Cowley,
his allegiances are more Continental than English. At his best,
Crashaw has a superbly rich commanding tone – as in 'Love
thou art absolute, sole Lord/Of life and death' – but often there's

124

something too hectically ingenious about his exaltations and adorations, or so I find. But I do respond, even if rather unwillingly, to the magnificent rhetoric of one of his several poems addressed to St Teresa – in particular to those lines towards the end when the excitement really catches fire. Here are the last thirty or so lines of 'The Flaming Heart – Upon the Book and Picture of the Seraphical Saint Teresa':

O *Heart*! the equal poise of love's both parts
Big alike with wound and darts.
Live in these conquering leaves; live all the same;
And walk through all tongues one triumphant *Flame*.
Live here, great *Heart*; and love and die and kill;
And bleed and wound; and yield and conquer still.
Let this immortal life where'er it comes
Walk in a crowd of loves and Martyrdoms.
Let mystic Deaths wait on't; and wise souls be
The love-slain witnesses of this life of thee.
O sweet incendiary! show here thy art,
Upon this carcass of a hard, cold, heart,
Let all thy scatter'd shafts of light, that play
Among the leaves of thy large Books of day,
Combin'd against this Breast at once break in
And take away from me my self and sin,
This gracious Robbery shall thy bounty be;
And my best fortunes such fair spoils of me.
O thou undaunted daughter of desires!
By all thy dow'r of Lights and Fires;
By all the eagle in thee, all the dove;
By all thy lives and deaths of love;
By thy large draughts of intellectual day,
And by thy thirsts of love more large then they;
By all thy brim-fill'd Bowls of fierce desire
By the last Morning's draught of liquid fire;
By the full kingdom of that final kiss
That seiz'd thy parting Soul, and seal'd thee his;
By all the heav'ns thou hast in him
(Fair sister of the Seraphim!)
By all of *Him* we have in *Thee*;
Leave nothing of my *Self* in me.

Let me so read thy life, that I
Unto all life of mine may die.

Thomas Traherne's poems weren't discovered until the very
end of the nineteenth century, and were first published in 1903.
When they were first found they were thought to be more poems
by Vaughan, and in a way one can see why; but some clever
detective work established them as Traherne's, and so a hitherto
unknown seventeenth-century poet was given currency. Tra-
herne, like Vaughan, had Welsh connections, and was a clergy-
man. He was also a notable writer of meditative and lyrical
devotional prose – the *Centuries of Meditations* – and the spirit
and substance of both prose and verse is much the same: the
goodness and beauty of created things, the innocence of child-
hood, and a sense of wonder at God's glory. All of these come
through in his poem 'The Salutation':

These little limbs,
These eyes and hands which here I find,
These rosy cheeks wherewith my life begins,
Where have ye been? behind
What curtain were ye from me hid so long,
Where was, in what abyss, my speaking tongue?

When silent I
So many thousand, thousand years
Beneath the dust did in a chaos lie,
How could I smiles or tears,
Or lips or hands or eyes or ears perceive?
Welcome ye treasures which I now receive.

I that so long
Was nothing from eternity,
Did little think such joys as ear or tongue
To celebrate or see:
Such sounds to hear, such hands to feel, such feet,
Beneath the skies on such a ground to meet.

New burnisht joys!
Which yellow gold and pearl excel!
Such sacred treasures are the limbs in boys,
In which a soul doth dwell;

Their organiséd joints and azure veins
More wealth include than all the world contains.

From dust I rise,
    And out of nothing now awake;
These brighter regions which salute mine eyes,
    A gift from God I take.
The earth, the seas, the light, the day, the skies,
The sun and stars are mine; if those I prize.

Long time before
    I in my mother's womb was born,
A God preparing did this glorious store,
    The world, for me adorne.
Into this Eden so divine and fair,
So wide and bright, I come His son and heir.

A stranger here
    Strange things doth meet, strange glories see;
Strange treasures lodg'd in this fair world appear,
    Strange all and new to me;
But that they mine should be, who nothing was,
That strangest is of all, yet brought to pass.

And here, finally, is something of the other side of the coin in
Traherne: childhood seen not just positively as the glory of
creation in a state of innocence, but negatively – a 'happy
ignorance' of all that, later, will spoil it. The poem is called
'Eden':

A learned and a happy ignorance
        Divided me
    From all the vanity,
From all the sloth, care, pain, and sorrow that
    advance
        The madness and the misery
Of men. No error, no distraction I
Saw soil the earth or overcloud the sky.

I knew not that there was a serpent's sting
        Whose poison shed
        On men, did overspread

The world; nor did I dream of such a thing
　　　As sin, in which mankind lay dead.
They all were brisk and living wights to me,
Yea, pure and full of immortality.

Joy, pleasure, beauty, kindness, glory, love,
　　　Sleep, day, life, light,
　　Peace, melody, my sight,
My ears and heart did fill and freely move.
　　All that I saw did me delight.
The Universe was then a world of treasure,
To me an universal world of pleasure.

Unwelcome penitence was then unknown,
　　　Vain costly toys,
　　Swearing and roaring boys,
Shops, markets, taverns, coaches, were un-
　　shewn;
　　　So all things were that drowned my joys:
No thorns choked up my path, nor hid the face
Of bliss and beauty, nor eclipsed the place.

Only what Adam in his first estate,
　　　Did I behold;
　　Hard silver and dry gold
As yet lay under ground; my blessed fate
　　Was more acquainted with the old
And innocent delights which he did see
In his original simplicity.

Those things which first his Eden did adorn,
　　　My infancy
　　Did crown. Simplicity
Was my protection when I first was born.
　　Mine eyes those treasures first did see
Which God first made. The first effects of Love
My first enjoyments upon earth did prove;

And were so great, and so divine, so pure,
　　　So fair and sweet,
　　So true; when I did meet

Them here at first, they did my soul allure,
   And drew away my infant feet
Quite from the works of men; that I might see
The glorious wonders of the Deity.

Robert Herrick (1591–1674)
Richard Lovelace (1618–1657)
Charles Cotton (1630–1687)
Andrew Marvell (1621–1678)
Samuel Butler (1612–1680)
John Wilmot, Earl of Rochester (1647–1680)   P.P.

———————————◆———————————

The seventeenth century is probably the richest of all centuries
in English poetry. It begins with Shakespeare and his followers
in full flower, it continues with the School of Donne, dividing
neatly into the secular and religious poets of the Caroline Age,
goes underground during the Civil War and the Common-
wealth, and re-emerges in a new and ribald splendour at the
Restoration, to end with the superb decorum of the first
Augustans. It's a century which abounds in great names –
Shakespeare and Donne at its head, Dryden at its end, and the
young Alexander Pope turning his first rhymes. In the middle
comes John Milton, grandest and most self-conscious of English
poets. The reign of King James I, at the century's start, saw the
publication of the two most influential books in English – the
Authorised Version of the Bible in 1611 and the First Folio
of Shakespeare's Plays in 1623. There's no doubt that this is the
high-water mark of the English language. In the previous
chapters Anthony Thwaite dealt with the followers of Donne
who used his metaphysical style to praise their God – most of
them, like Herbert, plainer and more wholehearted than Donne
himself – and the next chapter deals with the poetry of Milton.
This section is devoted to the poets who accepted Donne's
revolution of sensibility, but were more attracted by his amorous
conceits than by his religious ingenuities. Of course, every
poet of quality is his own man and the trends and influences we
notice do not detract from his originality. Among courtly poets
of King Charles's reign, there is always some distinguishing mark,
130

however closely they followed the prevailing conventions of love poetry or of pastoral, derived from the Greek and Roman classics. Robert Herrick, for instance, was a clergyman friend of Ben Jonson, who took his religious duties lightly. He is a sort of English Ronsard – a writer of feather-light lyrics, entirely dependent on expert placing of words to keep the charm from becoming insipid. When he writes well, Herrick is as touching and natural as the country beauties he described. All his poems are conventional – short, attractive verses addressed to intelligent women, softly sententious about time and fading beauty, reconciled, melodious and warm of heart. Here's one called 'To Daisies, Not to Shut so Soon'.

> Shut not so soon; the dull-ey'd night
> Has not as yet begunne
> To make a seizure on the light,
> Or to seale up the Sun.
>
> No Marigolds yet closed are;
> No shadows great appeare;
> Nor doth the early Shepheards Starre
> Shine like a spangle here.
>
> Stay but till my Julia close
> Her life-begetting eye;
> And let the whole world then dispose
> It selfe to live or dye.

As the dispute between the King and Parliament grew more bitter, the poets began to take sides. Most were still courtiers and were loyal to their king, but this preponderance is offset by the two greatest poets of the Civil War, who were Parliament men – John Milton and Andrew Marvell. The Caroline writers have been called Cavalier Poets but the name doesn't fit them well. They were largely free from faction (there are exceptions, such as the embattled polemicist, John Cleveland), though they had little taste for Puritan manners and severities. Richard Lovelace, for instance, fought for King Charles until the Cavaliers were overwhelmed and he has had the misfortune to be known by some rather priggish verses addressed to his mistress Lucasta on going to the wars. But Lovelace had real intellect and he benefits from being read in his entirety. The simple and honourable soldier then appears a complex and doubting intelligence. This is a neglected aspect of Lovelace which shows up in the brief but baffling poem in three-line stanzas called 'La Bella Bona Roba'. It's as concentrated as Shakespeare's 'The Phoenix and the Turtle', and deals with the same matters – sexual love and the fall in the garden of Eden. Revulsion from sex has never been a bar to idealistic love. A bona roba is a whore and Lovelace is writing about the sex war:

> I cannot tell who loves the Skeleton
> Of a poor Marmoset, nought but boan, boan.
> Give me a nakednesse with her cloath's on.
>
> Such whose white-sattin upper coat of skin,
> Cuts upon velvet rich Incarnadin,
> Ha's yet a Body (and of Flesh) within.
>
> Sure it is meant good Husbandry in men,
> Who do incorporate with Aëry leane,
> T' repair their sides, and get their Ribb agen.
>
> Hard hap unto that Huntsman that Decrees
> Fat joys for all his swet, when as he sees,
> After his 'Say, nought but his Keepers Fees.
>
> Then Love I beg, when next thou tak'st thy Bow,
> Thy angry shafts, and dost Heart-Chasing go,
> Passe Rascall Deare, strike me the largest Doe.

John Cleveland was the most effective of the propagandists for the King's cause. Cleveland was a satirist with a love of extravagant language and a fine command of invective. Others on the King's side were Suckling and Carew; then there was Edmund Waller who served whichever side was winning. He and Abraham Cowley are important for introducing a new regularity and decorum into verse. This was later to culminate in the consummate smoothness of the poetry of Alexander Pope. Though these men wrote religious poems, they were not mystics like Vaughan, Crashaw and Traherne. Often they were country gentlemen, and if they used the love conventions of disdainful maids and amorous swains and called their mistresses Chloe, Delia and Amaryllis and invented pastoral lovers with names like Strephon and Dorcas in the classical manner of Theocritus and Virgil, none the less they knew the realities of country life well enough. But it pleased them to write about it good-humouredly. No one did this better than Charles Cotton, the close friend of Lovelace. Cotton's poem 'Evening' is like a painting of country life – it looks forward to the English school of Constable, with just a little classicism showing in its parody of the formal style.

> The Day's grown old, the fainting Sun
> Has but a little way to run,
> And yet his Steeds, with all his skill,
> Scarce lug the Chariot down the Hill.
>
> With Labour spent, and Thirst Opprest,
> Whilst they strain hard to gain the West,
> From Fetlocks hot drops melted light,
> Which turn the Meteors in the Night.
>
> The Shadows now so long do grow,
> That Brambles like tall Cedars show,
> Mole-hills seem Mountains, and the Ant
> Appears a monstrous Elephant.
>
> A very little little Flock
> Shades thrice the ground that it would stock;
> Whilst the small Stripling following them,
> Appears a mighty Polypheme.
>
> These being brought into their Fold,
> And by the thrifty Master told,
> He thinks his Wages are well paid,
> Since none are either lost, or stray'd.
>
> Now lowing Herds are each-where heard,
> Chains rattle in the Villains Yard,
> The Cart's on Tayl set down to rest,
> Bearing on high the Cuckold's Crest.
>
> The hedge is stript, the Clothes brought in,
> Nought's left without should be within,
> The Bees are hiv'd, and hum their Charm,
> Whilst every House does seem a Swarm.

The Cock now to the Roost is prest:
For he must call up all the rest;
The Sow's fast pegg'd within the Sty,
To still her squeaking Progeny.

Each one has had his Supping Mess,
The Cheese is put into the Press,
The Pans and Bowls clean scalded all,
Rear'd up against the Milk-House Wall.

And now on Benches all are sat
In the cool air to sit and chat,
Till Phoebus, dipping in the West,
Shall lead the World the way to Rest.

The English Civil War, which ended with the execution of Charles I and the virtual dictatorship of Oliver Cromwell, is an extraordinary event in European history. It would not be too assertive to say that England has escaped the various turmoils which have disturbed Europe since the French Revolution just because our landed gentry chopped off their king's head at the right moment in the seventeenth century. However, Cromwell's revolution did not produce much poetry. Milton was Latin Secretary to the Commonwealth and Andrew Marvell in turn was Milton's helper. But their great poems come either from before Cromwell's dictatorship, or after it. Milton is a law unto himself; Marvell's achievement is more relaxed. He was an ambitious young Puritan, with natural leanings to wit and extravagance, but capable of seeing the world clearly and acting with good sense and courage. For a while, he was tutor to Cromwell's only rival on the Parliamentary side, Lord Fairfax. Living in Fairfax's Yorkshire retreat, he wrote his longest and most exquisitely formal poem, 'Upon Appleton House'. It's an example of artificiality allied to natural observation: in it, he imagines the superworld of humans from the point of view of insects and denizens of the garden. The poem makes us see that we in our turn are miniatures in the eye of God. Marvell stood by his cause, though he was never a bigot. He first sat as Member for Hull in one of Cromwell's last parliaments. On Charles II's restoration, he continued his parliamentary career and never swerved from opposition to the King's policies. He is the perfect

moderator between Puritan excitability and Cavalier elegance –
nobody is more witty and yet no English poet has a better sense
of proportion in his work. One of his most celebrated poems is
entitled 'To His Coy Mistress'. Only a rare sensibility could have
contrived so beautiful a celebration of sexual desire. It fell to
the Puritan Marvell to write the most elegant poem in English on
love, the first principle of life and supreme opponent of death.

> Had we but world enough, and Time,
> This coyness Lady were no crime.
> We would sit down, and think which way
> To walk, and pass our long Love's Day.
> Thou by the Indian Ganges' side
> Should'st Rubies find: I by the Tide
> Of Humber would complain. I would
> Love you ten years before the Flood:
> And you should if you please refuse
> Till the Conversion of the Jews.
> My vegetable Love should grow
> Vaster than Empires, and more slow.
> An hundred years should go to praise
> Thine Eyes, and on thy Forehead gaze.
> Two hundred to adore each Breast:
> But thirty thousand to the rest.
> An Age at least to every part,
> And the last Age should show your Heart.
> For Lady you deserve this state;
> Nor would I love at lower rate.
>   But at my back I alwaies hear
> Times winged Chariot hurrying near:
> And yonder all before us lye
> Deserts of vast Eternity.
> Thy Beauty shall no more be found;
> Nor, in thy marble Vault, shall sound
> My echoing Song: then Worms shall try
> That long preserv'd Virginity:
> And your quaint Honour turn to dust;
> And into ashes all my Lust.
> The Grave's a fine and private place,
> But none I think do there embrace.

Now therefore, while the youthful hew
Sits on thy skin like morning dew,
And while thy willing Soul transpires
At every pore with instant Fires,
Now let us sport us while we may;
And now, like am'rous birds of prey,
Rather at once our Time devour,
Than languish in his slow-chapt pow'r.
Let us roll all our Strength, and all
Our Sweetness, up into one Ball:
And tear our Pleasures with rough strife,
Thorough the Iron gates of Life.
Thus, though we cannot make our Sun
Stand still, yet we will make him run.

Marvell is so attractive a poet, it would be agreeable to go on quoting him, but there is room for only one more poem. It harks back to the convention of Lovelace, though it surpasses him in depth of feeling. It's called 'The Definition of Love', and describes the unhappy randomness of human feelings. How often in our own lives has each of us realised that his love is, as Marvell says, 'begotten by despair upon impossibility'.

My Love is of a birth as rare
As 'tis for object strange and high:
It was begotten by despair
Upon Impossibility.

Magnanimous Despair alone
Could show me so divine a thing,
Where feeble Hope could ne'r have flown
But vainly flapt its Tinsel Wing.

And yet I quickly might arrive
Where my extended Soul is fixt,
But Fate does Iron wedges drive,
And alwaies crouds it self betwixt.

For Fate with jealous Eye does see
Two perfect loves; nor lets them close:
Their union would her ruine be,
And her Tyrannick pow'r depose.

And therefore her Decrees of Steel
Us as the distant Poles have plac'd,
(Though Loves whole World on us doth wheel)
Not by themselves to be embrac'd.

Unless the giddy Heaven fall,
And Earth some new convulsion tear;
And, us to joyn, the World should all
Be cramp'd into a Planisphere.

As Lines so Loves oblique may well
Themselves in every Angle greet:
But ours so truly Paralel,
Though infinite can never meet.

Therefore the Love which us doth bind,
But Fate so enviously debarrs,
Is the Conjunction of the Mind,
And Opposition of the Stars.

After Cromwell's death, the Protectorship collapsed and the nation turned with relief to the easy-going King Charles II. Charles wisely did not gloat over his defeated enemies. Quite soon, however, he was faced with a hostile Parliament and various anti-Papist plots. The Puritans had suppressed the theatres and all other signs of licentiousness. These now came back with double vehemence. Charles II's reign is the second great period of the English drama. Alas, it's not our concern here, since the plays were mostly comedies and written in prose. But the sensibility of this sceptical age – not just its rakehell courtiers, damning themselves with drink and debauchery, but also the resurgence of Science which culminated in the setting-up of Europe's first scientific academy, the Royal Society – produced a rash of doubting and sardonic poetry. The most redoubtable nihilist of the period was the Earl of Rochester, but sardonic credit should be paid to Samuel Butler, the only verse satirist who compares with Pope and Byron. He was a rather threadbare propagandist for the Royalist cause, and published his satirical masterpiece, *Hudibras*, only after the Restoration in 1660. Unfortunately, he received little reward for his loyalty and died in poverty. Yet his poem remains one of the best burlesques of solemn silliness in any language. It's almost as good as *Don*

Quixote and shares with Byron's *Don Juan* the distinction of being a readable long poem – something neither Milton or Wordsworth quite achieved. In this passage, Butler is describing a canting Christian, a holier-than-thou hypocrite, obviously a type he'd met often enough in his life and one he cordially detested.

> For his Religion it was fit
> To match his Learning and his Wit:
> 'Twas Presbyterian true blew,
> For he was of that stubborn Crew
> Of Errant Saints, whom all men grant
> To be the true Church Militant:
> Such as do build their Faith upon
> The holy text of Pike and Gun;
> Decide all Controversies by
> Infallible Artillery;
> And prove their Doctrine Orthodox
> By Apostolick Blows and Knocks;
> Call Fire and Sword and Desolation,
> A godly-thorough-Reformation,
> Which always must be carry'd on,
> And still be doing, never done:
> As if Religion were intended
> For nothing else but to be mended.
> A sect, whose chief Devotion lies
> In odd perverse Antipathies;
> In falling out with that or this,
> And finding somewhat still amiss;
> More peevish, cross, and spleenatick
> Than Dog distract, or Monky sick.
> That with more care keep Holy-Day
> The wrong, than others the right way:
> Compound for Sins, they are inclin'd to,
> By damning those they have no mind to;
> Still so perverse and opposite,
> As if they worshipp'd God for spight,
> The self-same thing they will abhor
> One way, and long another for.
> Free-will they one way disavow,

Another, nothing else allow.
All Piety consists therein
In them, in other Men all Sin.
Rather than fail, they will defie
That which they love most tenderly,
Quarrel with minc'd Pies, and disparage
Their best and dearest friend, Plum-porridge;
Fat Pig and Goose it self oppose,
And blaspheme Custard through the Nose.
Th'Apostles of this fierce Religion,
Like Mahomet's, were Ass and Widgeon,
To whom our Knight by fast instinct
Of Wit and Temper was so linkt,
As if Hypocrisy and Non-sense
Had got th'Advouson of his Conscience.

Two poets of the time have the same verve and realism which distinguishes such playwrights as Wycherley, Vanbrugh and Congreve. They are John Dryden and the Earl of Rochester. Rochester was highly precocious. He was a teenager at the Restoration and inherited great wealth while very young. His reaction was wholly in character – he whored and played up with enormous style so that he was quickly known as the worst libertine of the age. The character of Dorimant in Etherege's play, *The Man of Mode*, is a portrait of Rochester. He did this in earnest, yet he has a fair claim to be considered one of the most serious poets in English. He died young, as a result of his excesses, but also out of anti-authoritarian bravado. If the great French poet Rimbaud has a precursor, it must be Rochester. His lyrics are fiery and audacious. Here are two of them – the first almost loving, the second an example of cynical fraternisation in the Sex War. Their titles are 'Love and Life' and 'To a Lady in a Letter'.

All my past life is mine no more,
   The flying hours are gone;
Like transitory Dreams giv'n o're,
Whose Images are kept in store,
   By Memory alone.

What ever is to come is not,
   How can it then be mine?

The present Moment's all my Lot,
And that, as fast as it is got,
   Phillis, is wholly thine.

Then talk not of Inconstancy,
   False Hearts, and broken Vows.
If I by Miracle can be,
This live-long Minute true to thee,
   'Tis all that Heav'n allows.

*

Such Perfect Bliss, fair Cloris, we
   In our Enjoyment prove:
'Tis pity restless Jealousie
   Should mingle with our Love.

Let us, since Wit has taught us how,
   Raise Pleasure to the Top:
You Rival Bottle must allow,
   I'le suffer Rival Fop.

Think not in this that I design
   A Treason 'gainst Love's Charms,
When following the God of Wine
   I leave my Cloris' Arms.

Since you have that, for all your haste,
   At which I'le ne're repine,
Will take its Liquor off as fast,
   As I can take off mine.

There's not a brisk insipid Spark,
   That flutters in the Town:
But with your Wanton Eyes you mark
   Him out to be your own.

Nor do you think it worth your care
   How empty, and how dull,
The heads of your Admirers are,
   So that their Cods be full.

All this you freely must confess,
   Yet we ne're disagree:
For did you love your Pleasure less,
   You were no Match for me.

Whilst I, my Pleasure to pursue,
    Whole Nights am taking in
The lusty Juice of Grapes, take you
    The Juice of lusty Men.

If the stories of Rochester's death can be believed, he died
reconciled to the Church. Nevertheless the scepticism of his
poetry is absolute. We have no good reason to prefer sceptics to
believers, but equally we shouldn't turn away from clear-
sighted views of life's meaninglessness. Two more Rochester
poems make just this point. The first is a translation of a chorus
from a play by Seneca. It's pure Rochester and owes little to its
ostensible model.

    After Death, nothing is, and Nothing, Death,
    The utmost Limit of a Gasp of Breath:
    Let the ambitious Zealot lay aside,
His hopes of Heav'n (whose Faith is but his Pride)
    Let slavish souls lay by their Fear,
    Nor be concern'd, which way, or where
    After this life they shall be hurl'd;
Dead, we become the Lumber of the World;
And to that Mass of Matter shall be swept,
Where things Destroy'd, with things Unborn are kept.
    Devouring time swallows us whole,
Impartial Death confounds Body and Soul.
    For Hell, and the foul Fiend that rules
    God's everlasting fiery Goales,
    Devis'd by Rogues, dreaded by Fools;
(With his grim griezly Dog, that keeps the Door)
Are sensless Stories, idle Tales,
Dreams, Whimseys, and no more

And one of the most perfect of Rochester's poems, the one he
entitled 'Upon Nothing'. In it, his intelligence and invention
cancel out the despair he describes. The poem falls into a great
silence which for the poet was like death itself.

    Nothing! thou Elder Brother ev'n to Shade,
    Thou hadst a Being 'ere the World was made,
    And (well fixt) art alone of ending not afraid.

E're Time and Place were, Time and Place were not
When Primitive Nothing something strait begot,
Then all proceeded from the great united – What?

Something, the gen'ral Attribute of all,
Sever'd from thee, its sole Original,
Into thy boundless self, must undistinguish'd fall.

Yet something did the Mighty Pow'r command,
And from thy fruitful emptiness's hand,
Snatcht Men, Beasts, Birds, Fire, Water, Aire, and Land.

Matter, the wicked'st Offspring of thy Race,
By Forme assisted, flew from thy Embrace,
And Rebel Light obscur'd thy reverend dusky Face.

With Form and Matter, Time and Place did join,
Body, thy Foe, with these did Leagues combine,
To spoil thy peaceful Realm, and ruin all thy Line.

But Turn-Coat Time assists the Foe in vain,
And brib'd by thee, destroys thy short-liv'd Reign,
And to thy hungry Womb, drives back thy Slaves again.

Tho Mysteries are barr'd from Laick-Eyes,
And the Divine alone with Warrant pryes
Into thy Bosome, where the truth in private lyes,

Yet this of thee the wise may freely say,
Thou from the Virtuous, nothing dost delay,
And to be part of thee, the Wicked wisely pray.

Great Negative, how vainly would the Wise,
Enquire, define, distinguish, teach, devise,
Didst thou not stand to point their blind Philosophies!

Is or is not, the Two great ends of Fate,
And true, or false, the Subject of debate,
That perfect, or destroy, the vast designs of State,

When they have rack'd the Politician's Breast,
Within thy Bosome, most securely rest,
And when reduc'd to thee, are least unsafe, and best.

But Nothing, why does Something still permit,
That Sacred Monarchs shou'd at Councel sit,
With Persons highly thought, at best, for Nothing fit,

Whil'st weighty Something modestly abstains,
From Princes' Coffers, and from States-Men's Brains,
And Nothing there, like stately Something reigns?

Nothing who dwellst with Fools, in grave disguise,
From whom they Reverend Shapes and Forms devise,
Lawn-sleeves, and Furrs, and Gowns, when they like
 thee look wise.

French Truth, Dutch Prowess, British Policy,
Hybernian Learning, Scotch Civility,
Spaniards dispatch, Danes Wit, are mainly seen in thee.

The great Man's Gratitudes to his best Friend,
Kings' promises, Whores' Vows, towards thee they bend,
Flow swiftly into thee, and in thee ever end.

John Milton (1608-1674)   A.T.

———————◆———————

Milton stands like a great monument – or, to put it as T. S. Eliot once did, like the Great Wall of China – almost half-way through this book. The two similes may sound as if they're saying the same thing; but if you think about them, they're not really. Is Milton almost the greatest English poet, almost as great as Shakespeare, an unassailable and heartening and splendid force in our poetry? Or does he wind forbiddingly across the landscape, huge but awful, unignorable but somehow not admirable – and certainly not heartening and lovable?

We have to reckon here with a poet whose seriousness of purpose and grandeur of ambition can be matched only by Spenser and Wordsworth, and whose spiritual dedication outdoes theirs. Milton's seriousness, ambition and dedication are seen at their highest form in *Paradise Lost*; and in this section I've decided to choose only from that, ignoring all the other achievements – 'Lycidas', 'Comus', 'Samson Agonistes', and all the shorter poems and sonnets. It's *Paradise Lost* that's the great monument or Chinese wall.

Paradise Lost is an epic poem, and to say that is to say something other than that it's a long poem: *The Faerie Queene* is a long allegorical narrative, and Wordsworth's *Prelude* is a long philosophical autobiography, but neither is an epic. Nor – to define the ground more clearly – was Milton working the same field as Homer or Virgil, though he was very much aware of both as great examples and forebears. The closest one can get to a comparison is with Dante's *Divine Comedy* – and even then the comparison doesn't work for much of the way, because Dante was demonstrating an existing theological system, whereas Milton was designing a self-sufficient new one which (and this suggests the audacity of his scheme) would not only take root from the Bible but have Biblical resonance and authority.

144

To do this Milton developed a language and a cadence which quite deliberately ignored what most of his predecessors and all his contemporaries had done and were doing. The theme was to be the Fall of Man and War in Heaven, and from this the poet was to 'assert Eternal Providence, /And justify the ways of God to men'. The necessary technical instrument for this couldn't, in Milton's view, be what he called 'the jingling sound of like endings' – that is, rhyme – but the English equivalent of the unrhymed achievements of Homer in Greek and Virgil in Latin: Milton called it 'English heroic verse without rhyme.' The first twenty-six lines of Book I of *Paradise Lost* not only demonstrate this – they give you a synopsis of Milton's intention and a view of his ambition as well:

> Of Mans first disobedience, and the Fruit
> Of that Forbidden Tree, whose mortal tast
> Brought death into the world, and all our woe,
> With loss of Eden, till one greater Man
> Restore us, and regain the blissful seat,
> Sing Heav'nly Muse, that on the secret top
> Of Oreb, or of Sinai, didst inspire
> That shepherd, who first taught the chosen seed,
> In the beginning how the Heav'ns and earth
> Rose out of Chaos: Or if Sion Hill
> Delight thee more, and Siloa's brook that flow'd
> East by the oracle of God; I thence
> Invoke thy aid to my adventrous song,
> That with no middle flight intends to soar
> Above th'Aonian mount, while it pursues
> Things unattempted yet in Prose or Rhime.
> And chiefly Thou O Spirit, that dost prefer
> Before all temples th'upright heart and pure,
> Instruct me, for Thou know'st; Thou from the first
> Wast present, and with mighty wings outspread
> Dove-like satst brooding on the vast Abyss
> And mad'st it pregnant: what in me is dark
> Illumine, what is low raise and support;
> That to the highth of this great Argument
> I may assert Eternal Providence,
> And justifie the wayes of God to men.

'Things unattempted yet in prose or rhyme': there, at the
beginning, we have quite explicitly the exalted ambition Milton
had set himself. And what things! Soon after those introductory
lines, there is the first great speech of the poem: Satan, cast down
by God to Hell with the other rebel angels, sees close by him
'One next himself in power and next in crime' – Beelzebub –
and addresses him like this:

> If thou beest he; but O how fall'n! how chang'd
> From him, who in the happy realms of Light
> Cloth'd with transcendent brightness didst outshine
> Myriads though bright: If he whom mutual league,
> United thoughts and counsels, equal hope,
> And hazard in the Glorious Enterprize,
> Joynd with me once, now misery hath joyned
> In equal ruin; into what Pit thou seest
> From what highth fal'n, so much the stronger provd
> He with his Thunder: and till then who knew
> The force of those dire Arms? yet not for those
> Nor what the Potent Victor in his rage
> Can else inflict do I repent or change,
> Though chang'd in outward lustre; that fixt mind
> And high disdain, from sence of injur'd merit,
> That with the mightiest rais'd me to contend,
> And to the fierce contention brought along
> Innumerable force of Spirits arm'd
> That durst dislike his reign, and me preferring,
> His utmost power with adverse power oppos'd
> In dubious Battel on the Plains of Heav'n,
> And shook his throne. What though the field be lost?
> All is not lost; the unconquerable Will,
> And study of revenge, immortal hate,
> And courage never to submit or yield:
> And what is else not to be overcome?
> That Glory never shall his wrath or might
> Extort from me. To bow and sue for grace
> With suppliant knee, and deifie his power
> Who from the terrour of this Arm so late
> Doubted his empire, that were low indeed,
> That were an ignominy and shame beneath

This downfall; since by Fate the strength of Gods
And this Empyreal substance cannot fail,
Since through experience of this great event
In Arms not worse, in foresight much advanc't,
We may with more successful hope resolve
To wage by force or guile eternal Warr
Irreconcileable, to our grand Foe,
Who now triumphs, and in th'excess of joy
Sole reigning holds the Tyranny of Heav'n.

Many readers and commentators have seen Satan as the real hero of Milton's poem; certainly I'm inclined to say that this is an example of the Devil having all the best tunes. But the real *voice* of *Paradise Lost*, whoever is actually speaking, is Milton's: a complex, grand, conspicuously rhetorical voice, full of rich allusions, exotic place-names, and in complete control of a hovering, circling, weaving and serpentine syntax. Here is that voice at the beginning of Book III, speaking out of Milton's blindness, in a great hymn to light:

Hail holy light, offspring off Heav'n first-born,
Or of th'Eternal Coeternal beam
May I express thee unblam'd? since God is light,
And never but in unapproached light
Dwelt from Eternitie, dwelt then in thee,
Bright effluence of bright essence increate.
Or hear'st thou rather pure Ethereal stream,
Whose fountain who shall tell? before the Sun,
Before the Heavens thou wert, and at the voice
Of God, as with a Mantle didst invest
The rising world of waters dark and deep,
Won from the void and formless infinite.
Thee I re-visit now with bolder wing,
Escap't the Stygian pool, though long detain'd
In that obscure sojourn, while in my flight
Through utter and through middle darkness borne
With other notes then to th' Orphean Lyre
I sung of Chaos and Eternal Night,
Taught by the heaven'ly Muse to venture down
The dark descent, and up to reascend,
Though hard and rare: thee I revisit safe,

And feel thy sovran vital Lamp; but thou
Revisit'st not these eyes, that rowle in vain
To find thy piercing ray, and find no dawn;
So thick a drop serene hath quenched thir Orbs,
Or dim suffusion veild. Yet not the more
Cease I to wander where the Muses haunt
Cleer Spring, or shadie Grove, or Sunnie Hill,
Smit with the love of sacred song; but chief
Thee Sion and the flowrie Brooks beneath
That wash thy hallowd feet, and warbling flow,
Nightly I visit: nor somtimes forget
Those other two equal'd with me in Fate,
So were I equal'd with them in renown,
Blind Thamyris and blind Maeonides,
And Tiresias and Phineus Prophets old.
Then feed on thoughts, that voluntarie move
Harmonious numbers; as the wakeful Bird
Sings darkling, and in shadiest Covert hid
Tunes her nocturnal Note. Thus with the Year
Seasons return, but not to me returns
Day, or the sweet approach of Ev'n or Morn
Or sight of vernal bloom, or Summers Rose,
Or flocks, or herds, or human face divine;
But cloud in stead, and ever-during dark
Surrounds me, from the chearful waies of men
Cut off, and for the Book of knowledge fair
Presented with a Universal blanc
Of Natures works to mee expung'd and ras'd,
And wisdome at one entrance quite shut out.
So much the rather thou Celestial light
Shine inward, and the mind through all her powers
Irradiate, there plant eyes, all mist from thence
Purge and disperse, that I may see and tell
Of things invisible to mortal sight.

And here is that voice again, speaking even more directly from
Milton's sense of purpose and his both instinctive and highly
schooled awareness of his poetic gifts, this time much later on,
in Book IX, when Adam and Eve are about to eat the forbidden
fruit:

No more of talk where God or Angel guest
With Man, as with his Friend, familiar us'd
To sit indulgent, and with him partake
Rural repast, permitting him the while
Venial discourse unblam'd: I now must change
Those notes to Tragic; foul distrust, and breach
Disloyal on the part of Man, revolt,
And disobedience: on the part of Heav'n
Now alienated, distance and distaste,
Anger and just rebuke, and judgement giv'n,
That brought into this World a world of woe,
Sinne and her shadow Death, and Miserie
Death's harbinger: sad task, yet argument
Not less but more heroic then the wrauth
Of stern Achilles on his foe pursu'd
Thrice fugitive about Troy wall; or rage
Of Turnus for Lavinia disespous'd,
Or Neptun's ire or Junos, that so long
Perplex'd the Greek and Cytherea's son;
If answerable style I can obtaine
Of my celestial patroness, who deignes
Her nightly visitation unimplor'd,
And dictates to me slumbring, or inspires
Easie my unpremeditated Verse:
Since first this subject for Heroic Song
Pleas'd me long choosing, and beginning late
Not sedulous by Nature to indite
Warrs, hitherto the onely argument
Heroic deem'd, chief maistrie to dissect
With long and tedious havoc fabl'd Knights
In Battels feign'd; the better fortitude
Of Patience and heroic Martyrdom
Unsung; or to describe Races and Games,
Or tilting furniture, emblazon'd Shields,
Impreses quaint, Caparisons and Steeds;
Bases and tinsel trappings, gorgious Knights
At Joust and Torneament; then marshal'd feast
Serv'd up in Hall with Sewers, and Seneshals;
The skill of artifice or office mean,
Not that which justly gives heroic name

To Person or to Poem. Mee of these
Nor skilld nor studious, higher Argument
Remaines, sufficient of it self to raise
That name, unless an age too late, or cold
Climat, or Years damp my intended wing
Deprest, and much they may, if all be mine,
Not Hers who brings it nightly to my Ear.

The voice is more vigorous when it describes Satan surrounded by the angels during the war in heaven in Book IV:

While thus he spake, th' Angelic Squadron bright
Turnd fierie red, sharpning in mooned hornes
Thir Phalanx, and began to hemm him round
With ported Spears, as thick as when a field
Of Ceres ripe for harvest waving bends
Her bearded Grove of ears, which way the wind
Swayes them; the careful Plowman doubting stands
Least on the threshing floore his hopeful sheaves
Prove chaff. On th' other side Satan allarm'd
Collecting all his might dilated stood,
Like Teneriff or Atlas unremov'd:
His stature reacht the Skie, and on his Crest
Sat horror Plum'd; nor wanted in his graspe
What seemd both Spear and Shield: now dreadful deeds
Might have ensu'd, nor onely Paradise
In this commotion, but the Starrie Cope
Of Heav'n perhaps, or all the Elements
At least had gon to rack, disturbd and torne
With violence of this conflict, had not soon
Th' Eternal to prevent such horrid fray
Hung forth in Heav'n his golden Scales, yet seen
Betwixt Astrea and the Scorpion signe,
Wherein all things created first he weighd,
The pendulous round Earth with ballanc't Aire
In counterpoise, now ponders all events,
Battels and Realms: in these he put two weights
The sequel each of parting and of fight;
The latter quick up flew, and kickt the beam;

These extracts can't give you a full idea of the richness and range of the poem: they only hint at it, and even then that means leaving out some of the strangest and most compelling stuff, such as the great debate among the fallen angels in Hell about the recovery of heaven, or Satan's splendid speech towards the beginning of Book IV. But, since we've had the beginning of the poem, let's at least have the end as well: Book XII, from where the angel Michael leads Adam and Eve out of Paradise. Michael is speaking at the beginning:

This having learnt, thou hast attaind the summe
Of wisdome; hope no higher, though all the Starrs
Thou knewst by name, and all th'ethereal Powers,
All secrets of the deep, all natures works,
Or works of God in Heav'n, Air, Earth, or Sea,
And all the riches of this World enjoydst,
And all the rule, one Empire; onely add
Deeds to thy knowledge answerable, add Faith,
Add Vertue, Patience, Temperance, add Love,
By name to come call'd charitie, the soul
Of all the rest:
                then wilt thou not be loath
To leave this Paradise, but shalt possess
A Paradise within thee, happier farr.
Let us descend now therefore from this top
Of Speculation; for the hour precise
Exacts our parting hence; and see the guards,
By mee encampt on yonder Hill, expect
Thir motion, at whose front a flaming Sword,
In signal of remove, waves fiercely round;
We may no longer stay: go, waken Eve;
Her also I with gentle dreams have calm'd
Portending good, and all her spirits compos'd
To meek submission: thou at season fit
Let her with thee partake what thou hast heard,
Chiefly what may concern her Faith to know,
The great deliverance by her Seed to come
(For by the Womans Seed) on all Mankind.
That ye may live, which will be many dayes,
Both in one Faith unanimous though sad,
With cause for evils past, yet much more cheer'd
With meditation on the happie end.

He ended, and they both descend the Hill;
Descended, Adam to the Bowre where Eve
Lay sleeping ran before, but found her wak't;
And thus with words not sad she him receav'd.
　　Whence thou returnst, & whither wentst, I know;
For God is also in sleep, and dreams advise,
Which he hath sent propitious, some great good
Presaging, since with sorrow and hearts distress
Wearied I fell asleep: but now lead on;
In mee is no delay; with thee to goe,
Is to stay here; without thee here to stay,
Is to go hence unwilling; thou to mee
Art all things under Heav'n, all places thou,
Who for my wilful crime art banisht hence.
This further consolation yet secure
I carry hence; though all by mee is lost,
Such favour I unworthie am voutsaft,
By mee the Promis'd Seed shall all restore.
　　So spake our Mother Eve, and Adam heard
Well pleas'd, but answer'd not; for now too nigh
Th'Archangel stood, and from the other Hill
To thir fixt station, all in bright array
The Cherubim descended: on the ground
Gliding meteorous, as Ev'ning Mist
Ris'n from a River o're the marish glides,
And gathers ground fast at the Labourers heel
Homeward returning. High in Front advanc't,
The brandisht Sword of God before them blaz'd
Fierce as a comet; which with torrid heat,
And vapour as the Libyan air adjust,
Began to parch that temperate clime; whereat
In either hand the hastning Angel caught
Our lingring Parents, and to th'Eastern gate
Led them direct, and down the Cliff as fast
To the subjected Plaine; then disappeer'd.
They looking back, all th'Eastern side beheld
Of Paradise, so late thir happie seat,
Wav'd over by that flaming Brand, the Gate
With dreadful faces throng'd, and fierie armes:
Some natural tears they dropt', but wip'd them soon;

152

The World was all before them, where to choose
Thir place of rest, and Providence thir guide:
They hand in hand with wandring steps and slow,
Through Eden took thir solitarie way.

John Dryden (1631–1700)   A.T.

———————◆◆——————

Towards the end of his long life (he was almost 70 when he died) John Dryden wrote in a letter: 'They say my talent is satire. If it be so, 'tis a fruitful age, and there is an extraordinary crop to gather.' Certainly it's as a satirical poet that Dryden is best known, but he was a man of considerable range, who in his lifetime was as much known for his plays as for his poems, and whose satirical work was chiefly done in his middle and later years. In this section I want you to see some of the satire, but I want you to see some other parts of his output too. Because Dryden was a thoroughgoing *professional* writer, who earned his living – a pretty handsome living – by writing, and who could turn his hand to anything.

He was also very much a *public* writer, and his first notable verses were an elegy on Cromwell, published when he was 28. A year later, equally public and professional, he published a poem on the happy restoration and return of his sacred majesty, Charles II, and a year after that a Panegyric on Charles's coronation. His enemies didn't forget those verses on Cromwell, but he'd played his cards right, and before long he was appointed Poet Laureate.

To write public poetry a poet must have not only a sense of public sympathies but also must feel eager to memorialise, and be capable of recording, those events which catch the public mood. This is what Dryden did in his long poem *Annus Mirabilis* – the Wonderful Year – a poem which patriotically records the English exploits against the Dutch in 1666, but which is perhaps of more interest to us for its sections on the Great Fire of London. The poem has just celebrated the naval defeat of the Dutch (only a temporary defeat, incidentally) and now Dryden changes the mood from one of celebration to one of menace, a turn in the wheel of fortune:

154

But ah! how unsincere are all our joys!
  Which, sent from Heav'n, like Lightning make no stay.
Their palling taste the journeys length destroys,
  Or grief, sent post, o'r-takes them on the way.

Swell'd with our late successes on the Foe,
  Which France and Holland wanted power to cross:
We urge an unseen Fate to lay us low,
  And feed their envious eyes with English loss.

Each element his dread command obeys,
  Who makes or ruines with a smile or frown;
Who as by one he did our Nation raise,
  So now he with another pulls us down.

Yet, London, Empress of the Northern Clime,
  By an high fate thou greatly didst expire;
Great as the worlds, which at the death of time
  Must fall, and rise a nobler frame by fire.

As when some dire Usurper Heav'n provides,
  To scourge his country with a lawless sway:
His birth, perhaps, some petty village hides,
  And sets his cradle out of Fortune's way:

Till fully ripe his swelling fate breaks out,
  And hurries him to mighty mischiefs on:
His Prince supriz'd at first, no ill could doubt,
  And wants the pow'r to meet it when 'tis known.

Such was the rise of this prodigious fire,
  Which in mean buildings first obscurely bred,
From thence did soon to open streets aspire,
  And straight to Palaces and Temples spread.

The diligence of trades and noiseful gain,
  And luxury, more late, asleep were laid:
All was the nights, and in her silent reign,
  No sound the rest of Nature did invade.

In this deep quiet, from what source unknown,
  Those seeds of fire their fatal birth disclose:
And first, few scatt'ring sparks about were blown,
  Big with the flames that to our ruine rose.

Then, in some close-pent room it crept along,
　And, smouldering as it went, in silence fed:
Till th'infant monster, with devouring strong,
　Walk'd boldly upright with exalted head.

Now, like some rich or mighty Murderer,
　Too great for prison, which he breaks with gold:
Who fresher for new mischiefs does appear,
　And dares the world to tax him with the old.

So scapes th'insulting fire his narrow jail,
　And makes small out-lets into open air:
There the fierce winds his tender force assail,
　And beat him down-ward to his first repair.

The winds, like crafty Courtezans, with-held
　His flames from burning, but to blow them more:
And, every fresh attempt, he is repell'd
　With faint denials, weaker than before.

And now, no longer letted of his prey,
　He leaps up at it with inrag'd desire:
O'r-looks the neighbours with a wide survey,
　And nods at every house his threatning fire.

The ghosts of Traitors, from the Bridge descend,
　With bold fanatick spectres to rejoyce:
About the fire into a dance they bend,
　And sing their Sabbath notes with feeble voice.

Our Guardian Angel saw them where he sate
　Above the Palace of our slumbring King,
He sigh'd, abandoning his charge to Fate,
　And, drooping, oft looked back upon the wing.

At length the crackling noise and dreadful blaze,
　Call'd up some waking Lover to the sight:
And long it was ere he the rest could raise,
　Whose heavy eye-lids yet were full of night.

The next to danger, hot pursu'd by fate,
　Half-cloth'd, half naked, hastily retire:
And frighted Mothers strike their breasts, too late,
　For helpless infants left amidst the fire.

Their cries soon waken all the dwellers near:
  Now murmuring noises rise in every street:
The more remote run stumbling with their fear,
  And, in the dark, men justle as they meet.

So weary Bees in little cells repose:
  But if night-robbers lift the well-stor'd Hive,
An humming through their waxen city grows,
  And out upon each others wings they drive.

Now streets grow throng'd and busie as by day:
  Some run for Buckets to the hallow'd Quire:
Some cut the Pipes, and some the Engines play,
  And some more bold mount Ladders to the fire.

In vain: for, from the East, a Belgian wind,
  His hostile breath through the dry rafters sent:
The flames impell'd, soon left their foes behind,
  And forward, with a wanton fury went.

A key of fire ran all along the shore,
  And lighten'd all the river with the blaze:
The waken'd tydes began again to roar,
  And won'dring fish in shining waters gaze.

Old father Thames rais'd up his reverend head,
  But fear'd the fate of Simoeis would return:
Deep in his Ooze he sought his sedgy bed,
  And shrunk his waters back into his urn.

The fire, mean time, walks in a broader gross,
  To either hand his wings he opens wide:
He wades the streets, and straight he reaches cross,
  And plays his longing flames on th'other side.

At first they warm, then scorch, and then they take:
  Now with long necks from side to side they feed:
At length, grown strong, their Mother fire forsake,
  And a new colony of flames succeed.

To every nobler portion of the town,
  The curling billows roul their restless tyde:
In parties now they straggle up and down,
  As armies, unoppos'd, for prey divide.

One mighty Squadron, with a wide wind sped,
    Through narrow lanes his cumber'd fire does haste:
By pow'rful charms of gold and silver led,
    The Lombard Banquers and the Change to waste.

Another backward to the Tow'r would go,
    And slowly eats his way against the wind:
But the main body of the marching foe
    Against th'Imperial Palace is design'd. . .

Night came, but without darkness or repose,
    A dismal picture of the gen'ral doom:
Where souls distracted when the Trumpet blows,
    And half unready with their bodies come.

Those who have homes, when home they do repair,
    To a last lodging call their wand'ring friends.
Their short uneasie sleeps are broke with care,
    To look how near their own destruction tends.

Those who have none sit round where once it was,
    And with full eyes each wonted room require:
Haunting the yet warm ashes of the place,
    As murder'd men walk where they did expire.

Some stir up coals and watch the Vestal fire,
    Others in vain from sight of ruine run:
And, while through burning lab'rinths they retire,
    With loathing eyes repeat what they would shun.

The most, in fields, like herded beasts lie down;
    To dews obnoxious on the grassie floor:
And while their babes in sleep their sorrows drown,
    Sad parents watch the remnants of their store.

While by the motion of the flames they ghess
    What streets are burning now, and what are near,
An infant, waking, to the paps would press
    And meets, instead of milk, a falling tear.

That is clear, clean, supple, elegant verse, not striving for any
other effect than the dignified recording of an experience shared
by a large number of his audience. Though I think it's very

beautifully done, and I'm a great admirer of the *Annus Mirabilis*, what it lacks is energy; and it was energy that Dryden brought to his satirical poetry – in particular the vituperative and wounding energy which he perfected in the rhyming couplet, the so-called 'heroic' couplet. But before we come to the satires themselves, let's look at a poem in which Dryden enumerated some of the qualities he looked for in satire. He does this in an elegy he wrote on the premature death of a young poet who admired Dryden and whom Dryden admired in turn: John Oldham. It's a poem of genuine personal feeling, I think, but it also has the cool, classic quality of Dryden at his best:

> Farewel, too little and too lately known,
> Whom I began to think and call my own;
> For sure our souls were near ally'd; and thine
> Cast in the same Poetick mould with mine.
> One common note on either lyre did strike,
> And knaves and fools we both abhorr'd alike:
> To the same goal did both our studies drive,
> The last set out the soonest did arrive,
> Thus Nisus fell upon the slippery place,
> While his young friend perform'd and won the race.
> O early ripe! to thy abundant store
> What could advancing age have added more?
> It might (what nature never gives the young)
> Have taught the numbers of thy native tongue.
> But Satyr needs not those, and Wit will shine
> Through the harsh cadence of a rugged line.
> A noble error, and but seldom made,
> When poets are by too much force betray'd.
> Thy generous fruits, though gather'd ere their prime
> Still shew'd a quickness; and maturing time
> But mellows what we write to the dull sweets of Rime.
> Once more, hail and farewel; farewel thou young,
> But ah too short, Marcellus of our tongue;
> Thy brows with ivy, and with laurels bound;
> But Fate and gloomy Night encompass thee around.

'The harsh cadence of a rugged line' was not, in fact, an indulgence that Dryden often allowed himself: though he has a more

bludgeoning way with him than Pope, Dryden was usually
polished and smooth in his satire. One of his prime butts was
the poet Thomas Shadwell, and indeed Dryden devoted a whole
poem to demolishing Shadwell. Dryden imagines another bad
poet, Richard Flecknoe, lying on his death-bed and appointing
Shadwell his true heir. Here are the opening lines of Dryden's
poem *MacFlecknoe*:

> All human things are subject to decay,
> And, when Fate summons, Monarchs must obey:
> This Fleckno found, who, like Augustus, young
> Was call'd to empire, and had govern'd long:
> In prose and verse, was own'd, without dispute
> Through all the realms of Non-sense, absolute.
> This aged prince now flourishing in peace,
> And blest with issue of a large increase,
> Worn out with business, did at length debate
> To settle the succession of the state:
> And pond'ring which of all his sons was fit
> To reign, and wage immortal war with wit;
> Cry'd, 'tis resolv'd; for Nature pleads that he
> Should onely rule, who most resembles me:
> Shadwell alone my perfect image bears,
> Mature in dullness from his tender years.
> Shadwell alone, of all my sons, is he
> Who stands confirm'd in full stupidity.
> The rest to some faint meaning make pretence,
> But Shadwell never deviates into sense.
> Some beams of wit on other souls may fall,
> Strike through and make a lucid interval;
> But Shadwell's genuine night admits no ray,
> His rising fogs prevail upon the day:
> Besides his goodly fabrick fills the eye,
> And seems design'd for thoughtless majesty:
> Thoughtless as Monarch Oakes, that shade the plain,
> And, spread in solemn state, supinely reign.

Dryden's most striking achievement in satire, though, is
Absalom and Achitophel. Here, under an elaborate but transparent
code of Bibilical names, he used his satire as a direct political
weapon against the members of a court faction which seemed

dangerous to Charles II, in particular the Earl of Shaftesbury and the Duke of Buckingham, lightly disguised under the names of Achitophel and Zimri (Absalom in the title, by the way, is the Duke of Monmouth). It's said that Charles II himself encouraged Dryden to write the poem. This is the English satirical couplet at its best. Here is Achitophel:

> Of these the false Achitophel was first:
> A name to all succeeding ages curst.
> For close designs, and crooked counsels fit;
> Sagacious, bold, and turbulent of wit:
> Restless, unfixt in principles and place;
> In pow'r unpleas'd, impatient of disgrace.
> A fiery soul, which working out its way,
> Fretted the pigmy-body to decay:
> And o'r inform'd the tenement of clay,
> A daring pilot in extremity;
> Pleas'd with the danger, when the waves went high
> He sought the storms; but for a calm unfit,
> Would steer too nigh the sands, to boast his wit.
> Great wits are sure to madness near alli'd;
> And thin partitions do their bounds divide:
> Else, why should he, with wealth and honour blest,
> Refuse his age the needful hours of Rest?
> Punish a body which he coud not please;
> Bankrupt of life, yet prodigal of ease?
> And all to leave, what with his toil he won,
> To that unfeather'd, two-legg'd thing, a Son:
> Got, while his soul did huddled notions trie;
> And born a shapeless lump, like anarchy.
> In friendship false, implacable in Hate:
> Resolv'd to ruine or to rule the state.
> To compass this, the triple bond he broke;
> The pillars of the publick safety shook:
> And fitted Israel for a foreign yoke.

Finally, even more witheringly and contemptuously, here is what Dryden makes of Buckingham, under the guise of Zimri: Buckingham was himself a wit and playwright, and had already satirised Dryden in a play. But through its tough vigour,

Dryden's portrait survives, and whatever Buckingham said is forgotten:

> Such were the tools; but a whole hydra more
> Remains, of sprouting heads too long, to score.
> Some of their chiefs were princes of the land:
> In the first rank of these did Zimri stand:
> A man so various, that he seem'd to be
> Not one, but all Mankind's epitome.
> Stiff in opinions, always in the wrong;
> Was every thing by starts, and nothing long:
> But, in the course of one revolving moon,
> Was chymist, fidler, states-man, and buffoon:
> Then all for women, painting, rhiming, drinking;
> Besides ten thousand freaks that dy'd in thinking.
> Blest Madman, who coud every hour employ,
> With something New to wish, or to enjoy!
> Railing and praising were his usual theams;
> And both (to shew his judgement) in extreams;
> So over violent, or over civil,
> That every man, with him, was God or Devil.
> In squandering wealth was his peculiar art:
> Nothing went unrewarded, but desert.
> Begger'd by fools, whom still he found too late:
> He had his jest, and they had his estate.
> He laugh'd himself from court; then sought relief
> By forming parties, but could ne'r be chief:
> For, spight of him, the weight of business fell
> On Absalom and wise Achitophel:
> Thus, wicked but in will, of means bereft,
> He left not Faction, but of that was left.

Jonathan Swift (1667-1745)
Alexander Pope (1688-1744)   P.P.

———————◆———————

The half-century between the accession of Queen Anne and the
death of King George II is known in literary history as the
Augustan age. The name was bestowed on it by the age itself –
its statesmen and artists were conscious of a new confidence and
stability, and they likened their times to the great days at the
beginning of the Roman Empire when the Emperor Augustus
restored the glory of Rome after fifty years' civil war. Not only
did Augustus set the state in order, he endeavoured to reform
literature – even to use it as a tool of official policy. His minister,
Maecenas, was patron to Virgil and Horace and the poetry
written in this first Augustan age was in turn the inspiration of
the English poets of the eighteenth century. The Greek and
Roman classics had always been admired and imitated in England,
but the English Augustans now went much further. They saw
themselves as not just the heirs of Virgil and Horace, but almost as
reincarnations of them. The Florentine Humanists of the fifteenth
century had thought very similarly, but by this time England
was a great power, not merely a city-state in Tuscany. The Duke
of Marlborough, Queen Anne's general, was the most successful
of all the English soldiers to invade the Continent, surpassing
in achievement such other commanders as Edward III, Henry
V, the Duke of Wellington and Lord Montgomery. England
was firmly launched on a policy of expansion which was to
culminate in the Empire of Queen Victoria. And Imperial
virtues and patriotism were universally popular, even with
Jonathan Swift and Alexander Pope, who were Tories and
opposed to the war policy of Marlborough. The change in
literary climate which occurred in a matter of two decades was
extreme. The Restoration wits, with their self-conscious
Satanism, were replaced by responsible and serious writers,

163

determined to substitute a sonorous professionalism for the lightweight amateurism of their courtly predecessors. Congreve and Vanbrugh were the last great Restoration dramatists and Congreve's masterpiece, *The Way of the World*, was produced the year John Dryden died, in 1700. The way was clear for Swift and Pope to take over the leadership of letters in England. These two men dominate English poetry for almost a century, long after their deaths, in fact. All poetry written up to Wordsworth bears the stamp of their style, especially Pope's style. They were only two of the growing number of professional writers, but they were supreme in invention and in their insistence on the highest aims for literature. Ranged against them were the journalists of the age – men whose pens could be bought, the hacks of Grub Street, and literary fights were continual and bitter. Many of these mercenaries, such as Daniel Defoe, were themselves very good writers, but they did not share Swift's and Pope's sense of the high calling of poetry. Though party men, Swift and Pope were more independent than their rivals. They lived on terms of intimate acquaintance with the statesmen of the age and addressed them familiarly in poems and letters. Indeed, Pope's various epistles and dedications to members of the nobility are object lessons of formal good manners coupled with lively self-esteem. Pope never grovelled and never flattered – he knew his own superiority too well.

Swift is admired today largely for his prose works, and almost everybody has read *Gulliver's Travels*, at least the first part, the Voyage to Lilliput. His command of English prose has led to his being underestimated as a poet. There are two other reasons why his poetry is not sufficiently esteemed – he is thought too down-to-earth, not elevated enough in language and sentiment; and he is credited with a pathological distaste for human bodily functions, especially in women. But the fact that he nearly always wrote in four-foot couplets (a form which today we associate with Hilaire Belloc's *Cautionary Tales* and much amateur verse on greetings cards and the like) does not prevent his being an absolute master of poetic form. His material is perhaps the most deliberately unelevated of any major poet's – gossip, scandal, humdrum everyday events, servants' hall chat, etc. – yet from it he produces poetry marked with unmistakable signs of genius. His conversational

164

manner and commonsense tone enable him to leap from the ordinary to the striking in one line and to control the development of his verse with complete precision. Poems such as 'The Furniture of a Woman's Mind' and 'A Beautiful Young Nymph going to Bed' are notorious for their scabrous references to female sexuality, but you can set beside them some of the most tender poems ever produced in praise of women – Swift's birthday poems for Stella and Vanessa, the two women in his life. The following poem is Swift's birthday offering to Esther Johnson, the Stella of his journals, in 1710.

> All Travellers at first incline
> Where'er they see the fairest Sign;
> And if they find the Chambers neat,
> And like the liquor, and the Meat,
> Will call again, and recommend
> The Angel-Inn to ev'ry Friend:
> What though the Painting grows decay'd,
> The House will never lose its Trade:
> Nay, tho' the treach'rous Tapster Thomas
> Hangs a new Angel two doors from us,
> As fine as Dawbers Hand can make it,
> In hopes that Strangers may mistake it;
> We think it both a Shame and Sin
> To quit the true old Angel-Inn.
>
> Now, this is Stella's Case in fact,
> An Angel's face, a little crack'd:
> (Could Poets, or could Painters fix
> How Angels look at Thirty-six):
> This drew us in at first, to find
> In such a Form an Angel's Mind;
> And ev'ry Virtue now supplies
> The fainting rays of Stella's Eyes.
> See, at her Levee crowding Swains;
> Whom Stella freely entertains
> With Breeding, Humour, Wit and Sense:
> And puts them to so small Expence:
> Their Mind so plentifully fills,
> And makes such reasonable Bills;
> So little gets for what she gives,

We really wonder how she lives!
And had her Stock been less, no doubt,
She must have long ago run out.

Then who can think we'll quit the Place,
When Doll hangs out a newer Face;
Or stop and light at Cloe's Head,
With Scraps and Leavings to be fed.

Then Cloe, still go on to prate
Of Thirty-six and Thirty-eight:
Pursue your Trade of Scandal-Picking,
Your Hints, that Stella is no Chicken:
Your Innuendo's, when you tell us,
That Stella loves to talk with Fellows:
And let me warn you to believe
A Truth, for which your Soul should grieve:
That should you live to see the Day
When Stella's Locks must all be grey:
When Age must print a furrow'd Trace
On ev'ry Feature of her Face:
Though you, and all your senseless Tribe,
Could Art, or Time, or Nature Bribe,
To make you look like Beauty's Queen,
And hold for ever at Fifteen:
No Bloom of Youth can ever blind
The Cracks and Wrinkles of your Mind:
All Men of Sense will pass your Door,
And crowd to Stella's at Fourscore.

In *Gulliver's Travels*, *A Modest Proposal* and *A Tale of a Tub*, Swift looks at human weakness without mercy. He is always more acerbic in prose than in poetry. The misanthropy of these books is almost wholly black, although they remain outwardly true to the polite conventions of satire. But Swift kept a different part of his imagination for his verse. He wrote a great deal of it, and there is ample evidence throughout of his fondness for people, whatever their follies. The next poem, 'On Poetry, a Rhapsody', is a burlesque recipe for writing fashionable verse. Swift was out to knock hacks and dunces, just as Pope was. The following extract is limited to a couple of self-contained episodes. As Swift knew (and as most of us ruefully admit), in poetry many are called but few are chosen. The pitfalls are numerous and the dilemmas the poetaster can get himself into are described with wicked accuracy.

> All Humane Race would fain be Wits,
> And Millions miss, for one that hits.
> Young's Universal Passion, Pride,
> Was never known to spread so wide.
> Say, Britain, cou'd you ever boast,
> Three Poets in an Age at most?
> Our chilling Climate hardly bears
> A Sprig of Bays in Fifty Years:
> While ev'ry Fool his Claim alledges,
> As if it grew in common Hedges.
> What Reason can there be assign'd
> For this Perverseness in the Mind!
> Brutes find out where their Talents lie:
> A Bear will not attempt to fly:
> A founder'd Horse will oft debate,
> Before he tries a five-barr'd Gate:
> A Dog by instinct turns aside,
> Who sees the Ditch too deep and wide,
> But Man we find the only Creature,
> Who, led by Folly, combats Nature:
> Who, when she loudly cries, Forbear
> With Obstinacy fixes there;
> And, where his Genius least inclines,
> Absurdly bends his whole Designs.
>
> Not Empire to the Rising-Sun,
> By Valour, Conduct, Fortune won;
> Not highest Wisdom in Debates
> For framing Laws to govern States;
> Not Skill in Sciences profound,
> So large to grasp the Circle round;
> Such Heav'nly Influence require,
> As how to strike the Muses Lyre.
>
> Not Beggar's Brat on Bulk begot;
> Not Bastard of a Pedlar Scot;
> Not Boy brought up to cleaning Shoes;

The Spawn of Bridewell, or the Stews;
Not Infants dropt, the spurious Pledges
Of Gypsies litt'ring under Hedges,
Are so disqualify'd by Fate
To rise in Church, or Law, or State,
As he, whom Phoebus in his Ire
Hath blasted with Poetick Fire.

Hobbes clearly proves that ev'ry Creature
Lives in a State of War by Nature.
The Greater for the Smaller watch,
But meddle seldom with their Match.
A Whale of mod'rate Size will draw
A Shole of Herrings down his Maw;
A Fox with Geese his Belly crams;
A Wolf destroys a thousand Lambs.
But, search among the rhiming Race,
The Brave are worry'd by the Base.
If, on Parnassus' Top you sit,
You rarely bite, are always bit:
Each Poet of inferior Size
On you shall rail and criticize;
And try to tear you Limb from Limb,
While others do as much for him:
The Vermin only teaze and pinch
Their Foes superior by an Inch.
So, Nat'ralists observe, a Flea
Hath smaller Fleas than on him prey,
And these have smaller yet to bite 'em,
And so proceed ad infinitum:
Thus ev'ry Poet in his Kind,
Is bit by him that comes behind;
Who, tho' too little to be seen,
Can Teaze, and gall, and give the Spleen;
Call Dunces, Fools, and Sons of Whores,
Lay Grub-Street at each others Doors:
Extol the Greek and Roman Masters,
And curse our modern Poetasters:
Complain, as many an ancient Bard did,
How Genius is no more rewarded:

How wrong a Taste prevails among us;
How much our Ancestors out-sung us;
Can personate an aukward Scorn
For those who are not Poets born:
And all their Brother Dunces lash,
Who crowd the Press with hourly Trash.

Swift was born in Dublin of English parents in 1667: the majority of his best poems come from late in his life, after he had retired from practical politics and pamphleteering. He had been made Dean of St Patrick's Cathedral, Dublin, when he expected some better post in England. The hostility of the court stood in the way of his ultimate preferment. He greatly missed his English friends, but this didn't make him hostile to Ireland. The Irish people have never had a truer friend, and Swift used his pen to fight for their rights throughout his life. It's remarkable how unembittered this old man, a prey to many diseases and disappointments, was. His greatest poem was written in his Irish exile – the 'Verses on the Death of Dr Swift'. There's nothing confessional about it, yet it is one of the most moving poems in the language. It's much too long to quote entire, but the passages printed here can be read one after the other without disturbing the general argument.

Behold the fatal Day arrive!
How is the Dean? He's just alive.
Now the departing Pray'r is read:
    He hardly breathes. The Dean is dead.
Before the Passing-Bell begun,
The News thro' half the Town has run.
O, may we all for Death prepare!
What has he left? And Who's his Heir?
I know no more than what the News is,
'Tis all bequeath'd to Publick Uses.
To Publick Use! a perfect Whim!
What had the Publick done for him!
Mere Envy, Avarice, and Pride!
He gave it all: – But, first he dy'd.
And had the Dean, in all the Nation,
No worthy Friend, no poor Relation?

So ready to do Strangers good,
Forgetting his own Flesh and Blood?

Here shift the Scene, to represent
How those I love, my Death lament,
Poor POPE will grieve a Month; and GAY
A WEEK; and ARBUTHNOT a Day.

St John himself will scarce forbear
To bite his Pen, and drop a Tear.
The rest will give a Shrug, and cry,
I'm sorry; but we all must dye.

My female Friends, whose tender Hearts
Have better learn'd to act their Parts,
Receive the News in doleful Dumps,
The Dean is dead (and what is Trumps?)
The Lord have Mercy on his Soul
(Ladies I'll venture for the Vole)
Six Deans they say must bear the Pall,
(I wish I knew what King to call.)
Madam, your Husband will attend
The Funeral of so good a friend.
No Madam, 'tis a shocking Sight,
And he's engag'd Tomorrow Night!
My Lady Club wou'd take it ill
If he shou'd fail her at Quadrill.
He lov'd the Dean. (I led a Heart.)
But, dearest Friends, they say, must part.
His Time was come, he ran his Race;
We hope he's in a better Place.

Perhaps I may allow, the Dean
Had too much Satyr in his Vein;
And seem'd determined not to starve it,
Because no Age could more deserve it.
Yet, Malice never was his Aim;
He lash'd the Vice, but spar'd the Name.
No Individual could resent,
Where Thousands equally were meant:
His Satyr points at no Defect,

But what all Mortals may correct;
For, he abbhor'd that senseless Tribe
Who call it Humour when they jibe:
He spar'd a Hump or crooked Nose,
Whose owners set not up for Beaux.
True genuine Dulness mov'd his Pity,
Unless it offer'd to be witty.
Those, who their Ignorance confess'd,
He ne'er offended with a Jest;
But, laugh'd to hear an Idiot quote
A Verse from Horace, learn'd by Rote.

He knew an hundred pleasant Stories,
With all the turns of Whigs and Tories:
Was chearful to his dying Day,
And Friends would let him have his Way.

He gave the little Wealth he had,
To build a House for Fools and Mad:
And shew'd by one satyric Touch,
No Nation wanted it so much;
That Kingdom he hath left his Debtor,
I wish it soon may have a Better.

Alexander Pope was Swift's junior by twenty years, but their
friendship is a rare example of two men of genius seeing eye to
eye. Pope is the most precocious poet in English. His *Essay on
Criticism*, possibly the most polished long poem in the language,
was written when he was twenty-one. Before that, he had
perfected the heroic couplet with exemplary virtuosity in his
Pastorals, products of his teens. Pope was born writing well. He
also had the faculty of understanding things without having
experienced them. His material needs were all in books, and
from his earliest years he absorbed the literature and philosophy
of the past. He served up a compendium of his reading in *An
Essay on Criticism*, but instead of producing a dry-as-dust academic
poem or an impudent piece of showing-off, he achieved the pro-
digious feat of defining the art of good judging in both literature
and life. The classics were his watchwords, but he used them to
instil a love of what was excellent, not to do away with original
observation. In this extract, Pope is amusing himself by giving

examples of clichéd writing and then going on to offer a formula
for adding good taste to imagination.

> But most by Numbers judge a Poet's song,
> And smooth or rough, with them, is right or wrong;
> In the bright Muse tho' thousand Charms conspire,
> Her Voice is all these tuneful Fools admire,
> Who haunt Parnassus but to please their Ear,
> Not mend their Minds; as some to Church repair,
> Not for the Doctrine, but the Musick there.
> These equal Syllables alone require,
> Tho' oft the Ear the open Vowels tire,
> While Expletives their feeble Aid do join,
> And ten low Words oft creep in one dull line,
> While they ring round the same unvary'd Chimes,
> With sure returns of still expected Rhymes.
> Where-e'er you find the cooling Western Breeze,
> In the next line, it whispers thro' the Trees.
> If Chrystal streams with pleasing Murmurs creep,
> The Reader's threaten'd (not in vain) with Sleep.
> Then, at the last, and only Couplet fraught
> With some unmeaning Thing they call a Thought,
> A needless Alexandrine ends the Song,
> That like a wounded Snake, drags its slow length along.
> Leave such to tune their own dull Rhimes, and know
> What's roundly smooth, or languishingly slow;
> And praise the Easie Vigor of a Line,
> Where Denham's Strength, and Waller's Sweetness join.
> True ease in writing comes from Art, not Chance,
> As those move easiest who have learn'd to dance.
> 'Tis not enough no Harshness give Offence,
> The Sound must seem an Echo to the Sense.
> Soft is the Strain when Zephyr gently blows,
> And the smooth Stream in smoother Numbers flows;
> But when loud Surges lash the Sounding Shore,
> The hoarse, rough Verse shou'd like the Torrent roar.
> When Ajax strives, some Rocks' vast Weight to throw,
> The Line too labours, and the Words move slow;
> Not so, when swift Camilla scours the Plain,
> Flies o'er th'unbending Corn, and skims along the Main.

Hear how Timotheus' vary'd Lays surprise,
And bid alternate Passions fall and rise!
While, at each Change, the Son of Lybian Jove
Now burns with Glory, and then melts with Love;
Now his fierce Eyes with sparkling Fury glow;
Now Sighs steal out, and Tears begin to flow:
Persians and Greeks like Turns of Nature found,
And the World's Victor stood subdu'd by Sound!
The Pow'r of Musick all our Hearts allow;
And what Timotheus was, is Dryden now.
Avoid Extreams; and shun the Fault of such
Who still are pleas'd too little, or too much.
At ev'ry trifle scorn to take Offence,
That always shows Great pride, or little Sense;
Those Heads as Stomachs are not sure the best
Which nauseate all, and nothing can digest.
Yet let not each gay Turn thy Rapture move,
For Fools admire, but Men of Sense approve;
As things seem large which we thro' Mists descry,
Dulness is ever apt to magnify.

Pope's most exquisite work is his heroicomical epic *The Rape
of the Lock*. It came about from a scandal of the day, when a
gentleman affronted a lady by snipping off one of her curls, and
Pope was asked to reconcile the families by treating the happen-
ing in a mock-heroic travesty of the Trojan War. The artificiality
is as light and yet as passionate as Mozart's opera *Cosi Fan Tutti*,
a work which this poem resembles closely. Real feelings are
enveloped in a serene swathe of style. In the course of the poem,
Pope finds time to comment on the manners and fashions of
polite society. Here's the beginning of the third Canto, as
another day dawns over smart London. Note the brief but grim
modulation at the introduction of the bored Judge and the
hungry Jurymen. Pope knew well enough the realities that lay
behind the Augustan calm.

Close by those meads for ever crown'd with flow'rs,
Where Thames with pride surveys his rising Tow'rs,
There stands a structure of Majestick frame,
Which from the neighb'ring Hampton takes its name.
Here Britain's statesmen oft the Fall foredoom

173

Of foreign tyrants, and of nymphs at home;
Here thou, great Anna! whom three realms obey,
Dost sometimes counsel take – and sometimes tea.
   Hither the heroes and the nymphs resort,
To taste awhile the pleasures of a court;
In various Talk th'instructive hours they past,
Who gave the ball, or paid the visit last:
One speaks the glory of the British queen,
And one describes a charming Indian screen;
A third interprets Motions, looks, and eyes;
At ev'ry word a reputation dies.
Snuff, or the fan, supply each pause of chat,
With singing, laughing, ogling, and all that.
   Mean while declining from the noon of day,
The sun obliquely shoots his burning ray;
The hungry judges soon the sentence sign,
And wretches hang that jury-men may dine;
The merchant from th'Exchange returns in Peace,
And the long Labours of the Toilette cease.

Pope offers us a rare glimpse into his private world in the Epistle
he wrote to his medical friend, Dr Arbuthnot. Here he goes
some way to disclosing his nature and temperament in the way
Swift did in the verses on his own death. For instance, he gives
an account of his early apprenticeship as a poet and lists the
authors and men of letters who had encouraged him in his youth.
Arbuthnot was a life-long friend and made up, with Swift and
Gay, the Scriblerus Club, which Pope wrote satirical poems for.
This autobiographical excerpt is followed by another part of the
work, his famous description of the character of Addison, whom
he calls Atticus. He had written this portrait many years
previously and incorporated it into the epistle almost unchanged.
The unflattering picture he draws of Addison is not unfair. That
sort of belletrist is still with us, pontificating from a chair in a
university or dictating opinion in a Sunday paper – the kind of
man whose taste is always up-to-date and whose enthusiasms are
the perfect average of everybody's views.

   Why did I write? what sin to me unknown
Dipt me in ink, my parents', or my own?
As yet a child, nor yet a fool to fame,

I lisp'd in numbers, for the numbers came.
I left no calling for this idle trade,
No duty broke, no father dis-obey'd.
The muse but serv'd to ease some friend, not wife,
To help me thro' this long disease, my life,
To second, Arbuthnot! thy art and care,
And teach, the being you preserv'd, to bear.

But why then publish? Granville the polite,
And knowing Walsh, would tell me I could write;
Well-natur'd Garth inflam'd with early praise,
And Congreve lov'd, and Swift endur'd my lays;
The courtly Talbot, Somers, Sheffield read,
Ev'n mitred Rochester would nod the head,
And St John's self (great Dryden's friends before)
With open arms receiv'd one poet more.
Happy my studies, when by these approv'd!
Happier the author, when by these belov'd!

*

Peace to all such! but were there One whose fires
True genius kindles, and fair fame inspires,
Blest with each talent and each art to please,
And born to write, converse, and live with ease:
Shou'd such a man, too fond to rule alone,
Bear, like the Turk, no brother near the throne,
View him with scornful, yet with jealous eyes,
And hate for arts that caus'd himself to rise;
Damn with faint praise, assent with civil leer,
And without sneering, teach the rest to sneer;
Willing to wound, and yet afraid to strike,
Just hint a fault, and hesitate dislike;
Alike reserv'd to blame, or to commend,
A tim'rous foe, and a suspicious friend,
Dreading ev'n fools, by flatterers besieg'd,
And so obliging that he ne'er oblig'd;
Like Cato, give his little Senate laws,
And sit attentive to his own applause;
While wits and templers ev'ry sentence raise,
And wonder with a foolish face of praise.
Who but must laugh, if such a man there be?
Who would not weep, if Atticus were he!

Pope's most extraordinary work is *The Dunciad*. This long poem in four books is his last campaign against the dunces of his generation, but it is also something more. It's an extended vision of the triumph of Dullness, a goddess Pope always fought. His invention becomes grotesque, he sees a world dislocated from its proper order by a whole horde of ambitious suitors to the uncreative goddess. Her kingdom on earth is to be tasteless, unquiet, extensive and eternal. In these lines which end the poem, Pope becomes Dantesque. After the horror wrought by the anarchy of Dullness, the epilogue shows the world buried under everlasting blackness. Nobody can say that the heroic couplet lacks force after experiencing the magnificence of Pope's use of it in *The Dunciad*.

> In vain, in vain, – the all-composing Hour
> Resistless falls: The muse obeys the pow'r.
> She comes! she comes! the sable Throne behold
> Of night Primaeval, and of Chaos old!
> Before her, Fancy's gilded clouds decay,
> And all its varying Rain-bows die away.
> Wit shoots in vain its momentary fires,
> The meteor drops, and in a flash expires.
> As one by one, at dread Medea's strain,
> The sick'ning stars fade off th'ethereal plain;
> As Argus' eyes by Hermes' wand opprest,
> Clos'd one by one to everlasting rest;
> Thus at her felt approach, and secret might,
> Art after art goes out, and all is Night.
> See skulking truth to her old cavern fled,
> Mountains of Casuistry heap'd over her head!
> Philosophy, that lean'd on Heav'n before,
> Shrinks to her second cause, and is no more.
> Physic of Metaphysic begs defence,
> And Metaphysic calls for aid on Sense!
>
> See mystery to mathematics fly!
> In vain! they gaze, turn giddy, rave, and die.
> Religion blushing veils her sacred fires,
> And unawares Morality expires.
> Nor public flame, nor private, dares to shine;
> Nor human spark is left, nor glimpse divine!

Lo! thy dread empire, chaos! is restor'd;
Light dies before thy uncreating word:
Thy hand, great Anarch! lets the curtain fall;
And universal darkness buries all.

Thomas Gray (1716–1771)
Samuel Johnson (1709–1784)
Christopher Smart (1722–1771)
William Cowper (1731–1800)   P.P.

———————————•———————————

Alexander Pope remained the ideal of English poets throughout
the eighteenth century – at least until the change in sensibility
which came in with Blake and Wordsworth. The course of
eighteenth-century poetry is a good example of what happens to
a movement when it runs down. Augustan discipline, decorum
and respect for the Classics were not the inventions of Swift and
Pope, but their skill confirmed these virtues in the minds of
succeeding generations. Almost every poet of the time wrote in
couplets in the manner of Pope. There's an amusing account in
James Boswell's *Journal* of a year spent in Utrecht in Holland,
where he was trying to reform himself of such pastimes as
wenching and idling in smart society by a course of serious study.
At Samuel Johnson's suggestion, Boswell set himself the task of
writing about twenty lines of poetry a day on some elevated
theme. The poems he turned out are, of course, directly imitated
from Pope, just as are Johnson's own heroic couplets in his
famous poems, 'London' and 'The Vanity of Human Wishes'.
Johnson got quite close to Pope at times, but his hectoring
tone and fondness for the plainest of plain speech kept his sights
too low. Of the thousands of lines in couplets written after
Pope, very few are of real value. Only one poet restored the
couplet to its former greatness – George Crabbe – but the form
itself is still alive today, if only for the purposes of satire or light
verse, as poets such as Roy Campbell and W. H. Auden have
demonstrated.

   But if their couplets were usually failures, eighteenth-century
poets had more success with the rhymed stanza (very often a
quatrain), blank verse and the ode. Odes are poems of moderate
178

length in rather rhetorical language, usually celebrating some special scene or occasion. They allow a mixture of different lengths of line and also permit changing metres, though only within a very elevated manner. The Greeks perfected them, Pindar of Thebes being universally admired among ancient authors for his odes. Thomas Gray, who lived from 1716 to 1771 and who gave English literature its best-known poem, 'An Elegy Written in a Country Churchyard', wrote several odes which he labelled Pindarick. The best is 'Ode on a Distant Prospect of Eton College'. The language is extremely formal, the sentiments entirely conventional and the tone deeply sententious. Yet it is a fine poem, in part because it says in a memorable way so many things we know already. A poet doesn't have to be original to be good, and Gray's generalisations are acceptable because of the great care he took in expressing them. It is a sort of genius to be able to make proverbial statements before they become proverbial. Gray himself was a studious, back-biting, melancholy man, who was only at ease in the atmosphere of Cambridge University. But he had been in the outside world and he could remember what it felt like. His 'Eton College' ode is simple enough. The poet is revisiting the school he went to as a boy. Looking over its buildings and playing-fields, he sees the present generation of boys doing the same things he did as a youth. He addresses everybody and everything in the conventional terms of his day – a small hollow is called 'a shade', the Thames Valley becomes 'a watery glade', and so on. His view of the schoolboys as a race of innocents blissfully unaware of disappointments to come seems antediluvian to us, and yet may be as true as the latest psychoanalytic projections of them as embryo Prometheuses and Oedipuses. One thing to listen for is the subtle measure of the rhythm: the altering lengths of line and easily shifting emphases are most cleverly arranged. If you dislike the way the poet addresses Father Thames and asks him to tell him who drives the hoop or tosses the ball and other poetic invocations, you have Dr Johnson on your side. But poetry isn't debate and the invoking of inanimate objects is a legitimate way of keeping a poem going. In the second half, Gray passes on to a vision of the whole human condition. Once again it is a gloomy summary of the ends of life and knowledge. The poem concludes with two of the most famous lines in English, but there is a splendid

line just before them, one which sums up the whole poem –
'thought would destroy their paradise'.

Ye distant spires, ye antique towers,
That crown the watery glade,
Where grateful Science still adores
Her Henry's holy shade;
And ye, that from the stately brow
Of Windsor's heights the expanse below
Of grove, of lawn, of mead survey,
Whose turf, whose shade, whose flowers among
Wanders the hoary Thames along
His silver-winding way:

Ah, happy hills! ah, pleasing shade!
Ah, fields beloved in vain!
Where once my careless childhood strayed,
A stranger yet to pain!
I feel the gales that from ye blow
A momentary bliss bestow,
As waving fresh their gladsome wing,
My weary soul they seem to soothe,
And, redolent of joy and youth,
To breathe a second spring.

Say, Father Thames, for thou hast seen
Full many a sprightly race
Disporting on thy margent green
The paths of pleasure trace;
Who foremost now delight to cleave,
With pliant arm, thy glassy wave?
The captive linnet which enthral?
What idle progeny succeed
To chase the rolling circle's speed,
Or urge the flying ball?

While some on earnest business bent
Their murmuring labours ply
'Gainst graver hours, that bring constraint
To sweeten liberty:
Some bold adventurers disdain
The limits of their little reign,

And unknown regions dare descry:
Still as they run they look behind,
They hear a voice in every wind,
And snatch a fearful joy.

Gay Hope is theirs by fancy fed,
Less pleasing when possessed;
The tear forgot as soon as shed,
The sunshine of the breast:
Theirs buxom Health, of rosy hue,
Wild Wit, Invention ever new,
And lively Cheer, of Vigour born;
The thoughtless day, the easy night,
The spirits pure, the slumbers light
That fly the approach of morn.

Alas! regardless of their doom
The little victims play;
No sense have they of ills to come,
Nor care beyond to-day:
Yet see, how all around them wait
The ministers of human fate
And black Misfortune's baleful train! ·
Ah, show them where in ambush stand,
To seize their prey, the murderous band!
Ah, tell them they are men!

These shall the fury Passions tear,
The vultures of the mind,
Disdainful Anger, pallid Fear,
And Shame that sculks behind;
Or pining Love shall waste their youth,
Or Jealousy, with rankling tooth,
That inly gnaws the secret heart,
And Envy wan, and faded Care,
Grim-visaged comfortless Despair,
And Sorrow's piercing dart.

Ambition this shall tempt to rise,
Then whirl the wretch from high,
To bitter Scorn a sacrifice,
And grinning Infamy.

The stings of Falsehood those shall try
And hard Unkindness' altered eye,
That mocks the tear it forced to flow;
And keen Remorse with blood defiled,
And moody Madness laughing wild
Amid severest woe.

Lo! in the Vale of Years beneath
A grisly troop are seen,
The painful family of Death,
More hideous than their Queen:
This racks the joints, this fires the veins,
That every labouring sinew strains,
Those in the deeper vitals rage:
Lo! Poverty, to fill the band,
That numbs the soul with icy hand,
And slow-consuming Age.

To each his sufferings: all are men,
Condemned alike to groan;
The tender for another's pain,
The unfeeling for his own.
Yet, ah! why should they know their fate,
Since sorrow never comes too late,
And happiness too swiftly flies?
Thought would destroy their paradise!
No more; – where ignorance is bliss,
'Tis folly to be wise.

Dr Johnson said that Eton College suggested nothing to Gray which every beholder doesn't equally think and feel, and also that Gray thought his language the more poetical the more remote it was from common use. These criticisms come badly from Johnson. The Great Lexicographer and supreme embodiment of the English spirit is rather a mediocre poet. His common-sense about people and his measured prose are admirable, but poor sycophantic Boswell is the more interesting writer. Johnson's *Dictionary* and his *Lives of the Poets* are the best of his original writings. He shared to the full the century's melancholy – the opposite of its overcharged love of reason. The 'black dog', as they called the migraine or spleen, perched on Johnson's shoulder while he wrote his poetry. But he was a generous man, and, after he became famous and reasonably well-off, he sheltered various unfortunates in his house. One was a physician, Robert Levet, who died not long before Johnson himself, in 1782. The great doctor, so near his own end, left some exemplary verses on the death of his friend. These represent him in a more emotional vein than do his better-known classicising poems. If the general feeling remains cold, that is the fault of eighteenth-century decorum: a considerable personal involvement lies behind this formal lament, 'On the Death of Dr Robert Levet':

> Condemn'd to hope's delusive mine,
> As on we toil from day to day,
> By sudden blasts, or slow decline,
> Our social comforts drop away.
>
> Well tried through many a varying year,
> See LEVET to the grave descend;
> Officious, innocent, sincere,
> Of ev'ry friendless name the friend.
>
> Yet still he fills affection's eye,
> Obscurely wise, and coarsely kind;
> Nor, letter'd arrogance, deny
> Thy praise to merit unrefin'd.
>
> When fainting nature call'd for aid,
> And hov'ring death prepar'd the blow,
> His vig'rous remedy display'd
> The power of art without the show.
>
> In misery's darkest caverns known,
> His useful care was ever nigh,
> Where hopeless anguish pour'd his groan,
> And lonely want retir'd to die.
>
> No summons mock'd by chill delay,
> No petty gain disdain'd by pride,
> The modest wants of ev'ry day
> The toil of every day supplied.
>
> His virtues walk'd their narrow round,
> Nor made a pause, nor left a void;
> And sure th'Eternal Master found
> The single talent well employed.

The busy day, the peaceful night,
Unfelt, uncounted, glided by;
His frame was firm, his powers were bright,
Tho' now his eightieth year was nigh.

Then with no throbbing fiery pain,
No cold gradations of decay,
Death broke at once the vital chain,
And free'd his soul the nearest way.

According to Boswell, Dr Johnson saw no reason why the poet Christopher Smart should have been locked up in Bedlam. Society thought otherwise, since Smart's insanity took the form of religious mania and the eighteenth century had small taste for such enthusiasm. While in Bedlam, where he appears to have been treated humanely, even by our standards, and allowed a room, a garden and a cat of his own, Smart wrote his great poem, 'Jubilate Agno' (Rejoice in the Lamb), probably the strangest single literary production of the century. Smart's career had begun orthodoxly enough at Cambridge, where he was a classical scholar and won a reputation as a wit but also as a heavy drinker. He tired of academic life and came to London to work in Grub Street. His many poems, articles and texts for London editors and musicians show that he overworked badly, and he also took to drinking more heavily. He married a bookseller's daughter, which further articled him to hack work. At the same time, he took his calling as a poet seriously and five times won the Seatonian Prize for Poetry, offered by Cambridge University. Most of his poetry before his breakdown is average eighteenth-century stuff: some of the lighter pieces are engaging and his blank-verse poem in imitation of *The Georgics*, entitled 'The Hop Garden', has a distinct feeling for the landscape of his childhood in Kent. But nothing prepares us for the impact of 'Jubilate Agno'. Smart was locked up some time in 1757, probably at the instigation of his family, and he was kept in asylums until 1763. He had begun to upset people by such conduct as urging them to join him in public prayer in unlikely places like St James's Park. 'Jubilate Agno' shows the strong influence of the rhapsodic prose-poetry of the Bible, especially the psalms. Today it does not seem mad, and not even very obscure. It was intended to be spoken aloud with an antiphonal
184

effect, rather like the responses in church. The whole manuscript (and less than half has survived, nothing from it being published before 1939) is divided into long lines beginning either with the word 'Let' or the word 'For'. Originally, there must have been one 'For' verse to answer each 'Let' verse. The 'Let' verses are mostly Biblical and constitute a litany of praise of God by the animal kingdom, whose names are coupled with characters from the Old Testament. Smart selected his creatures not only from natural histories of his time but also from the Latin of Pliny and legendary bestiaries. The 'For' verses are more personal and often refer to Smart's own circumstances, especially to his misfortunes. Fortunately for posterity, his paranoia took the form of manic elevation of spirit and his unhappy life is transmuted to love of God. The matching of verse and response is not always very close. Nor are the pairs of lines necessarily related to each other in sequence, though frequently Smart strikes a particular vein of concern which runs through a number of consecutive pairings. The following pairs are the best from the two hundred and fifty in the most complete section of the manuscript. They are not all consecutive in the original.

Let Achsah rejoice with the Pigeon who is an antidote to malignity and will carry a letter /
For I bless God for the Postmaster general and all conveyancers of letters under his care especially Allen & Shelvock

Let Tohu rejoice with the Grouse – the Lord further the cultivating of heaths and the peopling of deserts /
For my grounds in New Canaan shall infinitely compensate for the flats and maynes of Staindrop Moor.

Let Hillel rejoice with Ammodytes, whose colour is deceitful and he plots against the pilgrim's feet /
For the praise of God can give to a mute fish the notes of a nightingale.

Let Eli rejoice with Leucon – he is an honest fellow, which is a rarity /
For I have seen the White Raven and Thomas Hall of Willingham and am myself a greater curiosity than both.

Let Hushim rejoice with the King's Fisher, who is of royal beauty, tho' plebian size /

For in my nature I quested for beauty, but God, God hath sent
me to sea for pearls.

Let Bedan rejoice with Ossifrage – the bird of prey and the man
of prayer /
For nature is more various than observation tho' observers be
innumerable.

Let Bukki rejoice with the Buzzard, who is clever, with the
reputation of a silly fellow /
For Silly Fellow! Silly Fellow! is against me and belongeth
neither to me nor to my family.

Let Joram rejoice with the Water Rail, who takes his delight in
the river /
For I pray God bless the CAM – Mr. HIGGS & Mr. & Mrs.
WASHBOURNE as the drops of the dew.

Let Shephatiah rejoice with the little Owl, which is the winged
Cat /
For I am possessed of a cat, surpassing in beauty, from whom I
take occasion to bless Almighty God.

Let Zelophehad rejoice with Ascalabotes who casteth not his
coat till a new one is prepared for him /
For the Sun's at work to make me a garment and the Moon is at
work for my wife.

Let Andrew rejoice with the Whale, who is arrayd in beauteous
blue & is a combination of bulk & activity /
For they work upon me with their harping-irons, which is a
barbarous instrument, because I am more unguarded
than others.

Let Philip rejoice with Boca, which is a fish that can speak /
For the ENGLISH TOUNGUE shall be the language of the WEST.

Let Urbane rejoice with Glanis, who is a crafty fish who bites
away the bait and saves himself /
For the TRUMPET of God is a blessed intelligence & so are all
the instruments in Heaven.

Let Stachys rejoice with Glauciscus, who is good for Women's
milk /
For God the Father Almighty plays upon the HARP of stupen-
dous magnitude and melody.

Let Aristobulus rejoice with Glycymerides who is pure and
    sweet /
For at that time malignity ceases and the devils themselves are at
    peace.

Let Herodion rejoice with Holothuria which are prickly fishes /
For this time is perceptible to man by a remarkable stillness and
    serenity of soul.

It's doubtful that Smart ever intended publishing 'Jubilate
Agno'. As his spirits broke in confinement, the poem degenerated
into little more than a device for recording the passage of time –
he took to adding a line a day. Some time before the end, he
wrote the section which has become the most famous – his
praise of his cat Jeoffry. His cat is very Blakean – he says of it,
'For the Cherub Cat is a form of the Angel Tiger'.

For I will consider my cat Jeoffry.
For he is the servant of the Living God duly and daily
    serving him.
For at the first glance of the glory of God in the East he
    worships in his way.
For this is done by wreathing his body seven times round
    with elegant quickness.
For if he meets another cat he will kiss her in kindness.
For one mouse in seven escapes by his dallying.
For he counteracts the powers of darkness by his electrical
    skin & glaring eyes.
For he is an instrument for the children to learn bene-
    volence on.
For the English Cats are the best in Europe.
For he knows that God is his Saviour.
For there is nothing sweeter than his peace when at rest.
For he is of the Lord's poor and so indeed is he called by
    benevolence
perpetually – Poor Jeoffry! Poor Jeoffry! the rat has bit thy
    throat.
For I bless the name of the Lord Jesus that Jeoffry is
    better.
For by stroking him I have found out electricity.
For he can tread to all the measures upon the musick.

William Cowper has much in common with Smart. He too suffered mental derangement, but while Smart was manic Cowper felt sinful and depressed – partly because he had been indoctrinated into severe Evangelical Calvinism. A man of gentle and obliging character, he nevertheless believed he was outcast from God, a sinner whose only hope of evading damnation lay in Divine Redemption. The worst effect of Cowper's illness was that the less he had to reproach himself with, the more he believed himself guilty. It was at a period of his life when he felt his damnation was sure that he wrote his most powerful poem, 'The Castaway'. He hit upon exactly the right subject to portray his own sense of being totally lost. The poem is a classic statement of despair, a perfectly extended metaphor of the soul abandoned by God. Cowper had read how, when a British ship, commanded by Anson, was rounding Cape Horn, one of the sailors fell from the rigging into the sea. The crew were unable to help him but had to watch his struggles in the sea until he disappeared from sight. Cowper saw in this event an image of his own struggle against insanity and despair. Except at the beginning and end, he works only with the sailor's experience – he doesn't try to find stanza-by-stanza parallels with his own case. The poem has none of the overt psychology of a modern work with a similar theme, William Golding's novel, *Pincher Martin*. By the end, you feel Cowper has earned the right to link himself, in his quiet English house, with the terrible fate of the drowning sailor.

> Obscurest night involv'd the sky,
> Th'Atlantic billows roar'd,
> When such a destin'd wretch as I,
> Wash'd headlong from on board,
> Of friends, of hope, of all bereft,
> His floating home for ever left.
>
> No braver chief could Albion boast
> Than he with whom he went,
> Nor ever ship left Albion's coast,
> With warmer wishes sent.
> He lov'd them both, but both in vain,
> Nor him beheld, nor her again.

Not long beneath the whelming brine,
Expert to swim, he lay;
Nor soon he felt his strength decline,
Or courage die away;
But wag'd with death a lasting strife,
Supported by despair of life.

He shouted: nor his friends had fail'd
To check the vessel's course,
But so the furious blast prevail'd,
That, pitiless perforce,
They left their outcast mate behind,
And scudded still before the wind.

Some succour yet they could afford;
And such as storms allow,
The cask, the coop, the floated cord,
Delay'd not to bestow,
But he (they knew) nor ship, nor shore,
Whate'er they gave, should visit more.

Nor, cruel as it seemed, could he
Their haste himself condemn,
Aware that flight, in such a sea,
Alone could rescue them;
Yet bitter felt it still to die
Deserted, and his friends so nigh.

He long survives, who lives an hour
In ocean, self-upheld;
And so long he, with unspent pow'r,
His destiny repell'd;
And ever, as the minutes flew,
Entreated help, or cried – Adieu!

At length, his transient respite past,
His comrades, who before
Had heard his voice in ev'ry blast,
Could catch the sound no more.
For then, by toil subdued, he drank
The stifling wave, and then he sank.

No poet wept him: but the page
Of narrative sincere,

That tells his name, his worth, his age,
Is wet with Anson's tear.
And tears by bards or heroes shed
Alike immortalize the dead.

I therefore purpose not, or dream,
Descanting on his fate,
To give the melancholy theme
A more enduring date:
But misery still delights to trace
Its 'semblance in another's case.

No voice divine the storm allay'd,
No light propitious shone;
When, snatch'd from all effectual aid,
We perished, each alone:
But I beneath a rougher sea,
And whelm'd in deeper gulphs than he.

By way of postscript, there's a special irony in yoking Smart
and Cowper together. The preservation of the manuscript of
'Jubilate Agno' was due to friends of Cowper's, into whose
possession it passed, and who regarded Smart as an exemplary
case of poetic mania. They preserved it because of its relevance
to Cowper's own condition, though they thought it useless as
poetry. Reading it and 'The Castaway' together, it's easy to
conclude that in religion, as in so much else, mania is a more
fortunate state than despair.

Robert Burns (1759-1796)
George Crabbe (1754-1832)
William Blake (1757-1827)   P.P.

———————◆———————

The relationship between popular poetry and formal poetry
has never been as close as the similar relationship between folk
music and art music. The beautiful anonymous lyrics of the late
Middle Ages were genuinely popular poems which nevertheless
conformed to the highest standards of art. But during the next
three centuries, as English literature expanded, popular poetry
appeared only in songs and proverbial sayings in plays and
poems by formal masters. The day of that great poet, Anon,
seemed to be over. Music, however, still carried much popular
verse into literature. The persistence of a tune guaranteed life
to the words as well. Popular poetry not written to be sung
degenerated into such things as Broadside Ballads, where
murders, highwaymen's executions and bawdy scandals were
told in rough and ready verse, with clanging rhymes and
thumping rhythms. It's appropriate that the eighteenth century,
whose formal art is so obsessed with propriety of diction and
decorum of thought, should have its literary underground of
ballads, catches and pop songs, which are the very antithesis
of the literary purity admired by the cognoscenti. A great deal
of this stuff is worthless, though poets often used it for satirical
effect, as in Swift's amusing parody of an execution ballad –
'Clever Tom Clinch going to be Hanged'. The older tradition
survived in music. The eighteenth is the great musical century,
and though England has no one to match Bach, Haydn and
Mozart, this country, in its role of the United States of the time,
attracted many famous musicians, notably Handel, who wrote
most of his operas and oratorios for the London season. Popular
music both drew on and parodied this official music. John Gay's
The Beggar's Opera, was a hugely successful take-off of Italian

opera, using anything from Handel himself to traditional tunes like 'Lilliburlero'. In its turn, it led to the establishment in Germany of the popular operatic form known as *Singspiel*, which is father to Mozart's, Weber's and even Wagner's operas.

The decade which followed Johnson and Smart saw the break-up of Augustan order and the beginnings of Romanticism. This chapter is a rounding-off of the eighteenth century and shows how various tensions (including the political ones which led to the French Revolution) paved the way for the Romantic epoch. Three poets stand out as transitional figures: Robert Burns, William Blake and George Crabbe. Crabbe and Blake lived on into the nineteenth century, but both are firmly eighteenth-century in mind and personality. The third, the great Scots poet, Robert Burns, died in 1796. Music is the clue to the understanding of Burns's work. He was a very prolific poet, who in his short life wrote a large number of English poems, as well as the lyrics in Scots which have made him world-famous. Lowland Scots is a dialect of English, not really farther removed from Standard Southern English than, say, Northumbrian or Dorsetshire. But Burns printed his poems to spell out the Lowland dialect and gave his nation a new pride and poetical self-consciousness. Many of his longer rhyming poems in Scots are too loosely written, but some of his attacks on his Kirk- attending neighbours, such as 'Holy Willy's Prayer', are tours-de-force of satirical skill. But Burns's greatness lies in his lyrics. He wrote some hundreds of short lyrical poems, often to fit traditional melodies. Many of these are refinements of existing lyrics. To give an impression of Burns at his most rumbustious and yet economical, one cannot do better than go to the musical work he collaborated in, entitled *The Jolly Beggars*. It's a Lowland Scots relative of *The Beggar's Opera*. (A note on some of the Scots words: 'fou' is 'full' or 'drunk'; a 'hizzie' is a wench; a 'stirk' a bullock; 'daffin' is fun.)

> Sir Wisdom's a fool when he's fou;
> Sir Knave is a fool in a session;
> He's there but a prentice I trow,
> But I am a fool by profession.
>
> My grannie she bought me a beuk,
> An' I held awa to the school;

I fear I my talent misteuk,
  But what will ye hae of a fool?

For drink I would venture my neck;
  A hizzie's the half of my craft;
But what could ye other expect,
  Of ane that's avowedly daft?

I ance was ty'd up like a stirk,
  For civilly swearing and quaffing;
I ance was abus'd i' the kirk,
  For towsing a lass i' my daffin.

Poor Andrew that tumbles for sport,
  Let nae body name wi' a jeer;
There's even, I'm tauld, i' the Court
  A tumbler ca'd the Premier.

Observ'd ye yon reverend lad
  Mak faces to tickle the mob,
He rails at our mountebank squad,
  It's rivalship just i' the job.

And now my conclusion I'll tell,
  For faith I'm confoundedly dry:
The chiel that's a fool for himself,
  Guid Lord, he's far dafter than I.

In the next Chorus, the only dialect word is 'callets', who are
female children.

A fig for those by law protected!
  Liberty's a glorious feast!
Courts for cowards were erected,
  Churches built to please the priest.

What is title, what is treasure,
  What is reputation's care?
If we lead a life of pleasure,
  'Tis no matter how or where.
        A fig, etc.

With the rady trick and fable,
  Round we wander all the day,
And at night, in barn or stable,

Hug our doxies on the hay.
　　　A fig, etc.

Does the train-attended carriage
　　Thro' the country lighter rove?
Does the sober bed of marriage
　　Witness brighter scenes of love?
　　　A fig, etc.

Life is all a variorum,
　　We regard not how it goes;
Let them cant about decorum,
　　Who have character to lose.
　　　A fig, etc.

Here's to budgets, bags and wallets!
　　Here's to all the wandering train!
Here's our ragged brats and callets!
　　One and all cry out, Amen!
　　　A fig, etc.

Burns's lyrical talent shows up to fine account in two more short poems. There is a tradition that he inscribed the first stanza of 'I Murder Hate' on the window of a bedroom in a tavern with a diamond pen. The poet whimsically asks to die while making love to a woman (a common enough joke). The Biblical reference in the second stanza comes from the Book of Numbers. Zimri, while sleeping with a Midianite woman called Cozbi, was killed – a javelin being driven through them both in the act.

I murder hate by field or flood,
　　Tho' glory's name may screen us;
In wars at home I'll spend my blood,
　　Life-giving wars of Venus:
The deities that I adore
　　Are social Peace and Plenty;
I'm better pleased *to make one more*
　　Than be the death of twenty.

I would not die like Socrates,
　　For all the fuss of Plato;
Nor would I with Leonidas;

Nor yet would I with Cato.
The Zealots of the Church or State
Shall ne'er my mortal foes be,
But let me have bold Zimri's fate,
Within the arms of Cozbi!

The second is a beautiful lyric written for an already existing tune – 'O Whistle and I'll come to you, my Lad.' (Two words need explaining – 'tent' is watch; 'syne' is then.) It's a tender summons by a young girl to her lover.

Chorus –   O whistle, and I'll come to you, my lad,
O whistle, and I'll come to you, my lad;
Tho' father and mother and a' should gae mad,
O whistle, and I'll come to you, my lad.

But warily tent, when ye come to court me,
And come na unless the back-yett be a'jee;
Syne up the back-style, and let naebody see,
And come as ye were na coming to me,
And come as ye were na coming to me.

At kirk or at market, whene'er ye meet me,
Gang by me as tho' that ye car'd nae a flie;
But steal me a blink o' your bonie black e'e,
Yet look as ye were na looking at me,
Yet look as ye were na looking at me.

Ay vow and protest that ye carena for me,
And *whyles* ye may lightly my beauty a wee;
But court na anither, tho' joking ye be,
For fear that she wyle your fancy frae me,
For fear that she wyle your fancy frae me.

George Crabbe, alone of the poets who came after Pope, could rival his skill with the heroic couplet. But Crabbe put it to altogether different use; he is one of the most wholehearted realists in our literature. Writing at the end of the century, Crabbe was already old-fashioned: in fact, he was the reactionaries' favourite poet. Byron, for instance, whose tastes in verse were far from romantic, called him 'Nature's sternest painter, and the best'. Crabbe grew up in Aldeburgh, Suffolk. In his time, it was a poor fishing village, and, as the son of a local exciseman, he had ample opportunity to see the life of the people as it was actually lived. He was an amateur naturalist, and also trained in medicine. His accuracy of description may have come from his ability to look at people and society with the same detachment he preserved towards flowers and rocks. Crabbe's first great success as a poet was 'The Village', published in 1783. It's a brilliant work for a poet to establish himself with. Crabbe conceived the poem as an answer to the idealising of rural life in such poems as Goldsmith's *Deserted Village*, a picture of a rustic Arcadia before the Enclosures of the latter part of the eighteenth century. Crabbe was determined to tell the truth of village life as he knew it.

But if he was concerned with the sort of detail that conventional poets shunned, he was equally determined to make his poem a work of art. In the following passage, Crabbe is describing the fields and waste land on the outskirts of the village. The realistic picture takes on an unearthly menace, as though the very land was able to exemplify the stunted life of its people.

> Lo! where the heath, with withering brake grown o'er,
> Lends the light turf that warms the neighbouring poor;
> From thence a length of burning sand appears,
> Where the thin harvest waves its wither'd ears;
> Rank weeds, that every art and care defy,
> Reign o'er the land, and rob the blighted rye:
> There thistles stretch their prickly arms afar,
> And to the ragged infant threaten war;
> There poppies, nodding, mock the hope of toil;
> There the blue bugloss paints the sterile soil;
> Hardy and high, above the slender sheaf,
> The slimy mallow waves her silky leaf;
> O'er the young shoot the charlock throws a shade,
> And clasping tares cling round the sickly blade;
> With mingled tints the rocky coasts abound,
> And a sad splendour vainly shines around.

Once into the village proper, Crabbe's method is to describe the various inhabitants according to their occupations. Most are shown as wretched. He is in his element among the unfortunate, the drunk, the sick and the dying. This is his account of the parish poorhouse:

196

Theirs is yon house that holds the parish poor,
Whose walls of mud scarce bear the broken door;
There, where the putrid vapours, flagging, play,
And the dull wheel hums doleful through the day –
There children dwell, who know no parents' care;
Parents, who know no children's love, dwell there!
Heart-broken matrons on their joyless bed,
Forsaken wives, and mothers never wed;
Dejected widows with unheeded tears,
And crippled age with more than childhood fears;
The lame, the blind, and, far the happiest they!
The moping idiot and the madman gay.
Here too the sick their final doom receive,
Here brought, amid the scenes of grief, to grieve,
Where the loud groans from some sad chamber flow,
Mix'd with the clamours of the crowd below;
Here, sorrowing, they each kindred sorrow scan,
And the cold charities of man to man.

Crabbe was both doctor and parson in his time, but he had no high opinion of the general run of such men. He knew they neglected their patients and parishioners, and he portrayed them without sympathy. The next few lines draw a picture of the village doctor at his work among the poor:

Anon, a figure enters, quaintly neat,
All pride and business, bustle and conceit;
With looks unalter'd by these scenes of wo,
With speed that, entering, speaks his haste to go,
He bids the gazing throng around him fly,
And carries fate and physic in his eye:
A potent quack, long versed in human ills,
Who first insults the victim whom he kills;
Whose murd'rous hand a drowsy Bench protect,
And whose most tender mercy is neglect.

The best friend any villager could have was death. So Crabbe thought, anyway, as his description of a funeral making its way to the village graveyard shows. This passage has a solemnity which is a good note to leave Crabbe on. Already, in this poem of his youth, he had mapped out the right territory for his genius. But though he is melancholy, he cannot be called low-spirited. The power of these sombre but shining verses puts them among the most impressive examples of naturalism in English. As the last survivor of the eighteenth century, Crabbe makes an interesting contrast with Wordsworth, who also liked to draw pictures of the lives of simple men. Crabbe, for all his formality, has much the clearer view.

> Up yonder hill, behold how sadly slow
> The bier moves winding from the vale below;
> There lie the happy dead, from trouble free,
> And the glad parish pays the frugal fee.
> No more, O Death! thy victim starts to hear
> Churchwarden stern, or kingly overseer;
> No more the farmer claims his humble bow,
> Thou art his lord, the best of tyrants thou!

William Blake is a once-off figure in English literature. During the last decade, he has become the hero of the British and American Underground, the prophet of the Alternative Society, forerunner of Ginsberg, inspirer of Adrian Mitchell, Crown Prince of the anti-academic establishment. Grossly simplified as this hippy picture of Blake is, it fits him better than the scholar's does. Scholars concentrate on his Swedenborgian origins, they carefully index and cross-reference the symbols of his Prophetic Books, and their professional interpretation of his mysticism says that 'the dark Satanic mills' of the famous lyric from *Milton* are churches and not the factories of the Industrial Revolution everyone else takes them for. Blake is a writer of hard-edged lyrics, who has few rivals for power and memorability. He is also a premature Whitman, all too often an inspired bore who substitutes a personal vision for the accumulated knowledge and methodology of the Christian West.

He is that very popular modern figure, the aphorist or oracle, who knows how to throw us off balance with a brilliant paradox or a startling epigram. Popular taste is probably right in liking Blake's lyrics and songs best, his self-contradictory sayings from 'The Marriage of Heaven and Hell' next, and his mystical poems in rhyming short lines, such as 'The Auguries of Innocence' as third choice. His Prophetic Books should be left to the scholars: the rest of us can content ourselves with the superb watercolours and engravings he made for them. His early fantasies, 'The Island in the Moon' and 'The Marriage of Heaven and Hell', are among his most original creations. Similar to them in mood are the short poems in the two collections, *Songs of Innocence* and *Songs of Experience*. Of the two quoted here, the first, 'Nurse's Song', is a strange anticipation of depth psychology, and the second, 'The Sick Rose', the most perfect short lyric in English.

When the voices of children are heard on the green
And whisp'rings are in the dale,
The days of my youth rise fresh in my mind,
My face turns green and pale.

Then come home, my children, the sun is gone down,
And the dews of night arise;
Your spring & your day are wasted in play,
And your winter and night in disguise.

O Rose, thou art sick!
The invisible worm
That flies in the night,
In the howling storm,

Has found out thy bed
Of crimson joy,
And his dark secret love
Does thy life destroy.

Blake's purpose in *The Songs of Experience* is the profound one of calling up the various impulses of man contained in the paradox of living. Among his sayings from *The Proverbs of Hell* is this: 'If the fool would persist in his folly, he would become wise.' Then again, 'One law for the Lion and Ox is Oppression.' A further one, 'Drive your cart and plow over the bones of the dead.' And a fourth, 'The cut worm forgives the plow.' Common to all Blake's insights is a love of exuberance: 'The cistern contains; the fountain overflows.' He rejoiced in the first principle of life, that everything should be itself to the highest degree of its power. Therefore, paradox doesn't worry him, since God who made the lamb also made the tiger. In the next poem, 'A Poison Tree', he comes close to the Freudian doctrine

of the effects of emotional repression – one hundred years before
Freud's birth.

> I was angry with my friend:
> I told my wrath, my wrath did end.
> I was angry with my foe:
> I told it not, my wrath did grow.
>
> And I water'd it in fears,
> Night & morning with my tears;
> And I sunned it with smiles,
> And with soft deceitful wiles.
>
> And it grew both day and night,
> Till it bore an apple bright;
> And my foe beheld it shine,
> And he knew that it was mine,
>
> And into my garden stole
> When the night had veil'd the pole:
> In the morning glad I see
> My foe outstretch'd beneath the tree.

Blake wrote some more difficult, though still melodious
poems, in rhyming four-foot couplets. One such is 'The Ever-
lasting Gospel'. He was not a naïve man, but this poem illustrates
his home-made attitude to Christianity. He was psychologically
incapable of accepting any orthodoxy.

Consequently, he saw Christ in a completely original way, as
a revolutionary who fought his own Father, a sort of New
Testament Prometheus. And he thought there had been as many
Christs as there were readers of the Gospels. Here is a crucial
passage from the middle of 'The Everlasting Gospel':

> The Vision of Christ that thou dost see
> Is my Vision's Greatest Enemy:
> Thine has a great hook nose like thine,
> Mine has a snub nose like to mine:
> Thine is the friend of All Mankind,
> Mine speaks in parables to the Blind:
> Thine loves the same world that mine hates,
> Thy Heaven doors are my Hell Gates.
> Socrates taught what Meletus

Loath'd as a Nation's Bitterest Curse,
And Caiphas was in his own Mind
A benefactor to Mankind:
Both read the Bible day & night,
But thou read'st black where I read white.

Blake turned more to painting and illustrating at the end of his life. The poems which belong to this period are cryptic and mysterious, none more so than 'The Gates of Paradise'. It is represented here by its beautiful Epilogue.

To The Accuser who is
The God of This World

Truly, My Satan, thou art but a Dunce,
And dost not know the Garment from the Man.
Every Harlot was a Virgin once,
Nor can'st thou ever change Kate into Nan.

Tho' thou art Worship'd by the Names Divine
Of Jesus & Jehovah, thou art still
The Son of Morn in weary Night's decline,
The lost Traveller's Dream under the Hill.

William Wordsworth (1770–1850)
Samuel Taylor Coleridge (1772–1834)   A.T.

The tag that has always been hung round Wordsworth's neck
is one that reads 'Nature Poet'. Generations of schoolchildren
have been brought up on his poem 'The Daffodils', and indeed
I suppose it's his best-known poem. I think people tend to
imagine that most of Wordsworth is to do with flowers and hills
and lakes, a sort of Lake District of the mind, full of the beauties
of inanimate nature, with actual human beings rather thin on the
ground – just a scattering of gnarled old peasants and idiot boys.

The fact that Wordsworth is thought of this way is partly
attributable to Wordsworth himself: after all, he did call himself
a 'Worshipper of Nature'. But the real force, and I think the
powerful strangeness, of his poetry at its best comes through
because we are made aware of the *human* side of this: of human
nature as well as inanimate nature, and of man as an instrument
through which nature transmits its messages. The Wordsworth
poem that celebrates this most explicitly is 'Tintern Abbey', and
in particular these lines:

> For I have learned,
> To look on nature, not as in the hour
> Of thoughtless youth; but hearing oftentimes
> The still, sad music of humanity,
> Nor harsh, nor grating, though of ample power
> To chasten and subdue. And I have felt
> A presence that disturbs me with the joy
> Of elevated thoughts; a sense sublime
> Of something far more deeply interfused,
> Whose dwelling is the light of setting suns,
> And the round ocean and the living air,
> And the blue sky, and in the mind of man:

A motion and a spirit, that impels
All thinking things, all objects of all thought,
And rolls through all things.

Although Wordsworth's poetry has a firm moral intent to demonstrate this 'sense sublime', the way in which he saw the function of the poet was to emphasise the passivity, the receptiveness – as in these lines from 'A Poet's Epitaph':

He is retired as noontide dew,
Or fountain in a noon-day grove;
And you must love him, ere to you
He will seem worthy of your love.

The outward shows of sky and earth,
Of hill and valley, he has viewed;
And impulses of deeper birth
Have come to him in solitude.

In common things that round us lie
Some random truths he can impart –
The harvest of a quiet eye
That broods and sleeps on his own heart.

But he is weak; both Man and Boy
Hath been an idler in the land;
Contented if he might enjoy
The things which others understand.

This receptive view of the poet is seen most importantly in Wordsworth in his long poem, *The Prelude* – or as he called it, a poem about 'The Growth of the Poet's Mind'. It's a spiritual autobiography, in fact, comparable with the *Confessions* of St Augustine. It occupied Wordsworth for much of his life, and was not published until after his death in 1850; but it had its beginnings long before, and the germ of part of it can be seen in a poem written when he was twenty-nine, with the weighty title 'Influence of Natural Objects in Calling Forth and Strengthening the Imagination in Boyhood and Early Youth'. It was first published as a separate piece in a magazine edited by his friend Coleridge, but I want you to see the version as it appeared in context in the completed *Prelude*. The first part, up to and including the description of taking the boat out and being frightened, came later: the rest, from the line 'Wisdom and Spirit of the Universe!', is the original poem:

Dust as we are, the immortal spirit grows
Like harmony in music; there is a dark
Inscrutable workmanship that reconciles
Discordant elements, makes them cling together
In one society. How strange that all
The terrors, pains, and early miseries,
Regrets, vexations, lassitudes interfused
Within my mind, should e'er have borne a part,
And that a needful part, in making up
The calm existence that is mine when I
Am worthy of myself! Praise to the end!
Thanks to the means which Nature deigned to employ;
Whether her fearless visitings, or those
That came with soft alarm, like hurtless light
Opening the peaceful clouds; or she may use
Severer interventions, ministry
More palpable, as best might suit her aim.

One summer evening (led by her) I found
A little boat tied to a willow tree
Within a rocky cave, its usual home.
Straight I unloosed her chain, and stepping in
Pushed from the shore. It was an act of stealth
And troubled pleasure, nor without the voice
Of mountain-echoes did my boat move on;
Leaving behind her still, on either side,
Small circles glittering idly in the moon,
Until they melted all into one track
Of sparkling light. But now, like one who rows,
Proud of his skill, to reach a chosen point
With an unswerving line, I fixed my view
Upon the summit of a craggy ridge,
The horizon's utmost boundary; for above
Was nothing but the stars and the grey sky.
She was an elfin pinnace; lustily
I dipped my oars into the silent lake,
And, as I rose upon the stroke, my boat
Went heaving through the water like a swan;

When, from behind that craggy steep till then
The horizon's bound, a huge peak, black and huge,
As if with voluntary power instinct
Upreared its head. I struck and struck again,
And growing still in stature the grim shape
Towered up between me and the stars, and still,
For so it seemed, with purpose of its own
And measured motion like a living thing,
Strode after me. With trembling oars I turned,
And through the silent water stole my way
Back to the covert of the willow tree;
There in her mooring-place I left my bark, –
And through the meadows homeward went, in grave
And serious mood; but after I had seen
That spectacle, for many days, my brain
Worked with a dim and undetermined sense
Of unknown modes of being; o'er my thoughts
There hung a darkness, call it solitude
Or blank desertion. No familiar shapes
Remained, no pleasant images of trees,
Of sea or sky, no colours of green fields;
But huge and mighty forms, that do not live
Like living men, moved slowly through the mind
By day, and were a trouble to my dreams.

Wisdom and Spirit of the universe!
Thou Soul that art the eternity of thought,
That givest to forms and images a breath
And everlasting motion, not in vain
By day or star-light thus from my first dawn
Of childhood didst thou intertwine for me
The passions that build up our human soul;
Not with the mean and vulgar works of man,
But with high objects, with enduring things –
With life and nature – purifying thus
The elements of feeling and of thought,
And sanctifying, by such discipline,
Both pain and fear, until we recognise
A grandeur in the beatings of the heart.
Nor was this fellowship vouchsafed to me

With stinted kindness. In November days,
When vapours rolling down the valley made
A lonely scene more lonesome, among woods,
At noon and 'mid the calm of summer nights,
When, by the margin of the trembling lake,
Beneath the gloomy hills homeward I went
In solitude, such intercourse was mine;
Mine was it in the fields both day and night,
And by the waters, all the summer long.

And in the frosty season, when the sun
Was set, and visible for many a mile
The cottage windows blazed through twilight gloom,
I heeded not their summons: happy time
It was indeed for all of us – for me
It was a time of rapture! Clear and loud
The village clock tolled six, – I wheeled about,
Proud and exulting like an untired horse
That cares not for his home. All shod with steel,
We hissed along the polished ice in games
Confederate, imitative of the chase
And woodland pleasures, – the resounding horn,
The pack loud chiming, and the hunted hare.
So through the darkness and the cold we flew,
And not a voice was idle; with the din
Smitten, the precipices rang aloud;
The leafless trees and every icy crag
Tinkled like iron; while far distant hills
Into the tumult sent an alien sound
Of melancholy not unnoticed, while the stars
Eastward were sparkling clear, and in the west
The orange sky of evening died away.
Not seldom from the uproar I retired
Into a silent bay, or sportively
Glanced sideway, leaving the tumultuous throng,
To cut across the reflex of a star
That fled, and, flying still before me, gleamed
Upon the glassy plain; and oftentimes,
When we had given our bodies to the wind,
And all the shadowy banks on either side

Came sweeping through the darkness, spinning still
The rapid line of motion, then at once
Have I, reclining back upon my heels,
Stopped short; yet still the solitary cliffs
Wheeled by me – even as if the earth had rolled
With visible motion her diurnal round!
Behind me did they stretch in solemn train,
Feebler and feebler, and I stood and watched
Till all was tranquil as a dreamless sleep.

The strength of that passage from *The Prelude* lies in the way it moves exaltedly, even excitedly, from the circumstantial; and this is almost always the process in Wordsworth, and the source of his finest work. There are times when he seems to be moralising in a vacuum, and then the words trudge ploddingly on – but given some scene or incident that excites his memory, the rhythms and language become rapt and powerful. Think of 'The Solitary Reaper'. In 1803, Wordsworth went on a tour of Scotland; a couple of years later (remember Wordsworth's remark about poetry being the product of 'emotion recollected in tranquillity') he wrote this short poem – a scene caught and recorded and preserved forever, an emotion commemorated:

Behold her, single in the field,
Yon solitary Highland Lass!
Reaping and singing by herself;
Stop here, or gently pass!
Alone she cuts and binds the grain,
And sings a melancholy strain;
O listen! for the Vale profound
Is overflowing with the sound.

No Nightingale did ever chaunt
More welcome notes to weary bands
Of travellers in some shady haunt,
Among Arabian sands:
A voice so thrilling ne'er was heard
In spring-time from the Cuckoo-bird,
Breaking the silence of the seas
Among the farthest Hebrides.

Will no one tell me what she sings? –
Perhaps the plaintive numbers flow
For old, unhappy, far-off things,
And battles long ago:
Or is it some more humble lay,
Familiar matter of to-day?
Some natural sorrow, loss, or pain,
That has been, and may be again?

Whate'er the theme, the Maiden sang
As if her song could have no ending;
I saw her singing at her work,
And o'er the sickle bending; –
I listened, motionless and still;
And, as I mounted up the hill,
The music in my heart I bore,
Long after it was heard no more.

Wordsworth said of his work that it was 'a thing unprece-
dented in literary history that a man should talk so much about
himself'; and when we talk about the Romantic Revival or the
Romantic poets, this is partly what we mean – that the Romantic
poet himself was his own central subject-matter. This isn't
entirely so in Wordsworth, but it *is* so of his best poems. And
when we look at Coleridge, for so many years Wordsworth's
strange, powerfully gifted but essentially unfulfilled friend, we
see the dangers and extremes of this: twice – in 'The Rime of the
Ancient Mariner' and in 'Kubla Khan' – Coleridge moved
brilliantly away from Romantic self-absorption to Romantic
invention. The rest of his small body of poetry, though it has
very fine things in it, is the work of a man desperately short of a
reference point outside his own vast and unfocused energies.

My genial spirits fail;
And what can these avail
To lift the smothering weight from off my breast?
It were a vain endeavour,
Though I should gaze forever
On that green light that lingers in the west:
I may not hope from outward forms to win
The passion and the life, whose fountains are within.

Those lines from Coleridge's 'Dejection: an Ode' lead me to what is generally taken to be – and I agree – his masterpiece, 'Kubla Khan'. Because *that* is a poem which is wholly one whose 'fountains' are 'within'. Whatever the source, or rather sources – and it's been shown that 'Kubla Khan' is a poem which draws most subtly and strangely on Coleridge's reading – the force is that described by Coleridge in his sub-title: 'A Vision in a Dream'. We must also remember, I suppose, that Coleridge calls it 'a Fragment'; he was interrupted by that person from Porlock who called while he was composing it. But, in a sense, what Romantic poetry is *not* fragmentary?

In Xanadu did Kubla Khan
A stately pleasure-dome decree:
Where Alph, the sacred river, ran
Through caverns measureless to man
Down to a sunless sea.
So twice five miles of fertile ground
With walls and towers were girdled round:
And there were gardens bright with sinuous rills,
Where blossomed many an incense-bearing tree;
And here were forests ancient as the hills,
Enfolding sunny spots of greenery.

But oh! that deep romantic chasm which slanted
Down the green hill athwart a cedarn cover!
A savage place! as holy and enchanted
As e'er beneath a waning moon was haunted
By woman wailing for her demon-lover!
And from this chasm, with ceaseless turmoil seething,
As if this earth in fast thick pants were breathing,
A mighty fountain momently was forced:
Amid whose swift half-intermitted burst
Huge fragments vaulted like rebounding hail,
Or chaffy grain beneath the thresher's flail:
And 'mid these dancing rocks at once and ever
It flung up momently the sacred river.
Five miles meandering with a mazy motion
Through wood and dale the sacred river ran,
Then reached the caverns measureless to man,
And sank in tumult to a lifeless ocean:

And 'mid this tumult Kubla heard from far
Ancestral voices prophesying war!

The shadow of the dome of pleasure
Floated midway on the waves;
Where was heard the mingled measure
From the fountain and the caves.
It was a miracle of rare device,
A sunny pleasure-dome with caves of ice!

A damsel with a dulcimer
In a vision once I saw:
It was an Abyssinian maid,
And on her dulcimer she played,
Singing of Mount Abora.
Could I revive within me
Her symphony and song,
To such a deep delight 'twould win me,
That with music loud and long,
I would build that dome in air,
That sunny dome! those caves of ice!
And all who heard should see them there,
And all should cry, Beware! Beware!
His flashing eyes, his floating hair!
Weave a circle round him thrice,
And close your eyes with holy dread,
For he on honey-dew hath fed,
And drunk the milk of Paradise.

Percy Bysshe Shelley (1792–1822)
John Keats (1795–1821)
John Clare (1793–1864)   P.P.

———————◆———————

Romanticism is the one great movement in the history of European art which the British can claim to have invented. There had been the *Sturm und Drang* period in Germany, exemplified by Goethe's novel *The Sorrows of Werther*, and Rousseau in France advised a return to nature and away from the predominant artificiality of the eighteenth century, but it wasn't until the impact of poets like Byron and Wordsworth, novelists like Sir Walter Scott and Fennimore Cooper and painters such as Constable and Turner made itself felt that Romanticism came into its own. The 'back-to-nature' movement brought with it a taste for the exotic and the picturesque, and it was the Celtic fringe of Britain which became so popular. The bogus Scottish folk poems of Ossian were read and imitated all over the Continent, and throughout the nineteenth century it was accepted that if you wanted a good setting for your Romantic opera you put it in the wilder parts of the British Isles. Our literature and painting became the chief inspiration of the Continental avant-garde. Movements in literature can derive from misunderstandings and what the French, German and Russian writers made of Byron and the rest was based more on their romantic way of life (and the fact that Byron and Shelley were eccentric aristocrats) than on what they wrote.

Provided we interpret the word Romanticism freely, it will do to describe two of the three poets in this chapter – Percy Shelley and John Keats, men whose very names suggest 'poet' to us, so fully has our education and the taste for Romanticism conditioned our reactions. A belief that the poet is different from other men ('an unacknowledged legislator' Shelley called him), and a wholehearted preference for feelings over intellect, are two of the main psychological traits of Romanticism. The less adventurous side is in the language. At first, when Wordsworth and Coleridge propounded the reform of the artificiality of Augustan poetry, it looked as if Romanticism would widen the vocabulary and freshen the diction of poetry. All too soon, however, the Romantics got bogged down in a special language of their own – each had a sweet tooth, and no poet of the Romantic Era can match the poets of the seventeenth century for adventurous use of language. The chief fault of Romantic poetry is that it's too consciously 'poetic', too determined to draw a line between our experience of words as we go about our ordinary tasks and when we sit down to write poems. Shelley, though an arch-Romantic, had strong links with the classics. He had fluent Greek and Latin and he translated from German and Spanish. The best of his poems add a classical sharpness to their high emotions: during his exile in Italy he managed to introduce some of the clarity of the Italian light into his writing. Although he died in his thirtieth year, he wrote a vast quantity of poetry. Inevitably, much of it is inflated and poorly achieved, and, unlike Keats, he left few perfect poems. We find isolated lines of great power in the middle of hazy garrulity and abstract language. To show how simply Shelley could write, when he relaxed, here is a poem called 'With a Guitar, to Jane', which moves mellifluously through its rhyming four-foot lines.

> The artist who this idol wrought,
> To echo all harmonious thought,
> Felled a tree, while on the steep
> The woods were in their winter sleep,
> Rocked in that repose divine
> On the wind-swept Apennine;
> And dreaming, some of Autumn past,
> And some of Spring approaching fast,
> And some of April buds and showers,
> And some of songs in July bowers,
> And all of love; and so this tree, –
> O that such our death may be! –
> Died in sleep, and felt no pain,
> To live in happier form again:
> From which, beneath Heaven's fairest star,

The artist wrought this loved Guitar,
And taught it justly to reply,
To all who question skilfully,
In language gentle as thine own;
Whispering in enamoured tone
Sweet oracles of woods and dells,
And summer winds in sylvan cells;
For it had learned all harmonies
Of the plains and of the skies,
Of the forests and the mountains,
And the many-voicèd fountains;
The clearest echoes of the hills,
The softest notes of falling rills,
The melodies of birds and bees,
The murmuring of summer seas,
And pattering rain, and breathing dew,
And airs of evening; and it knew
That seldom-heard mysterious sound,
Which, driven on its diurnal round,
As it floats through boundless day,
Our world enkindles on its way.

The next two poems illustrate Shelley's peculiar brand of intellectual sensuality. He was a man of intense mental rigour, at home with the highest concepts of philosophy, as his friend Peacock's account of him shows, yet the chief feeling one gets from his poetry is of an impulsive extravagance, an attractive but immature dominance of mood over matter. The first poem, 'Stanzas written in Dejection near Naples', is a perfect expression of adolescent self-pity, but Shelley's observation of his own misery is set in a well-drawn natural landscape.

The sun is warm, the sky is clear,
    The waves are dancing fast and bright,
Blue isles and snowy mountains wear
The purple noon's transparent might,
    The breath of the moist earth is light,
Around its unexpanded buds;
    Like many a voice of one delight,
    The winds, the birds, the ocean floods,
The City's voice itself, is soft like Solitude's.

I see the Deep's untrampled floor
    With green and purple seaweeds strown;
I see the waves upon the shore,
    Like light dissolved in star-showers, thrown:
    I sit upon the sands alone, –
The lightning of the noontide ocean
    Is flashing round me, and a tone
Arises from its measured motion,
How sweet! did any heart now share in my emotion.

Alas! I have nor hope nor health,
    Nor peace within nor calm around,
Nor that content surpassing wealth
    The sage in meditation found,
    And walked with inward glory crowned –
Nor fame, nor power, nor love, nor leisure.
    Others I see whom these surround –
Smiling they live, and call life pleasure; –
To me that cup has been dealt in another measure.

Yet now despair itself is mild,
    Even as the winds and waters are;
I could lie down like a tired child,
    And weep away the life of care
    Which I have borne and yet must bear,
Till death like sleep might steal on me,
    And I might feel in the warm air
My cheek grow cold, and hear the sea
Breathe o'er my dying brain its last monotony.

Some might lament that I were cold,
    As I, when this sweet day is gone,
Which my lost heart, too soon grown old
    Insults with this untimely moan;
    They might lament – for I am one
Whom men love not, – and yet regret,
    Unlike this day, which, when the sun
Shall on its stainless glory set,
Will linger, though enjoyed, like joy in memory yet.

The second poem is a brief but famous lyric from Act One of

his fantasy-drama based on a lost play by Aeschylus, *Prometheus Unbound*. The voice speaking is that of a spirit of the air.

> On a poet's lips I slept
> Dreaming like a love-adept
> In the sound his breathing kept;
> Nor seeks nor finds he mortal blisses,
> But feeds on the aëreal kisses
> Of shapes that haunt thought's wildernesses.
> He will watch from dawn to gloom
> The lake-reflected sun illume
> The yellow bees in the ivy-bloom,
> Nor heed nor see, what things they be;
> But from these create he can
> Forms more real than living man,
> Nurselings of immortality!

Shelley was as absolute a revolutionary as William Blake, but he was an atheist too. He hated the reactionary governments which ruled Europe after the defeat of Napoleon, especially Castlereagh's in London and Metternich's in Vienna. When a working-class meeting at Manchester was shot down by troops in 1818, a massacre which became known as Peterloo, Shelley wrote 'The Mask of Anarchy' to express his loathing of the English tyranny and his sympathy with all aspirant republicans and democrats. Its power springs from its extreme simplicity of language as well as the vehemence of its feeling. Here are the first nine stanzas and then the final two from the poem.

> As I lay asleep in Italy
> There came a voice from over the Sea,
> And with great power it forth led me
> To walk in the visions of Poesy.
>
> I met Murder on the way –
> He had a mask like Castlereagh –
> Very smooth he looked, yet grim;
> Seven blood-hounds followed him:
>
> All were fat; and well they might
> Be in admirable plight,

For one by one, and two by two,
He tossed them human hearts to chew
Which from his wide cloak he drew.

Next came Fraud, and he had on,
Like Eldon, an ermined gown;
His big tears, for he wept well,
Turned to mill-stones as they fell.

And the little children, who
Round his feet played to and fro,
Thinking every tear a gem,
Had their brains knocked out by them.

Clothed with the Bible, as with light,
And the shadows of the night,
Like Sidmouth, next, Hypocrisy
On a crocodile rode by.

And many more Destructions played
In this ghastly masquerade,
All disguised, even to the eyes,
Like Bishops, lawyers, peers, or spies.

Last came Anarchy: he rode
On a white horse, splashed with blood;
He was pale even to the lips,
Like Death in the Apocalypse.

And he wore a kingly crown;
And in his grasp a sceptre shone;
On his brow this mark I saw –
'I AM GOD, AND KING, AND LAW!'

'And these words shall then become
Like Oppression's thundered doom
Ringing through each heart and brain,
Heard again – again – again –

'Rise like Lions after slumber
In unvanquishable number –
Shake your chains to earth like dew

Which in sleep had fallen on you –
Ye are many – they are few.'

At the end of his life, Shelley was beginning to combine his abstract idealism with a new strength of concrete detail, and had he lived, he might have become a great poet. His was the sort of talent, like Yeats's, which needs time to develop. Unfortunately, he didn't get that time. But, as this extract from 'The Boat on the Serchio' shows, he had gone some way towards acquiring an individual voice when he died. The passage is the opening of the poem, a description of the break of day over the river and its surrounding countryside.

Our boat is asleep on Serchio's stream,
Its sails are folded like thoughts in a dream,
The helm sways idly, hither and thither;
  Dominic, the boatman, has brought the mast,
  And the oars, and the sails; but 'tis sleeping fast,
Like a beast, unconscious of its tether.

The stars burnt out in the pale blue air,
And the thin white moon lay withering there;
To tower, and cavern, and rift, and tree,
The owl and the bat fled drowsily.
Day had kindled the dewy woods,
  And the rocks above and the stream below,
And the vapours in their multitudes,
  And the Apennine's shroud of summer snow,
And clothed with light of aëry gold
The mists in their eastern caves uprolled.

Day had awakened all things that be,
The lark and the thrush and the swallow free,
  And the milkmaid's song and the mower's scythe,
And the matin-bell and the mountain bee:
Fireflies were quenched on the dewy corn,
  Glow-worms went out on the river's brim,
  Like lamps which a student forgets to trim:
The beetle forgot to wind his horn,
  The crickets were still in the meadow and hill:
Like a flock of rooks at a farmer's gun

Night's dreams and terrors, every one,
Fled from the brains which are their prey
From the lamp's death to the morning ray.

John Keats died at twenty-six but, unlike Shelley, his talent
was fully formed at his death. The next most precocious poet in
English after Pope, Keats was Pope's opposite in almost every
way. He had a prodigious love of beautiful language, excessively
beautiful it can seem sometimes. Fortunately, he was equipped
with an excellent ear for the cadences of spoken verse, and a
much better eye for surface detail than most poets. Keats had
the sort of talent which the American poet Wallace Stevens
described as 'essential gaudiness'. Just as 'poetic' as Shelley, he
was superior to Shelley in organisation and control of sound. A
mature Keats poem goes about as far in the voluptuous use of
words as poetry will allow – at the same time, it remains a
consciously worked artifact, always under control. Keats's letters
reveal him as sharp-witted and acute. He knew his genius was
menaced by morbidity and excess and that his tuberculosis would
increase the death-intoxication of his mind. So he kept the
example of the Jacobean poets before him; beauty remained his
justification, but he was determined not to let even the sweeetest
poems become over-ripe. He didn't have Shelley's classical
training, but he loved the legacy of the ancient world, especially
as he found it reflected in the great English poets. He wrote his
own poems with Lemprière's Classical Dictionary beside him,
and even his richest lines show the influence of the classics in
their proportion and harmony. For instance, his sonnet 'To
Sleep' is so saturated with sweetness that only its marvellous
judgment as sound saves it from being sickly.

O soft embalmer of the still midnight,
    Shutting, with careful fingers and benign,
Our gloom-pleas'd eyes, embower'd from the light,
    Enshaded in forgetfulness divine:
O soothest Sleep! if so it please thee, close
    In midst of this thine hymn my willing eyes,
Or wait the 'Amen', ere thy poppy throws
    Around my bed its lulling charities.
Then save me, or the passed day will shine
Upon my pillow, breeding many woes, –

Save me from curious Conscience, that still lords
Its strength for darkness, burrowing like a mole;
  Turn the key deftly in the oiled wards,
And seal the hushed Casket of my Soul.

Another poem where Keats pulls out all the stops to achieve an unheard-of richness is the one addressed 'To Autumn'. One of his most original discoveries was the use to which that rather frigid if rhapsodical form, the ode, could be put. In a letter, he defined the power of the imagination to make any subject its own – what he called 'negative capability'. Thus he was able to meditate upon a given subject in the manner required of odes without losing himself in argument or boring his reader with too much information. The cast of his mind was sensuous rather than reflective, and his rhetoric turns into true poetry. His style is miles from Wordsworth's 'language of men' – in fact, it is almost wholly artificial, yet generations of readers have recognised in Keats's famous poems the true voice of human feeling.

Season of mists and mellow fruitfulness,
  Close bosom-friend of the maturing sun;
Conspiring with him how to load and bless
  With fruit the vines that round the thatch-eaves run;
To bend with apples the moss'd cottage-trees,
  And fill all fruit with ripeness to the core;
    To swell the gourd, and plump the hazel shells
With a sweet kernel; to set budding more,
And still more, later flowers for the bees,
Until they think warm days will never cease,
    For Summer has o'er-brimm'd their clammy cells.

Who hath not seen thee oft amid thy store?
  Sometimes whoever seeks abroad may find
Thee sitting careless on a granary floor,
  Thy hair soft-lifted by the winnowing wind;
Or on a half-reap'd furrow sound asleep,
  Drows'd with the fume of poppies, while thy hook
    Spares the next swath and all its twined flowers:
And sometimes like a gleaner thou dost keep
  Steady thy laden head across a brook;
  Or by a cyder-press, with patient look,
    Thou watchest the last oozings hours by hours.

Where are the songs of Spring? Ay, where are they?
    Think not of them, thou hast thy music too, –
While barred clouds bloom the soft-dying day,
    And touch the stubble-plains with rosy hue;
Then in a wailful choir the small gnats mourn
    Among the river sallows, borne aloft
        Or sinking as the light wind lives or dies;
And full-grown lambs loud bleat from hilly bourn;
    Hedge-crickets sing; and now with treble soft
    The red-breast whistles from a garden-croft;
        And gathering swallows twitter in the skies.

Byron, who was in most respects a good judge of his fellow-men, made a bad miscalculation about Keats. At first he called him 'a miserable self-polluter of the mind', and then, influenced by Shelley, came to regard him as a victim of villainous literary reviewers in England. As he put it: ''Tis strange the mind, that fiery particle/Should let itself be snuffed out by an article.' But Keats was far tougher than Byron thought, and was not moved overmuch by the unfavourable reviews his poems received. He died in 1821 in Rome, hopelessly seeking a cure from his tuberculosis. Had he lived, he would probably have moved towards a style less lush and more concentrated. His unfinished blank verse poem 'Hyperion' is almost Miltonic, but with a luminousness foreign to Milton. Keats found in the Titans, the pre-Olympian gods of Greece, a subject on which his deeper imagination could work. The poem is still sensual but it is also a meditation on the place of intellectual power in the natural world. Here is the end of Book One as his father Saturn urges Hyperion to set out to take up the cause of the dispossessed Titans:

'Divine ye were created, and divine
In sad demeanour, solemn, undisturb'd,
Unruffled, like high Gods, ye liv'd and ruled:
Now I behold in you fear, hope, and wrath;
Actions of rage and passion; even as
I see them, in the mortal world beneath,
In men who die. – This is the grief, O Son!
Sad sign of ruin, sudden dismay, and fall!
Yet do thou strive; as thou art capable,
As thou canst move about, an evident God;

And canst oppose to each malignant hour
Ethereal presence: – I am but a voice,
My life is but the life of winds and tides,
No more than winds and tides can I avail: –
But thou canst. – Be thou therefore in the van
Of circumstance; yea, seize the arrow's barb
Before the tense string murmur. – To the earth!
For there thou wilt find Saturn, and his woes.
Meantime I will keep watch on thy bright sun,
And of thy seasons be a careful nurse.'–
Ere half this region-whisper had come down,
Hyperion arose, and on the stars
Lifted his curved lids, and kept them wide
Until it ceas'd; and still he kept them wide:
And still they were the same bright, patient star.
Then with a slow incline of his broad breast,
Like to a diver in the pearly seas,
Forward he stoop'd over the airy shore,
And plung'd all noiseless into the deep night.

John Clare hardly fits under the heading of Romanticism at
all, except that, living in its heyday and being aware of literary
fashion, he couldn't escape its effects entirely. Clare has been
misrepresented as a sort of country bumpkin among poets, but
like all geniuses he had as much sophistication as he needed for
his art. He was the son of a failed farmer in Northamptonshire,
and was brought up in severe poverty. His first poems showed
obvious talent and he became an overnight success among the
London literati. They patronised him, and found his sprinkling
of dialect words as well as his marvellously transparent language
a cause for wonder. As he was a farm boy, the fact that he wrote
poetry at all amazed them. The sad effect of this early popularity,
followed by inevitable neglect, was Clare's madness. He was
mad more in Cowper's vein than in Smart's, and had he had
enough money, he might never have been put in an asylum. He
suffered delusions during his confinement – one of them was to
think himself Lord Byron and to turn out extra cantos for *Don
Juan* as well as *Childe Harold*. This confirms that Clare was
interested in the public face of Romanticism, and, also, that he
recognised, as few people at that time did, where Byron's

greatness lay. Clare will always be loved for his poems about the English countryside. Not since the seventeenth century had there been so natural a combination of direct observation and poetic sympathy. Clare knew the birds, insects and animals of Northamptonshire by heart, and throughout his life he celebrated them in hundreds of brief and lyrical poems. His descriptions are as accurate as a naturalist's drawings, but his spirit is much more poetic. His concern for outcasts was intense; for instance, for the gypsies who camped in the fields near his home and the badger hunted down by dogs. Four poems follow which illustrate Clare's special qualities. The first, 'Clock-a-Clay', celebrates the ladybird. It's almost a child's poem, a delicate vignette honouring one of the smallest and most vulnerable of creatures.

> In the cowslip pips I lie,
> Hidden from the buzzing fly,
> While green grass beneath me lies,
> Pearled with dew like fishes' eyes,
> Here I lie, a clock-a-clay,
> Waiting for the time of day.
>
> While grassy forest quakes surprise,
> And the wild wind sobs and sighs,
> My gold home rocks as like to fall,
> On its pillar green and tall;
> When the pattering rain drives by
> Clock-a-clay keeps warm and dry.
>
> Day by day and night by night,
> All the week I hide from sight;
> In the cowslip pips I lie,
> In rain and dew still warm and dry;
> Day and night, and night and day,
> Red, black-spotted clock-a-clay.
>
> My home shakes in wind and showers,
> Pale green pillar topped with flowers,
> Bending at the wild wind's breath,
> Till I touch the grass beneath;
> Here I live, lone clock-a-clay,
> Watching for the time of day.

Next a sonnet entitled 'Emmonsail's Heath in Winter', where, by the simplest means, Clare draws a picture of the English countryside in its most characteristic season.

> I love to see the old heath's withered brake
> Mingle its crimpled leaves with furze and ling,
> While the old heron from the lonely lake
> Starts slow and flaps his melancholy wing,
> And oddling crow in idle motions swing
> On the half-rotten ash-tree's topmost twig,
> Beside whose trunk the gipsy makes his bed.
> Up flies the bouncing woodcock from the brig
> Where a black quagmire quakes beneath the tread;
> The fieldfares chatter in the whistling thorn
> And for the haw round fields and closen rove,
> And coy bumbarrels, twenty in a drove,
> Flit down the hedgerows in the frozen plain
> And hang on little twigs and start again.

Clare's use of the sonnet is unusual. Ever since Shakespeare and Milton, the sonnet had been chosen by English poets for their most profound and elevated thoughts. Having only fourteen lines to work in, they considered it appropriate to load each line with as much weight as it could carry and in consequence their sonnets were marmoreal and dignified. This is true of Keats's famous sonnets and Shelley's 'Ozymandias'. Clare did something quite different. He looked on the sonnet as the perfect receptacle for his direct observations of nature. The previous poem is a regular sonnet: the next, 'Gipsies', is certainly in fourteen lines, but Clare does a revolutionary thing, he largely dispenses with rhymes, except for the clinching couplet.

> The snow falls deep; the forest lies alone;
> The boy goes hasty for his load of breaks,
> Then thinks upon the fire and hurries back;
> The gipsy knocks his hands and tucks them up,
> And seeks his squalid camp, half hid in snow,
> Beneath the oak which breaks away the wind,
> And bushes close in snow like hovel warm;
> There tainted mutton wastes upon the coals,
> And the half-wasted dog squats close and rubs,

Then feels the heat too strong, and goes aloof;
He watches well, but none a bit can spare,
And vainly waits the morsel thrown away.
'Tis thus they live – a picture to the place,
A quiet, pilfering, unprotected race.

The last of these four poems is extremely simple. Clare
wrote it in his old age in the asylum. It's called 'I Am' and is about
the infinite sadness of being oneself – an emotion often over-
whelming in the insane. Clare wrote in an album two of the
most desolate lines in English –

Language has not the power to speak what love indites
The soul lies buried in the ink that writes.

'I am' extends this into three stanzas, which are epitaphs on three
things – the unhappiness of life, the mutability of fate and the
beauty of the natural world.

I am: yet what I am none cares or knows,
    My friends forsake me like a memory lost;
I am the self-consumer of my woes,
    They rise and vanish in oblivious host,
Like shades in love and death's oblivion lost;
And yet I am, and live with shadows tost

Into the nothingness of scorn and noise,
    Into the living sea of waking dreams,
Where there is neither sense of life nor joys,
    But the vast shipwreck of my life's esteems;
And e'en the dearest – that I loved the best –
Are strange – nay, rather stranger than the rest.

I long for scenes where man has never trod,
    A place where woman never smiled or wept;
There to abide with my Creator, God,
    And sleep as I in childhood sweetly slept:
Untroubling and untroubled where I lie,
The grass below – above the vaulted sky.

George Gordon, Lord Byron (1788–1824)
Thomas Hood (1799–1845)
Winthrop Mackworth Praed (1802–1839)   P.P.

Italy in the 1820s was rather like Paris after the First World War. The English poets who lived out their brief and feverish lives up and down the Italian peninsula had their counterpart in expatriate writers like Hemingway, Scott Fitzgerald and Ezra Pound who arrived in France in the 1920s. Each group was escaping from a stifling atmosphere at home; the philistinism of England after the Napoleonic War resembled the heyday of American materialism before the Wall Street crash. The England of George III's last years also appeared to the expatriate English poets as the chief upholder of overseas tyrannical regimes, rather as America does now to her revolutionary writers. The parallel can't be pressed too far, but it will help to explain the curious phenomenon of Byron and Shelley writing some of the most famous poems in English while living in exile in Italy. This fondness for Italy persisted through the nineteenth century, and generations of English poets, of whom the most notable is Robert Browning, settled there and sent their poetry home to a ready market in England.

George Gordon, Lord Byron, is probably the most famous English poet after Shakespeare among Continental readers. He established single-handed the special aura of Romanticism which excited whole generations of poets, including such remarkable men as Gérard de Nerval and Pushkin. Even Goethe, already an old man, felt the force of Byron's influence. Byron had every advantage in the business of image-making: he was an hereditary aristocrat, lame but nevertheless a fine athlete; he was very good-looking and had a strong and indiscriminate sexual drive; he was rich, witty and a good companion; highly educated and a born traveller, almost without fear; most important of all, his melancholy fitted him like a specially made suit of clothes. Nowadays, we see him as really very different from the contemporary view of him as the supreme Romantic. Working from his best poems, *English Bards & Scotch Reviewers*, *The Vision of Judgement*, *Beppo* and *Don Juan*, we esteem him as the last great champion of eighteenth-century classicism, with its social tone and sceptical temperament – steering a course, like his hero Pope, between the dullness of the academy and the self-intoxication Shelley foundered in. But this wisdom after the event goes too far in the other direction. Byron wrote a formidable body of poetry for a man who died in his thirty-seventh year and the bulk of it (if not the best of it) is highly Romantic. In addition to *Childe Harold's Pilgrimage*, the poem which made him famous all over Europe, there are also many passionate lyrics, heaven-storming verse dramas such as *Cain*, *Sardanapalus* and *Marino Faliero*, and long poems with exotic settings such as *The Giaour* and *The Bride of Abydos*.

There is ample evidence that Byron *was* an arch-Romantic, though it remains true that, in his finest poems and in his letters, he punctured that spirit of Byronism which was his own most successful creation. The one part of his Romanticism which he took wholly seriously was his love of freedom and his espousal of the cause of Greek independence. His earlier, fashionable self (the consciously 'Byronic' vein) is best represented by *Childe Harold's Pilgrimage*. This enormously influential poem is put together by the simplest and most effective means. As soon as he could leave England, Byron travelled through Europe to the Mediterranean and got to know not only Italy and Greece but also Turkey and the Levant. Although he hated the Turkish overlordship of Greece, he liked Turkish exoticism. He dressed in the national costume and enjoyed himself in the brothels and stews of the Aegean and Anatolia. These European and Levantine travels form the background to *Childe Harold*. Harold is just a peg for Byron to hang his observations on: in so far as Harold has any character, it's a fashionable mixture of melancholy and regret. He broods on lost love, lost innocence and lost glory – but he's little more than a poetical guide to the vanished splendour of European and Mediterranean culture. Canto Four opens with a description of Venice, which is accurate, attractive and atmospheric. Byron was only one of the many

English writers who fell in love with Venice. Not even Ruskin, Corvo or Hemingway has portrayed the city so affectionately.

I stood in Venice, on the Bridge of Sighs;
A palace and a prison on each hand:
I saw from out the wave her structures rise
As from the stroke of the enchanter's wand:
A thousand years their cloudy wings expand
Around me, and a dying Glory smiles
O'er the far times, when many a subject land
Look'd to the winged Lion's marble piles,
Where Venice sate in state, throned on her hundred isles!

She looks a sea Cybele, fresh from ocean,
Rising with her tiara of proud towers
At airy distance, with majestic motion,
A ruler of the waters and their powers:
And such she was; her daughters had their dowers
From spoils of nations, and the exhaustless East
Pour'd in her lap all gems in sparkling showers.
In purple was she robed, and of her feast
Monarchs partook, and deem'd their dignity increased.

In Venice Tasso's echoes are no more,
And silent rows the songless gondolier;
Her palaces are crumbling to the shore,
And music meets not always now the ear:
Those days are gone – but Beauty still is here.
States fall, arts fade – but Nature doth not die,
Nor yet forget how Venice once was dear,
The pleasant place of all festivity,
The revel of the earth, the masque of Italy!

But unto us she hath a spell beyond
Her name in story, and her long array
Of mighty shadows, whose dim forms despond
Above the Dogeless city's vanish'd sway;
Ours is a trophy which will not decay
With the Rialto; Shylock and the Moor,
And Pierre, cannot be swept or worn away –
The keystones of the arch! though all were o'er,
For us repeopled were the solitary shore.

The spouseless Adriatic mourns her lord;
And, annual marriage now no more renew'd,
The Bucentaur lies rotting unrestored,
Neglected garment of her widowhood!
St Mark yet see his lion where he stood
Stand, but in mockery of his wither'd power,
Over the proud Place where an Emperor sued,
And monarchs gazed and envied in the hour
When Venice was a queen with an unequall'd dower.

Before St Mark still glow his steeds of brass,
Their gilded collars glittering in the sun;
But is not Doria's menace come to pass?
Are they not bridled? – Venice, lost and won,
Her thirteen hundred years of freedom done,
Sinks, like a seaweed, unto whence she rose!
Better be whelm'd beneath the waves, and shun,
Even in destruction's depth, her foreign foes,
From whom submission wrings an infamous repose.

Statues of glass – all shiver'd – the long file
Of her dead Doges are declined to dust;
But where they dwelt, the vast and sumptuous pile
Bespeaks the pageant of their splendid trust;
Their sceptre broken, and their sword in rust,
Have yielded to the stranger: empty halls,
Thin streets, and foreign aspects, such as must
Too oft remind her who and what enthrals,
Have flung a desolate cloud o'er Venice' lovely walls.

Byron's sex life has been all too thoroughly researched. The
number of his conquests runs to hundreds, but so aristocratic
and famous a figure had no trouble getting women. Apart from
sensible and obliging girls like his last mistress, Teresa Guiccioli,
he seems to have loved only his half-sister Augusta. However, it
was not his love affairs which got him snubbed in England, but
the bitter court-case which raged around his marriage. It was a
ridiculous marriage and Byron was probably lucky to be banished
by the scandal and forced to live the last years of his life in Italy.
There he met Shelley, who was an inspired judge of poetry and
who encouraged him to persist with his long poem *Don Juan*,
when everyone in England, from his publisher John Murray to

the famous courtesan Harriet Wilson, was trying to get him to
abandon it as unworthy of his genius. At last, tired and sick as
he was, Byron managed to purge his work and his personality
of the last traces of 'Byronism'. Shelley's death and the increasing
tempo of the War of Independence in Greece brought Byron a
premonition of his own end. It came, not on the battlefield but
on the sickbed at Missolonghi, Northern Greece, where he was
trying to get the factious Greek parties to fight the Turks rather
than each other. On his last birthday, he wrote a poem which
distils the best of his world-weariness. What had been a pose was
now a reality, as this moving but unself-pitying poem, with its
half-hinted quotation from Shakespeare, shows. It's called 'On
this Day I Complete my 36th Year'.

> 'Tis time this heart should be unmoved,
> Since others it hath ceased to move:
> Yet, though I cannot be beloved,
> Still let me love.
>
> My days are in the yellow leaf;
> The flowers and fruits of love are gone;
> The worm, the canker, and the grief
> Are mine alone.
>
> The fire that on my bosom preys
> Is lone as some volcanic isle;
> No torch is kindled at its blaze –
> A funeral pile.
>
> The hope, the fear, the jealous care,
> The exalted portion of the pain
> And power of love, I cannot share,
> But wear the chain.
>
> But 'tis not thus – and 'tis not here –
> Such thoughts should shake my soul,
>   nor now,
> Where glory decks the hero's bier,
> Or binds his brow.
>
> The sword, the banner, and the field,
> Glory and Greece, around me see!
> The Spartan, borne upon his shield,
> Was not more free.

Awake! (not Greece – she *is* awake!)
Awake, my spirit! Think through whom
Thy life-blood tracks its parent lake,
And then strike home.

Tread those reviving passions down,
Unworthy manhood! – unto thee
Indifferent should the smile or frown
Of beauty be.

If thou regrett'st thy youth, why live?
The land of honourable death
Is here: up to the field, and give
Away thy breath.

Seek out – less often sought than found –
A soldier's grave, for thee the best;
Then look around, and choose thy ground,
And take thy rest.

By an irony that Byron might have relished, the work of freeing
Greece, which he was unable to accomplish, was done by the
tyranny-supporting hand of England herself. England kept a
fleet in the Mediterranean and this fleet totally destroyed the
Turks at the battle of Navarino, not long after Byron's death.
Although King George IV's Ministry was not keen to act on
Greece's behalf, the stir caused by Byron's death made British
public opinion pro-Greek. Byron's death therefore was not in
vain, and to this day he is honoured throughout Greece as the
greatest of Englishmen. Before he died, he managed to complete
sixteen cantos of his satirical masterpiece, *Don Juan*, the most
eminently readable long poem in the English language. For *Don
Juan*, he invented a beautifully mobile stanza, from the ancient
form of 'Rime Royale', consisting of six lines rhyming AB, AB, AB,
followed by a clinching couplet, the whole thing in standard five-
foot iambics. He employed this verse form with immense resource
and cavalier freedom. *Don Juan* has all the virtues of *Childe Harold*
and none of its faults. The story tells how the young Spanish
aristocrat Juan gets involved with a married woman in Seville, is
sent abroad to travel, and it then goes on to relate his various
adventures on the way. Byron's Juan had little in common with
the character invented by Tirso de Molina and elaborated by

Molière, Mozart and Shaw. He is an amorist but has none of the God-defying demonism of the Don Giovanni sort. Like Childe Harold, he is the skewer on which Byron hangs comment of every sort, ribald, satirical and delicate by turn. The virtuosity of the writing, including the brilliantly perverse rhyming, is amazing. Conversational yet elevated, discursive yet supremely aphoristic, *Don Juan* raises light verse to the highest level of artistry. It's the greatest satire in our language since Pope. The first of three extracts following is from Canto One – two stanzas poking fun at Byron's enemies, the Lake Poets. He hated them for selling out, and accepting Government pensions to write anti-Jacobin poems. Shelley and Peacock thought the same as Byron about them.

> If ever I should condescend to prose,
> I'll write poetical commandments, which
> Shall supersede beyond all doubt all those
> That went before; in these I shall enrich
> My text with many things that no one knows,
> And carry precept to the highest pitch:
> I'll call the work 'Longinus o'er a Bottle,
> Or, Every Poet his own Aristotle.'

> Thou shalt believe in Milton, Dryden, Pope;
> Thou shalt not set up Wordsworth, Coleridge, Southey;
> Because the first is crazed beyond all hope,
> The second drunk, the third so quaint and mouthy:
> With Crabbe it may be difficult to cope,
> And Campbell's Hippocrene is somewhat drouthy:
> Thou shalt not steal from Samuel Rogers, nor
> Commit – flirtation with the muse of Moore.

The second extract is from Canto Two, the emotional heart of the poem, which describes Juan's love affair with Haidée, a young girl from the Greek Islands. Byron modifies his bantering tone and writes of youthful love with sympathy and candour which is miles away from the posing he'd used in his early love poetry. Perhaps only a man as experienced as Byron could bring off so unmawkish a picture of romantic love.

> They looked up to the sky, whose floating glow
> Spread like a rosy ocean, vast and bright;

They gazed upon the glittering sea below,
Whence the broad moon rose circling into sight;
They heard the waves splash, and the wind so low,
And saw each other's dark eyes darting light
Into each other – and, beholding this,
Their lips drew near, and clung into a kiss;

A long, long kiss, a kiss of youth, and love,
And beauty, all concentrating like rays
Into one focus, kindled from above;
Such kisses as belong to early days,
Where heart, and soul, and sense, in concert move,
And the blood's lava, and the pulse a blaze,
Each kiss a heart-quake, – for a kiss's strength,
I think it must be reckon'd by its length.

They were alone, but not alone as they
Who shut in chambers think it loneliness;
The silent ocean, and the starlight bay,
The twilight glow, which momently grew less,
The voiceless sands, and dropping caves, that lay
Around them, made them to each other press,
As if there were no life beneath the sky
Save theirs, and that their life could never die.

They fear'd no eyes nor ears on that lone beach,
They felt no terrors from the night; they were
All in all to each other; though their speech
Was broken words, they thought a language there, –
And all the burning tongues the passions teach
Found in one sigh the best interpreter
Of nature's oracle – first love, that all
Which Eve has left her daughters since her fall.

Haidée's father was an Aegean pirate, and her love and Juan's ends
unhappily. Byron carries his hero on to a Turkish harem where
he has many odd adventures, thence to the Russian court and
finally to England, the grandest (and to Byron) the most hypo-
critical country in Europe. Through all Juan's adventures
Byron allows himself free comment on any subject that takes his
fancy, whether it's germane to the story or not – so that Canto
Nine, for instance, begins with a sustained philippic against the

Duke of Wellington, chief prop of the European legitimists and restorer of the *ancien régime*. *Don Juan* achieves its highest flights of satire once its hero arrives in England. Everything Byron remembered about English society is pilloried – the London season with its parties and its marriageable young ladies, the hypocrisy of the merchant class about money, the landed gentry and their appalling country life, the snobbery and jobbery of the literary world. The following seven stanzas from Canto Thirteen enumerate the guests at a country house party, watched over by their equally unspeakable ancestors, pictured on the walls. Under the geniality, we can recognise Byron's seriousness and his kinship with Alexander Pope.

> Steel barons, molten the next generation
> To silken rows and gay and garter'd earls,
> Glanced from the walls in goodly preservation:
> And Lady Marys blooming into girls,
> With fair young locks, had also kept their station:
> And countesses mature in robes and pearls:
> Also some beauties of Sir Peter Lely,
> Whose drapery hints we may admire them freely.
>
> Judges in very formidable ermine
> Were there, with brows that did not much invite
> The accused to think their lordships would determine
> His cause by learning much from might to right:
> Bishops, who had not left a single sermon;
> Attorneys-general, awful to the sight,
> As hinting more (unless our judgements warp us)
> Of the 'Star Chamber' than of 'Habeas Corpus'.
>
> The noble guests, assembled at the Abbey,
> Consisted of – we give the sex the pas –
> The Duchess of Fitz-Fulke; the Countess Crabby;
> The Ladies Scilly, Busey; – Miss Eclat,
> Miss Bombazeen, Miss Mackstay, Miss O'Tabby,
> And Mrs Rabbi, the rich banker's squaw;
> Also the honourable Mrs Sleep,
> Who look'd a white lamb, yet was a black sheep:
>
> There was Dick Dubious, the metaphysician,
> Who loved philosophy and a good dinner;

Angle, the soi-disant mathematician;
Sir Henry Silvercup, the great race winner.
There was the Reverend Rodomont Precisian,
Who did not hate so much the sin as sinner;
And Lord Augustus Fitz-Plantagenet,
Good at all things, but better at a bet.

There was Jack Jargon, the gigantic guardsman;
And General Fireface, famous in the field,
A great tactician, and no less a swordsman,
Who ate, last war, more Yankees than he kill'd.
There was the waggish Welsh Judge, Jefferies Hardsman,
In his grave office so completely skill'd,
That when a culprit came for condemnation,
He had his judge's joke for consolation.

If all these seem an heterogenous mass
To be assembled at a country seat,
Yet think, a specimen of every class
Is better than an humdrum tête-à-tête.
The days of Comedy are gone, alas!
When Congreve's fool could vie with Molière's bête:
Society is smooth'd to that excess,
That manners hardly differ more than dress.

Our ridicules are kept in the back ground –
Ridiculous enough, but also dull;
Professions, too, are no more to be found
Professional; and there is nought to cull
Of folly's fruit; for though your fools abound,
They're barren, and not worth the pains to pull.
Society is now one polish'd horde,
Form'd of two mighty tribes, The Bores and Bored.

Byron is the greatest writer of light verse in English, though he
is much more besides. But he was followed by two poets who
were also masters of a similar sort – Thomas Hood and Winthrop
Mackworth Praed. Hood is a virtuoso of clever rhymes and
bizarre metres, the founding father of *Comic and Curious Verse*.
His serious poetry is highly romantic and was much esteemed
in Germany in his day, but it is not really first-rate. His verses
attacking the exploitation of the poor, especially 'The Song of

the Shirt' and 'The Bridge of Sighs', are much admired, though they seem sentimental to modern taste. His greatest originality is to be found in those poems describing London life, the day-to-day suburban scene which he put into grotesque verse with impressive realism. Take, for instance, the 'Sonnet to Vauxhall'. It is a celebration of the famous London Pleasure Gardens, but in its weird, spasmic writing it leaps outside its century to join hands with some of the Surrealist poems of the twentieth century.

> The cold transparent ham is on my fork –
>   It hardly rains – and hark the bell! ding-dingle –
> Away, Three thousand feet at gravel work,
> Mocking a Vauxhall shower! – married and single
> Crush – rush! Soaked silks with wet white satin mingle.
> Hengler! Madame! round whom all bright sparks lurk,
> Calls audibly on Mr and Mrs Pringle
> To study the sublime, &c. (vide Burke)
> All noses are upturn'd! Whish-ish! On high
> The rocket rushes – trails – just steals in sight –
> Then droops and melts in bubbles of blue light –
> And Darkness reigns – Then balls flare up and die –
> Wheels whiz – smack crackers – serpents twist – and then
> Back to the cold transparent ham again.

Praed modestly declined to call himself a poet at all, but only a writer of *vers de société*. Yet nobody wrote such frothy doggerel so skilfully. Praed was a Member of Parliament, the only poet-MP since Andrew Marvell. He was a man of great charm and geniality, so there is no malice or indignation in his satire. But his poems of the London Season are never insipid or fawning. Part of his secret lay in his beautifully organised prosody – the metre ticking over, the rhymes not too *outré* and always nicely in place, the social detail enlivened by the right word in the right circumstance. Above all, Praed could draw recognisable pictures of the middle classes: he is as finely pointed and accurate as a good cartoonist. His effects always come off: his tone is never uncertain. Light verse of this character is undoubtedly true art. Here is one of Praed's most affecting vignettes, called 'Good-Night to the Season'.

Good-night to the Season! 'tis over!
Gay dwellings no longer are gay;
The courtier, the gambler, the lover,
Are scatter'd like swallows away:
There's nobody left to invite one,
Except my good uncle and spouse;
My mistress is bathing at Brighton,
My patron is sailing at Cowes:
For want of a better employment,
Till Ponto and Don can get out,
I'll cultivate rural enjoyment,
And angle immensely for trout.

Good-night to the Season! – the lobbies,
Their changes, and rumours of change,
Which startled the rustic Sir Bobbies,
And made all the Bishops look strange:
The breaches, and battles, and blunders,
Perform'd by the Commons and Peers;
The Marquis's eloquent thunder,
The Baronet's eloquent ears:
Denouncing of Papists and treasons,
For foreign dominion and oats;
Misrepresentation of reasons,
And misunderstanding of notes.

Good-night to the Season! – the buildings
Enough to make Inigo sick;
The paintings, and plasterings, and gildings
Of stucco, and marble, and brick;
The orders deliciously blended,
From love of effect, into one;
The club-houses only intended,
The palaces only begun;
The hell where the fiend, in his glory,
Sits staring at putty and stones,
And scrambles from story to story,
To rattle at midnight his bones.

Good-night to the Season! – the dances,
The fillings of hot little rooms,

The glancings of rapturous glances,
The fancyings of fancy costumes;
The pleasures which Fashion makes duties,
The praisings of fiddles and flutes,
The luxury of looking at beauties,
The tedium of talking to mutes;
The female diplomatists, planners
Of matches for Laura and Jane,
The ice of her Ladyship's manners,
The ice of his Lordship's champagne.

Good-night to the season! – the rages
Led off by the chiefs of the throng,
The Lady Matilda's new pages,
The Lady Eliza's new song;
Miss Fennel's macaw, which at Boodle's
Is held to have something to say;
Mrs Splenetic's musical poodles,
Which bark 'batti batti' all day;
The pony Sir Araby sported,
As hot and as black as a coal,
And the Lion his mother imported,
In bearskins and grease, from the Pole.

Good-night to the Season! – the Toso,
So very majestic and tall;
Miss Ayton, whose singing was so-so,
And Pasta, divinest of all;
The labour in vain of the Ballet,
So sadly deficient in stars;
The foreigners thronging the Alley,
Exhaling the breath of cigars;
The 'loge' where some heiress, how killing,
Environ'd with Exquisites sits,
The lovely one out of her drilling,
The Silly ones out of their wits.

Good-night to the Season! – the splendour
That beam'd in the Spanish Bazaar;
Where I purchased – my heart was so tender –
A card-case, – a pasteboard guitar, –

A bottle of perfume, – a girdle, –
A lithograph'd Riego full-grown,
Whom Bigotry drew on a hurdle
That artists might draw him on stone, –
A small panorama of Seville, –
A trap for demolishing flies, –
A caricature of the Devil, –
And a look from Miss Sheridan's eyes.

Good-night to the Season! – the flowers
Of the grand horticultural fête,
When boudoirs were quitted for bowers,
And the fashion was not to be late;
When all who had money and leisure
Grew rural o'er ices and wines,
All pleasantly toiling for pleasure,
All hungrily pining for pines,
And making of beautiful speeches,
And marring of beautiful shows,
And feeding on delicate peaches,
And treading on delicate toes.

Good-night to the Season! – another
Will come with its trifles and toys,
And hurry away, like its brother,
In sunshine, and odour, and noise.
Will it come with a rose or a briar?
Will it come with a blessing or curse?
Will its bonnets be lower or higher?
Will its morals be better or worse?
Will it find me grown thinner or fatter,
Or fonder of wrong or of right,
Or married, – or buried? – no matter,
Good-night to the season, Good-night!

Alfred, Lord Tennyson (1809–1892)

Philip Larkin once wrote that he was pretty certain that the general reader would sooner be wrecked on a desert island with a complete Tennyson than with a complete Wordsworth. I think I can see what he meant. With Wordsworth, you have to let yourself be drawn into the spirit of the man himself, you have to let him take you over, you have to submit to the Wordsworthian universe; and we aren't always in the mood for that. Whereas with Tennyson there's a great variety of experiences and moods, and the most interesting thing about them isn't the poet but the poem. There's Victorian Arthurian legend, there's lyricism of as pure and also as decorative a kind as you'll find anywhere, there are poems in dialect, philosophical meditations, sombre reflections on death, unashamedly patriotic stuff, narrative – and large quantities of all varieties. In fact, I can pick up the collected Tennyson as I do an anthology, and choose from many moods and many styles. Not all are equally attractive, and sometimes Tennyson can be boring or silly. But he sets out to entertain; and remember that this was the great age of the novel too, of Dickens in particular. Dickens and Tennyson are the great Victorian literary entertainers.

Sometimes a single Tennyson poem itself contains several different kinds: 'The Princess', for example, which is a long blank-verse narrative, has embedded in it some of his best-known lyrics: 'Tears, idle tears', 'The splendour falls on castle walls', 'Sweet and low', 'Ask me no more', 'Now sleeps the crimson petal, now the white', and this Idyll (Tennyson used the word), written in Switzerland:

> Come down, O maid, from yonder mountain height:
> What pleasure lives in height (the shepherd sang)
> In height and cold, the splendour of the hills?

But cease to move so near the Heavens, and cease
To glide a sunbeam by the blasted Pine,
To sit a star upon the sparkling spire;
And come, for Love is of the valley, come,
For Love is of the valley, come thou down
And find him; by the happy threshold, he,
Or hand in hand with Plenty in the maize,
Or red with spirted purple of the vats,
Or foxlike in the vine; nor cares to walk
With Death and Morning on the silver horns,
Nor wilt thou snare him in the white ravine,
Nor find him dropt upon the firths of ice,
That huddling slant in furrow-cloven falls
To roll the torrent out of dusky doors:
But follow; let the torrent dance thee down
To find him in the valley; let the wild
Lean-headed Eagles yelp alone, and leave
The monstrous ledges there to slope, and spill
Their thousand wreaths of dangling water-smoke,
That like a broken purpose waste in air:
So waste not thou; but come; for all the vales
Await thee; azure pillars of the hearth
Arise to thee; the children call, and I
Thy shepherd pipe, and sweet is every sound,
Sweeter thy voice, but every sound is sweet;
Myriads of rivulets hurrying through the lawn,
The moan of doves in immemorial elms,
And murmuring of innumerable bees.

From one kind of idyll to another: among Tennyson's most
ambitious efforts were *The Idylls of the King*, an epic cycle based
on the legends of King Arthur. Although they naturally draw
on Malory, and are deliberately archaic in tone, they're also very
Victorian too: late in his life, Tennyson said that he 'intended
Arthur to represent the Ideal Soul of Man coming into contact
with the warring elements of the flesh' – a notion that would
hardly have occurred to Malory. Tennyson also said that he
'could hardly light upon a finer close than that ghostlike passing
away of the king' – the last hundred lines of 'The Passing of
Arthur':

Then murmured Arthur, 'Place me in the barge.'
So to the barge they came. There those three Queens
Put forth their hands, and took the King, and wept.
But she, that rose the tallest of them all
And fairest, laid his head upon her lap,
And loosed the shattered casque, and chafed his hands,
And called him by his name, complaining loud,
And dropping bitter tears against a brow
Striped with dark blood: for all his face was white
And colourless, and like the withered moon
Smote by the fresh beam of the springing east;
And all his greaves and cuisses dashed with drops
Of onset; and the light and lustrous curls –
That made his forehead like a rising sun
High from the dais-throne – were parched with dust;
Or, clotted into points and hanging loose,
Mixed with the knightly growth that fringed his lips.
So like a shattered column lay the King;
Not like that Arthur who, with lance in rest,
From spur to plume a star of tournament,
Shot through the lists at Camelot, and charged
Before the eyes of ladies and of kings.

Then loudly cried the bold Sir Bedivere:
'Ah! my Lord Arthur, whither shall I go?
Where shall I hide my forehead and my eyes?
For now I see the true old times are dead,
When every morning brought a noble chance,
And every chance brought out a noble knight.
Such times have been not since the light that led
The holy elders with the gift of myrrh.
But now the whole Round Table is dissolved
Which was an image of the mighty world,
And I, the last, go forth companionless,
And the days darken round me, and the years,
Among new men, strange faces, other minds.'

And slowly answered Arthur from the barge:
'The old order changeth, yielding place to new,
And God fulfils himself in many ways,
Lest one good custom should corrupt the world.

Comfort thyself: what comfort is in me?
I have lived my life, and that which I have done
May He within himself make pure! but thou,
If thou shouldst never see my face again,
Pray for my soul. More things are wrought by prayer
Than this world dreams of. Wherefore, let thy voice
Rise like a fountain for me night and day.
For what are men better than sheep or goats
That nourish a blind life within the brain,
If, knowing God, they lift not hands of prayer
Both for themselves and those who call them friend?
For so the whole round earth is every way
Bound by gold chains about the feet of God.

But now farewell. I am going a long way
With these thou seest – if indeed I go
(For all my mind is clouded with a doubt) –
To the island-valley of Avilion;
Where falls not hail, or rain, or any snow,
Nor ever wind blows loudly; but it lies
Deep-meadowed, happy, fair with orchard lawns
And bowery hollows crowned with summer sea,
Where I will heal me of my grievous wound.'

So said he, and the barge with oar and sail
Moved from the brink, like some full-breasted swan
That, fluting a wild carol ere her death,
Ruffles her pure cold plume, and takes the flood
With swarthy webs. Long stood Sir Bedivere
Revolving many memories, till the hull
Looked one black dot against the verge of dawn,
And on the mere the wailing died away.

But when that moan had past for evermore,
The stillness of the dead world's winter dawn
Amazed him, and he groaned, 'The King is gone.'
And therewithal came on him the weird rhyme,
'From the great deep to the great deep he goes.'

Whereat he slowly turned and slowly clomb
The last hard footstep of that iron crag;
Thence marked the black hull moving yet, and cried,

'He passes to be King among the dead,
And after healing of his grievous wound
He comes again; but – if he come no more –
O me, be yon dark Queens in yon black boat,
Who shrieked and wailed, the three whereat we gazed
On that high day, when, clothed with living light,
They stood before his throne in silence, friends
Of Arthur, who should help him at his need?'

    Then from the dawn it seemed there came, but faint
As from beyond the limit of the world,
Like the last echo born of a great cry,
Sounds, as if some fair city were one voice
Around a king returning from his wars.

    Thereat once more he moved about, and clomb
Even to the highest he could climb, and saw,
Straining his eyes beneath an arch of hand,
Or thought he saw, the speck that bare the King,
Down that long water opening on the deep
Somewhere far off, pass on and on, and go
From less to less and vanish into light.
And the new sun rose bringing the new year.

So far we've seen Tennyson handling, in different ways, the
blank verse line; but his technical range was as wide as his moods,
and he was a great inventor and developer of stanzaic and metrical
forms. Here's one he used early in his life, in 'Mariana': it
carries an epigraph from Shakespeare's play *Measure for Measure* –
'Mariana in the moated grange' – but that was simply the
starting point; there's no other clear reference to Shakespeare or
the play in it. It's a strange, intricately patterned, mesmerised
and mesmerising poem:

    With blackest moss the flower-plots
        Were thickly crusted, one and all:
    The rusted nails fell from the knots
        That held the pear to the gable-wall.
    The broken sheds looked sad and strange:
        Unlifted was the clinking latch;
        Weeded and worn the ancient thatch
    Upon the lonely moated grange.

She only said, 'My life is dreary,
    He cometh not,' she said;
She said, 'I am aweary, aweary,
    I would that I were dead!'

Her tears fell with the dews at even;
    Her tears fell ere the dews were dried;
She could not look on the sweet heaven,
    Either at morn or eventide.
After the flitting of the bats,
    When thickest dark did trance the sky,
    She drew her casement-curtain by,
And glanced athwart the glooming flats.
    She only said, 'The night is dreary,
        He cometh not,' she said;
    She said, 'I am aweary, aweary,
        I would that I were dead!'

Upon the middle of the night,
    Waking she heard the night-fowl crow:
The cock sung out an hour ere light:
    From the dark fen the oxen's low
Came to her: without hope of change,
    In sleep she seemed to walk forlorn,
    Till cold winds woke the gray-eyed morn
About the lonely moated grange.
    She only said, 'The day is dreary,
        He cometh not,' she said;
    She said, 'I am aweary, aweary,
        I would that I were dead!'

About a stone-cast from the wall
    A sluice with blackened waters slept,
And o'er it many, round and small,
    The clustered marish-mosses crept.
Hard by a poplar shook alway,
    All silver-green with gnarlèd bark:
    For leagues no other tree did mark
The level waste, the rounding gray.
    She only said, 'My life is dreary,
        He cometh not,' she said;

She said, 'I am aweary, aweary,
    I would that I were dead!'

And ever when the moon was low,
    And the shrill winds were up and away,
In the white curtain, to and fro,
    She saw the gusty shadow sway.
But when the moon was very low,
    And wild winds bound within their cell,
    The shadow of the poplar fell
Upon her bed, across her brow.
    She only said, 'The night is dreary,
        He cometh not,' she said;
    She said, 'I am aweary, aweary,
        I would that I were dead!'

All day within the dreamy house,
    The doors upon their hinges creaked;
The blue fly sung in the pane; the mouse
    Behind the mouldering wainscot shrieked,
Or from the crevice peered about.
    Old faces glimmered through the doors,
    Old footsteps trod the upper floors,
Old voices called her from without.
    She only said, 'My life is dreary,
        He cometh not,' she said;
    She said, 'I am aweary, aweary,
        I would that I were dead!'

The sparrow's chirrup on the roof,
    The slow clock ticking, and the sound
Which to the wooing wind aloof
    The poplar made, did all confound
Her sense; but most she loathed the hour
    When the thick-moted sunbeam lay
    Athwart the chambers, and the day
Was sloping towards his western bower.
    Then, said she, 'I am very dreary,
        He will not come,' she said;
        She wept, 'I am aweary, aweary,
        Oh God, that I were dead!'

The great emotional wound in Tennyson's life was the death of his close friend Arthur Hallam when Tennyson was twenty-four. Several of his poems drew their inspiration from this loss, but the most substantial monument is the long cycle of quatrains called *In Memoriam*. Tennyson probably began *In Memoriam* within a few weeks of Hallam's death, but it occupied him on and off for the next dozen or fifteen years, and was eventually published – anonymously – in 1850. Late in his life, Tennyson said of the poem:

> It is rather the cry of the whole human race than mine. In the poem altogether private grief swells out into thought of, and hope for, the whole world. It begins with a funeral and ends with a marriage – begins with death and ends in promise of a new life – a sort of Divine Comedy, cheerful at the close. It is a very impersonal poem as well as personal.

The whole poem is written in over 130 sections of varying length: what I've tried to do is to give some of the flavour of it through stringing together several of the sections, sometimes widely separated ones. *In Memoriam* has been called 'dully abstract', but I find that judgment hard to take: to me, it's the most impressive, and often the most moving, elegy in the English language:

> Dark house, by which once more I stand
> Here in the long unlovely street,
> Doors, where my heart was used to beat
> So quickly, waiting for a hand,
>
> A hand that can be clasped no more –
> Behold me, for I cannot sleep,
> And like a guilty thing I creep
> At earliest morning to the door.
>
> He is not here; but far away
> The noise of life begins again,
> And ghastly through the drizzling rain
> On the bald street breaks the blank day.
>
> The path by which we twain did go,
> Which led by tracts that pleased us well,

Through four sweet years arose and fell,
From flower to flower, from snow to snow:

And we with singing cheered the way,
    And, crowned with all the season lent,
    From April on to April went,
And glad at heart from May to May:

But where the path we walked began
    To slant the fifth autumnal slope,
    As we descended following Hope,
There sat the Shadow feared of man;

Who broke our fair companionship,
    And spread his mantle dark and cold,
    And wrapt thee formless in the fold,
And dulled the murmur on thy lip,

And bore thee where I could not see
    Nor follow, though I walk in haste,
    And think, that somewhere in the waste
The Shadow sits and waits for me.

Be near me when my light is low,
    When the blood creeps, and the nerves prick
    And tingle; and the heart is sick,
And all the wheels of Being slow.

Be near me when the sensuous frame
    Is racked with pangs that conquer trust;
    And Time, a maniac scattering dust,
And Life, a Fury slinging flame.

Be near me when my faith is dry,
    And men the flies of latter spring,
    That lay their eggs, and sting and sing
And weave their petty cells and die.

Be near me when I fade away,
    To point the term of human strife,
    And on the low dark verge of life
The twilight of eternal day.

Unwatched, the garden bough shall sway,
  The tender blossom flutter down,
  Unloved, that beech will gather brown,
This maple burn itself away;

Unloved, the sun-flower, shining fair,
  Ray round with flames her disk of seed,
  And many a rose-carnation feed
With summer spice the humming air;

Unloved, by many a sandy bar,
  The brook shall babble down the plain,
  At noon or when the lesser wain
Is twisting round the polar star;

Uncared for, gird the windy grove,
  And flood the haunts of hern and crake;
  Or into silver arrows break
The sailing moon in creek and cove;

Till from the garden and the wild
  A fresh association blow,
  And year by year the landscape grow
Familiar to the stranger's child;

As year by year the labourer tills
  His wonted glebe, or lops the glades:
  And year by year our memory fades
From all the circle of the hills.

Doors, where my heart was used to beat
  So quickly, not as one that weeps
  I come once more: the city sleeps;
I smell the meadow in the street;

I hear a chirp of birds; I see
  Betwixt the black fronts long-withdrawn
  A light-blue lane of early dawn,
And think of early days and thee,

And bless thee, for thy lips are bland,
  And bright the friendship of thine eye;
  And in my thoughts with scarce a sigh
I take the pressure of thine hand.

Robert Browning (1812-1889)
Eugene Lee-Hamilton (1845-1907)

———————◆———————

Of the three great poets of the Victorian Age, the more con-
servative, Tennyson and Arnold, introduced contemporary life
into their poetry more than Robert Browning did. Yet there's
no doubt that Browning was a powerful innovator in his life-
time, the prime Modernist in English poetry in the nineteenth
century. And since then, he has been the biggest single influence
on the great Moderns of the twentieth century. Browning is a
great poet – you can feel it in your bones – but he is a very
extraordinary one. At every level, his work is paradoxical. A by-
word among his contemporaries for newness and difficulty, his
poetry is nonetheless stuffed with archaisms and scenes from the
past. Like the Latin tag which so delighted the Renaissance
Humanists (*festina lente*), Browning made haste by slowing
down, and travelled into a new world of verse by going back to
the past. While Tennyson and Arnold stayed at home, Browning
lived the most productive years of his life in Tuscany, Venice
and Rome, the stamping-grounds of the first generation of
British Romantic poets thirty years previously. Unlike them,
however, he made full use of the history and culture of these
places in his poems. Where Shelley and even Byron had used
Italy as a backdrop to their emotions, clarifying their poems by
setting them against the picturesque world of the Mediterranean,
Browning undertook the enormous task of bringing a whole
great civilisation back to life in his poetry. This is the reality
which underlies his adoption of the dramatic monologue and
dramatic lyric. Figures from late Medieval and Renaissance
times start out from Browning's poems in speaking likenesses –
passionate men and women from a time of uninhibited self-
expression. There's an element of escapism in this – Browning
turned his eyes away from Industrial England back to the Italy

249

of art-loving princes, *condottiere* and worldly prelates. He even went deep into the first decade of Italian decadence, the seventeenth century, for his longest single work, *The Ring and the Book*, the details of which are drawn from a sordid murder case which he might have matched any day in London or Birmingham. His Renaissance figures are self-explaining Victorians under their patina from the past. He also manages to work a great deal of himself into these supposedly autonomous portraits. The story of Browning's elopement with Elizabeth Barrett is romantic enough; more remarkable is the devotion of their twenty years in Italy, sharing the excitement of recreating high European culture in a new kind of poetry. This is summed up in some lines from the Epilogue to *Men & Women*, his book of 1855. A small point – the metre of this poem is not the usual English one of iambics, but the more urgent trochaics. This is a very hard metre to handle in English, but Browning does so with great success in 'One Word More':

> There they are, my fifty men and women
> Naming me the fifty poems finished!
> Take them, Love, the book and me together.
> Where the heart lies, let the brain lie also.
>
> Rafael made a century of sonnets,
> Made and wrote them in a certain volume
> Dinted with the silver-pointed pencil
> Else he only used to draw Madonnas:
> These, the world might view – but One, the volume.
> Who that one, you ask? Your heart instructs you.
> Did she live and love it all her life-time?
> Did she drop, his lady of the sonnets,
> Die, and let it drop beside her pillow
> Where it lay in place of Rafael's glory,
> Rafael's cheek so duteous and so loving –
> Cheek, the world was wont to hail a painter's,
> Rafael's cheek, her love had turned a poet's?
>
> Dante once prepared to paint an angel:
> Whom to please? You whisper 'Beatrice'.
> While he mused and traced it and retraced it,
> (Peradventure with a pen corroded

Still by drops of that hot ink he dipped for,
When, his left-hand i' the hair o' the wicked,
Back he held the brow and pricked its stigma,
Bit into the live man's flesh for parchment,
Loosed him, laughed to see the writing rankle,
Let the wretch go festering thro' Florence) –
Dante, who loved well because he hated,
Hated wickedess that hinders loving,
Dante standing, studying his angel, –
In there broke the folk of his Inferno.
Says he – 'Certain people of importance'
(Such he gave his daily, dreadful line to)
Entered and would seize, forsooth, the poet.
Says the poet – 'Then I stopped my painting.'

This I say of me, but think of you, Love!
This to you – yourself my moon of poets!
Ah, but that's the world's side – there's the wonder –
Thus they see you, praise you, think they know you.
Out of my own self, I dare to phrase it.
But the best is when I glide from out them,
Cross a step or two of dubious twilight,
Come out on the other side, the novel
Silent silver lights and darks undreamed of.
Where I hush and bless myself with silence.

Oh, their Rafael of the dear Madonnas,
Oh, their Dante of the dread Inferno,
Wrote one song – and in my brain I sing it,
Drew one angel – borne, see, on my bosom!

One way of thinking of the dramatic monologue, which
Browning used so often, is to postulate a play in which the poem
concerned is a key soliloquy or speech. But the poet has the
difficulty of including enough information to explain the poem's
emotional significance, and he must do so credibly without
making the speaker seem too obviously confessional. Too
often, dramatic monologues become condensations of the
speaker's whole life and achievement. Browning does not wholly
escape this temptation to give his characters 'highly character-
istic' things to say, but in his best monologues he hits the right

balance between essential information and poetical rhetoric. He always makes sure his speakers are properly placed against their age and background, and his eye for significant detail is original and dramatic. He is as much at home with real historical persons as with fictional ones, so that the monologues given to the Florentine painters Fra Filippo Lippi and Andrea del Sarto, the keyboard ruminations of the Abbé Vogler and the forlorn communings of King Saul, are not different in kind from Bishop Blougram's apology, Mr Sludge the Medium's self-justification or the chilly revelations of a Renaissance potentate, entitled 'My Last Duchess'. This poem, which is one of Browning's most effective inventions, is set in Ferrara, seat of the d'Este family and home town of Savonarola. Everything Browning tells us is made up, but the portrait of a petty Italian prince, both unscrupulous and snobbish, is the most fruitful look at innate cruelty since the time of Webster. The Duke is showing the picture of his late wife to a representative of his prospective wife's family, who has come to discuss details of the dowry with him. The odious courtliness and insensitivity is beautifully rendered.

That's my last Duchess painted on the wall,
Looking as if she were alive. I call
That piece a wonder, now: Frà Pandolf's hands
Worked busily a day, and there she stands.
Will't please you sit and look at her? I said
'Frà Pandolf' by design, for never read
Strangers like you that pictured countenance,
The depth and passion of its earnest glance,
But to myself they turned (since none puts by
The curtain I have drawn for you, but I)
And seemed as they would ask me, if they durst,
How such a glance came there; so, not the first
Are you to turn and ask thus. Sir, 'twas not
Her husband's presence only, called that spot
Of joy into the Duchess' cheek: perhaps
Frà Pandolf chanced to say 'Her mantle laps
Over my lady's wrist too much,' or 'Paint
Must never hope to reproduce the faint
Half-flush that dies along her throat': such stuff

Was courtesy, she thought, and cause enough
For calling up that spot of joy. She had
A heart – how shall I say? – too soon made glad,
Too easily impressed; she liked whate'er
She looked on, and her looks went everywhere.
Sir, 'twas all one! My favour at her breast,
The dropping of the daylight in the West,
The bough of cherries some officious fool
Broke in the orchard for her, the white mule
She rode with round the terrace – all and each
Would draw from her alike the approving speech,
Or blush, at least. She thanked men, – good! but thanked
Somehow – I know not how – as if she ranked
My gift of a nine-hundred-years-old name
With anybody's gift. Who'd stoop to blame
This sort of trifling? Even had you skill
In speech – (which I have not) – to make your will
Quite clear to such an one, and say, 'Just this
Or that in you disgusts me; here you miss,
Or there exceed the mark' – and if she let
Herself be lessened so, nor plainly set
Her wits to yours, forsooth, and made excuse,
– E'en then would be some stooping; and I choose
Never to stoop. Oh sir, she smiled, no doubt,
Whene'er I passed her; but who passed without
Much the same smile? This grew; I gave commands
Then all smiles stopped together. There she stands
As if alive. Will't please you rise? We'll meet
The company below, then. I repeat,
The Count your master's known munificence
Is ample warrant that no just pretence
Of mine for dowry will be disallowed;
Though his fair daughter's self, as I avowed
At starting, is my object. Nay, we'll go
Together down, sir. Notice Neptune, though,
Taming a sea-horse, thought a rarity,
Which Claus of Innsbruck cast in bronze for me!

The dramatic lyric, as practised by Browning, differs from the
dramatic monologue only in its protagonist. It does not demand

a central speaker who must buttonhole the reader. Instead, it can be a piece of reportage by the poet or a god's-eye view of the world. But it has the same dramatic purpose, the same intention of using significant detail to open up a wider territory. One such is 'A Toccata of Galuppi's'. We're in Venice, this time in the early years of the eighteenth century, when the Serene Republic had already ceased to be important politically, but was still one of the artistic and commercial capitals of Europe. Opera flourished, Goldoni was writing his plays, Casanova seducing his women – Venice was held to be the most fashionable city in Europe. Baldassare Galuppi was a composer who wrote bravura keyboard pieces which were enormously popular with the pleasure-loving Venetians. He specialised in Liberace-like swooning effects – the 'lesser thirds, sixths diminished, commiserating sevenths' mentioned in the poem. Galuppi was no Scarlatti, but he serves Browning well enough for his picture of a worldly society and the end which awaits it in death – probably on the cemetery island of San Michele. Again, Browning uses trochaics, but to quite different effect.

Oh, Galuppi, Baldassaro, this is very sad to find!
I can hardly misconceive you; it would prove me deaf and
  blind;
But although I give you credit, 'tis with such a heavy
  mind!

Here you come with your old music, and here's all the
  good it brings.
What, they lived once thus at Venice, where the merchants
  were the kings,
Where St Mark's is, where the Doges used to wed the sea
  with rings?

Ay, because the sea's the street there; and 'tis arched by
  . . . what you call
. . . Shylock's bridge with houses on it, where they kept
  the carnival!
I was never out of England – it's as if I saw it all!

Did young people take their pleasure when the sea was
  warm in May?

Balls and masks begun at midnight, burning ever to mid-
day,
When they made up fresh adventures for the morrow, do
you say?

Was a lady such a lady, cheeks so round and lips so red, –
On her neck the small face buoyant, like a bell-flower on
its bed,
O'er the breast's superb abundance where a man might
base his head?

Well (and it was graceful of them) they'd break talk off
and afford
– She, to bite her mask's black velvet, he to finger on his
sword,
While you sat and played Toccatas, stately at the clavi-
chord?

What? Those lesser thirds so plaintive, sixths diminished,
sigh on sigh,
Told them something? Those suspensions, those solu-
tions – 'Must we die?'
Those commiserating sevenths – 'Life might last! we can
but try!'

'Were you happy?' – 'Yes.' – 'And are you still as happy?'
– 'Yes – And you?'
– 'Then more kisses' – 'Did I stop them, when a million
seemed so few?'
Hark – the dominant's persistence, till it must be answered
to!

So an octave struck the answer. Oh, they praised you, I
dare say!
'Brave Galuppi! that was music! good alike at grave and
gay!
I can always leave off talking, when I hear a master play.'

Then they left you for their pleasure: till in due time, one
by one,
Some with lives that came to nothing, some with deeds as
well undone,
Death came tacitly and took them where they never see the
sun.

But when I sit down to reason, – think to take my stand
    nor swerve
Till I triumph o'er a secret wrung from nature's close
    reserve,
In you come with your cold music, till I creep thro' every
    nerve.

Yes, you, like a ghostly cricket, creaking where a house
    was burned –
'Dust and ashes, dead and done with, Venice spent what
    Venice earned!
The soul, doubtless, is immortal! – where a soul can be
    discerned.

'Yours for instance, you know physics, something of
    geology,
Mathematics are your pastime; souls shall rise in their
    degree;
Butterflies may dread extinction, – you'll not die, it cannot
    be!

'As for Venice and its people, merely born to bloom and
    drop,
Here on earth they bore their fruitage, mirth and folly were
    the crop.
What of soul was left, I wonder, when the kissing had to
    stop?

'Dust and ashes!' So you creak it, and I want the heart to
    scold.
Dear dead women, with such hair, too – what's become of
    all the gold
Used to hang and brush their bosoms? I feel chilly and
    grown old.

A good poem to leave Browning with is one of his most
adventurous pieces, 'Caliban upon Setebos', subtitled 'Natural
Theology on the Island'. His experimenting with poems based
on already existing works of art is another of his anticipations of
modern poetic practice: here all Browning's characters come
from Shakespeare's last play, *The Tempest*. Caliban is thinking
aloud about God and what God must be like. His mother, the

witch Sycorax, had taught him to worship Setebos, the aboriginal god of the island. Now that Prospero is in control, Caliban is trying to understand from natural and familiar sights the disposal and provision of happiness in the world. Browning uses Shakespeare's characters to fill out a Victorian internal monologue about religion and doubt. 'Caliban upon Setebos' is too long to quote entire, but these extracts illustrate the technique.

Setebos, Setebos, and Setebos!
'Thinketh, He dwelleth i' the cold o' the moon.

'Thinketh He made it, with the sun to match,
But not the stars; the stars came otherwise;
Only made clouds, winds, meteors, such as that:
Also this isle, what lives and grows thereon,
And snaky sea which rounds and ends the same.

'Thinketh, it came of being ill at ease:
He hated that He cannot change His cold,
Nor cure its ache. 'Hath spied an icy fish
That longed to 'scape the rock-stream where she lived,
And thaw herself within the lukewarm brine
O' the lazy sea her stream thrusts far amid,
A crystal spike 'twixt two warm walls of wave;
Only, she ever sickened, found repulse
At the other kind of water, not her life,
(Green-dense and dim-delicious, bred o' the sun)
Flounced back from bliss she was not borne to breathe,
And in her old bounds buried her despair,
Hating and loving warmth alike: so He.

'Thinketh, such shows nor right nor wrong in Him,
Nor kind, nor cruel: He is strong and Lord.
'Am strong myself compared to yonder crabs
That march now from the mountain to the sea,
'Let twenty pass, and stone the twenty-first,
Loving not, hating not, just choosing so.
'Say, the first straggler that boasts purple spots
Shall join the file, one pincer twisted off;
'Say, this bruised fellow shall receive a worm,
And two worms he whose nippers end in red;
As it likes me each time, I do: so He.

'Conceiveth all things will continue thus,
And we shall have to live in fear of Him
So long as He lives, keeps his Strength: no change,
If He have done His best, make no new world
To please Him more, so leave off watching this, –
If He surprise not even the Quiet's self
Some strange day, – or, suppose, grow into it
As grubs grow butterflies; else, here we are,
And there is He, and nowhere help at all.

'Believeth with the life, the pain shall stop.
His dam held different, that after death
He both plagued enemies and feasted friends:
Idly! He doth His worst in this our life,
Giving just respite lest we die through pain,
Saving last pain for worst, – with which, an end.
Meanwhile, the best way to escape His ire
Is, not to seem too happy. 'Sees, himself,
Yonder two flies, with purple films and pink,
Bask on the pompion bell above: kills both.
'Sees two black painful beetles roll their ball
On head and tail as if to save their lives:
Moves them the stick away they strive to clear.

Even so, 'would have Him misconceive, suppose
This Caliban strives hard and ails no less,
And always, above all else, envies Him;
Wherefore he mainly dances on dark nights,
Moans in the sun, gets under holes to laugh,
And never speaks his mind save housed as now:
Outside, 'groans, curses. If He caught me here,
O'erheard this speech, and asked 'What chuckles at?'
'Would, to appease Him, cut a finger off,
Or of my three kid yearlings burn the best,
Or let the toothsome apples rot on tree,
Or push my tame beast for the orc to taste:
While myself lit a fire, and made a song
And sung it, 'What I hate, be consecrate
To celebrate Thee and Thy state, no mate
For Thee; what see for envy in poor me?'
Hoping the while, since evils sometimes mend,

Warts rub away and sores are cured with slime,
That some strange day, will either the Quiet catch
And conquer Setebos, or likelier He
Decrepit may doze, as good as die.

(What what? A curtain o'er the world at once!
Crickets stop hissing; not a bird – or, yes,
There scuds His raven that has told Him all!
It was fool's play, this prattling! Ha! The wind
Shoulders the pillared dust, death's house o' the move,
And fast invading fires begin! White blaze –
A tree's head snaps – and there, there, there, there, there,
His thunder follows! Fool to gibe at Him!
Lo! 'Lieth flat and loveth Setebos!
'Maketh his teeth meet through his upper lip,
Will let those quails fly, will not eat this month
One little mess of whelks, so he may 'scape!)

Browning's influence is greater in the twentieth century
than in his lifetime and his immediate progeny was not great.
Among those of his contemporaries who derived much from his
work, the odd figure of Eugene Lee-Hamilton stands out. He
too lived in Florence and wrote dramatic reconstructions of the
past. An invalid for much of his life, he is more morbid and less
inventive than Browning, but he deserves to be remembered.
He had the Englishman's ready identification with Tuscany, and
took many of his subjects from Italy in the Browning manner.
The next poem, a sonnet, is called 'Lucca Signorelli to his Son'.
Signorelli was an Italian Quattrocento painter with a particularly
sculptured style. His pictures exaggerate anatomical detail for
deliberate effect, almost as if he were exposing the muscle case
underneath. Vasari tells how Signorelli stayed up all night to
sketch his own dead son.

They brought thy body back to me quite dead,
  Just as thou hadst been stricken in the brawl.
  I let no tear, I let no curses fall,
But signed to them to lay thee on the bed.

Then, with clenched teeth, I stripped thy clothes soaked
    red;
  And taking up my pencil at God's call,

All night I drew thy features, drew them all,
And every beauty of thy pale chill head.

For I required the glory of thy limbs,
    To lend it to archangel and to saint,
And of thy brow for brows with halo rims;

And thou shalt stand, in groups that I shall paint
    Upon God's walls; till, like procession hymns
Lost in the distance, ages make them faint.

Matthew Arnold (1822–1888)
Arthur Hugh Clough (1819–1861)

A.T.

My co-editor, Peter Porter, once used in a poem of his a phrase that always haunts me: 'the laureates of low spirits'. He used the phrase to characterise some poets of our own time, and very aptly too; but when I was re-reading the poets with whom this section deals, it suddenly occurred to me that it fitted them pretty aptly too – not just disparagingly, but with an accurate assessment of the driving force and the very subject-matter of Matthew Arnold and Arthur Hugh Clough. I like both these poets; but I must say that part of their appeal to me is that very often they catch a mood we've not yet encountered in this book: a sense not of horror or nobility or brutality, but of blankness, greyness, something too wan to be called despair, with a loss of energy and a realisation of failure. Here is one face of it, in Arnold's poem, 'Growing Old':

> What is it to grow old?
> Is it to lose the glory of the form,
> The lustre of the eye?
> Is it for beauty to forego her wreath?
> – Yes, but not this alone.
>
> Is it to feel our strength –
> Not our bloom only, but our strength – decay?
> Is it to feel each limb
> Grow stiffer, every function less exact,
> Each nerve more loosely strung?
>
> Yes, this, and more; but not
> Ah, 'tis not what in youth we dream'd 'twould be!
> 'Tis not to have our life
> Mellow'd and soften'd as with sunset-glow,
> A golden day's decline.

'Tis not to see the world
As from a height, with rapt prophetic eyes,
And heart profoundly stirr'd;
And weep, and feel the fulness of the past,
The years that are no more.

It is to spend long days
And not once feel that we were ever young;
It is to add, immured
In the hot prison of the present, month
To month with weary pain.

It is to suffer this,
And feel but half, and feebly, what we feel.
Deep in our hidden heart
Festers the dull remembrance of a change,
But no emotion – none.

It is – last stage of all –
When we are frozen up within, and quite
The phantom of ourselves,
To hear the world applaud the hollow ghost
Which blamed the living man.

Both Arnold and Clough were products of the high-minded, duty-ridden early Victorian intellectual aristocracy, dissatisfied with the bland Anglicanism of their day but unable to find any firm substitute for it. Classicising and mythologising were ways of trying to create a subject-matter and a style which would survive their loss of energy and loss of faith, but I don't feel that their best or most interesting work comes out of this. Matthew Arnold's 'Sohrab and Rustum', for instance, is an attempt at a sort of mini-epic (it's about 900 lines long), in which an old Persian legend about a warrior father unknowingly killing his warrior son is handled with the same stately, literary decorum we saw in Tennyson's Arthurian poems. Of course, it can be very beautiful: here are the last fifty or so lines of 'Sohrab and Rustum', after Sohrab has been fatally wounded and father and son have, too late, recognised one another:

He spoke; and Sohrab smiled on him, and took
The spear, and drew it from his side, and eased
His wound's imperious anguish; but the blood

Came welling from the open gash, and life
Flow'd with the stream; – all down his cold white side
The crimson torrent ran, dim now and soil'd,
Like the soil'd tissue of white violets
Left, freshly gather'd, on their native bank,
By children whom their nurses call with haste
Indoors from the sun's eye; his head droop'd low,
His limbs grew slack; motionless, white, he lay –
White, with eyes closed; only when heavy gasps,
Deep heavy gasps quivering through all his frame,
Convulsed him back to life, he open'd them,
And fix'd them feebly on his father's face;
Till now all strength was ebb'd, and from his limbs
Unwillingly the spirit fled away,
Regretting the warm mansion which it left,
And youth, and bloom, and this delightful world.
    So, on the bloody sand, Sohrab lay dead;
And the great Rustum drew his horseman's cloak
Down o'er his face, and sat by his dead son.
As those black granite pillars, once high-rear'd
By Jemshid in Persepolis, to bear
His house, now 'mid their broken flights of steps
Lie prone, enormous, down the mountain side –
So in the sand lay Rustum by his son.
    And night came down over the solemn waste,
And the two gazing hosts, and that sole pair,
And darken'd all; and a cold fog, with night,
Crept from the Oxus. Soon a hum arose,
As of a great assembly loosed, and fires
Began to twinkle through the fog; for now
Both armies moved to camp, and took their meal;
The Persians took it on the open sands
Southward, the Tartars by the river marge;
And Rustum and his son were left alone.
    But the majestic river floated on,
Out of the mist and hum of that low land,
Into the frosty starlight, and there moved,
Rejoicing, through the hush'd Chorasmian waste,
Under the solitary moon; – he flow'd
Right for the polar star, past Orgunje,

Brimming, and bright, and large; then sands begin
To hem his watery march, and dam his streams,
And split his currents; that for many a league
The shorn and parcell'd Oxus strains along
Through beds of sand and matted rushy isles –
Oxus, forgetting the bright speed he had
In his high mountain cradle in Pamere,
A foil'd circuitous wanderer – till at last
The long'd-for dash of waves is heard, and wide
His luminous home of waters opens, bright
And tranquil, from whose floor the new-bathed stars
Emerge, and shine upon the Aral Sea.

There were other ways of dealing with nostalgia and loss in their poetry of course: Arnold's poem 'The Scholar Gypsy', though just as literary as 'Sohrab and Rustum' – even more so in its language, actually – faces its spiritual mood more directly, as does 'Thyrsis', which was Arnold's elegy on the death of Clough. And most directly of all, yet very subtly too, there's Arnold's most admired poem, 'Dover Beach': here the setting, the descriptiveness, the literariness, the moralising, all blend together with great authority:

The sea is calm tonight.
The tide is full, the moon lies fair
Upon the straits; – on the French coast the light
Gleams and is gone; the cliffs of England stand,
Glimmering and vast, out in the tranquil bay.
Come to the window, sweet is the night-air!
Only, from the long line of spray
Where the sea meets the moon-blanch'd land,
Listen! you hear the grating roar
Of pebbles which the waves draw back, and fling,
At their return, up the high strand,
Begin, and cease, and then again begin,
With tremulous cadence slow, and bring
The eternal note of sadness in.

Sophocles long ago
Heard it on the Aegean, and it brought
Into his mind the turbid ebb and flow

Of human misery; we
Find also in the sound a thought,
Hearing it by this distant northern sea.

The Sea of Faith
Was once, too, at the full, and round earth's shore
Lay like the folds of a bright girdle furl'd.
But now I only hear
Its melancholy, long, withdrawing roar,
Retreating, to the breath
Of the night-wind, down the vast edges drear
And naked shingles of the world.

Ah, love, let us be true
To one another! for the world, which seems
To lie before us like a land of dreams,
So various, so beautiful, so new,
Hath really neither joy, nor love, nor light,
Nor certitude, nor peace, nor help for pain;
And we are here as on a darkling plain
Swept with confused alarms of struggle and flight,
Where ignorant armies clash by night.

In Arnold, there never seems to be for a moment a relaxation
of that resolute, hard-driven, scrupulous seriousness. Clough,
on the other hand, has a running line of grace-notes and whimsies,
along with preoccupations and glooms which he shares with
Arnold. The best-known of the poems in this lighter vein is
'The Latest Decalogue' – and it belies the grave tone of the
section-title Clough gave it, 'Poems on Life and Duty':

Thou shalt have one God only; who
Would be at the expense of two?
No graven images may be
Worshipped, except the currency:
Swear not at all; for, for thy curse
Thine enemy is none the worse:
At church on Sunday to attend
Will serve to keep the world thy friend:
Honour thy parents; that is, all
From whom advancement may befall;
Thou shalt not kill; but need'st not strive

Officiously to keep alive:
Do not adultery commit;
Advantage rarely comes of it:
Thou shalt not steal; an empty feat,
When it's so lucrative to cheat:
Bear not false witness; let the lie
Have time on its own wings to fly:
Thou shalt not covet, but tradition
Approves all forms of competition.

That's good light verse – light and bitter. But Clough's most ambitious and I think best work is much more wide-ranging than this. 'Amours de Voyages' is really a novel in verse, and though it's tempting to call it an autobiographical novel, Clough himself emphatically denied the suggestion with the words 'extremely not so'. Still, the fact remains that much of the poem describes in detail the events of the spring of 1849 in Rome, when Clough was staying in Italy on holiday. He was thirty at the time, and very like this description of the poem's central character, Claude, which appeared in a contemporary review:

A young English gentleman, well born and well connected, but naturally shy and rather satirical. His education has rendered him fastidious, and he is by temperament inclined to dream and meditate and question rather than to act.

'Amours de Voyage' weaves together, in a series of verse letters written in English hexameters, a personal story of a frustrated love affair and Claude's observation of the war between the new Roman Republic, under Mazzini, and the French, who invaded the city in an attempt to reinstate the banished Pope. Here is Claude writing to his correspondent Eustace after an incident which he characteristically describes in his wry, slightly supercilious but also slightly shocked fashion:

So, I have seen a man killed! An experience that, among
    others!
Yes, I suppose I have; although I can hardly be certain,
And in a court of justice could never declare I had seen it.
But a man was killed, I am told, in a place where I saw
Something; a man was killed, I am told, and I saw some-
    thing.

I was returning home from St. Peter's; Murray, as usual,
Under my arm, I remember; had crossed the St. Angelo
bridge, and
Moving towards the Condotti, had got to the first barricade,
when
Gradually, thinking still of St. Peter's, I became conscious
Of a sensation of movement opposing me, – tendency this
way
(Such as one fancies may be in a stream when the wave of
the tide is
Coming and not yet come, – a sort of noise and retention);
So I turned, and, before I turned, caught sight of stragglers
Heading a crowd, it is plain, that is coming behind that
corner.
Looking up, I see windows filled with heads; the Piazza,
Into which you remember the Ponte St. Angelo enters,
Since I passed, has thickened with curious groups; and now
the
Crowd is coming, has turned, has crossed that last
barricade, is
Here at my side. In the middle they drag at something.
What is it?
Ha! bare swords in the air, held up? There seem to be
voices
Pleading and hands putting back; official, perhaps; but
the swords are
Many, and bare in the air. In the air? they descend; they
are smiting,
Hewing, chopping – At what? In the air once more up-
stretched? And –
Is it blood that's on them? Yes, certainly blood! Of whom,
then?
Over whom is the cry of this furor of exultation?
  While they are skipping and screaming, and dancing
    their caps on the points of
Swords and bayonets, I to the outskirts back, and ask a
Mercantile-seeming bystander, 'What is it?' and he, look-
ing always
That way, makes me answer, 'A Priest, who was trying to
fly to

The Neapolitan army,' – and thus explains the proceeding.
    You didn't see the dead man? No; I began to be doubtful;
I was in black myself, and didn't know what mightn't
    happen, –
But a National Guard close by me, outside of the hubbub,
Broke his sword with slashing a broad hat covered with
    dust, – and
Passing away from the place with Murray under my arm,
    and
Stooping, I saw through the legs of the people the legs of
    a body.
    You are the first, do you know, to whom I have mentioned
    the matter.
Whom should I tell it to else? – these girls? – the Heavens
    forbid it!
Quidnuncs at Monaldini's? – Idlers upon the Pincian?
    If I rightly remember, it happened on that afternoon
    when
Word of the nearer approach of a new Neapolitan army
First was spread. I began to bethink me of Paris
    Septembers,
Thought I could fancy the look of that old 'Ninety-two.
    On that evening
Three or four, or, it may be, five, of these people were
    slaughtered
Some declared they had, one of them, fired on a sentinel;
    others
Say they were only escaping; a Priest, it is currently stated,
Stabbed a National Guard on the very Piazza Colonna:
History, Rumour of Rumours, I leave to thee to determine!
    But I am thankful to say the government seems to have
    strength to
Put it down; it has vanished, at least; the place is most
    peaceful.
Through the Trastevere walking last night, at nine of the
    clock, I
Found no sort of disorder; I crossed by the Island-bridges,
So by the narrow streets to the Ponte Rotto, and onwards
Thence by the Temple of Vesta, away to the great Coliseum,
Which at the full of the moon is an object worthy a visit.

When it comes to his notions of love, Claude is very much the same over-cultivated, irresolute, half-amused creature. Here he is writing to Eustace about his feelings for Mary:

I am in love, meantime, you think; no doubt you would
    think so.
I am in love, you say; with those letters, of course, you
    would say so.
I am in love, you declare. I think not so; yet I grant you
It is a pleasure indeed to converse with this girl. Oh, rare
    gift,
Rare felicity, this! she can talk in a rational way, can
Speak upon subjects that really are matters of mind and of
    thinking,
Yet in perfection retain her simplicity; never, one moment,
Never, however you urge it, however you tempt her,
    consents to
Step from ideas and fancies and loving sensations to those
    vain
Conscious understandings that vex the minds of mankind.
No, though she talk, it is music; her fingers desert not the
    keys; 'tis
Song, though you hear in the song the articulate vocables
    sounded,
Syllabled singly and sweetly the words of melodious mean-
    ing.
    I am in love, you say: I do not think so, exactly.
There are two different kinds, I believe, of human attrac-
    tion:
One which simply disturbs, unsettles, and makes you un-
    easy,
And another that poises, retains, and fixes and holds you.
I have no doubt, for myself, in giving my voice for the
    latter.
I do not wish to be moved, but growing where I was
    growing,
There more truly to grow, to live where as yet I had
    languished.
I do not like being moved: for the will is excited; and
    action

Is a most dangerous thing; I tremble for something
    factitious,
Some malpractice of heart and illegitimate process;
We are so prone to these things, with our terrible notions
    of duty.

Finally, I don't want to try to avoid Clough's best-known poem
simply because it *is* his best-known: I like it in its own right. For
a moment it catches a stronger breath, fixes a firmer note, than
almost anything else in Arnold or Clough. One can see why
Churchill picked it – and not just for non-literary reasons – for
that wartime speech:

> Say not the struggle nought availeth,
>   The labour and the wounds are vain,
> The enemy faints not, nor faileth,
>   And as things have been they remain.
>
> If hopes were dupes, fears may be liars;
>   It may be, in yon smoke concealed,
> Your comrades chase e'en now the fliers,
>   And, but for you, possess the field.
>
> For while the tired waves, vainly breaking,
>   Seem here no painful inch to gain,
> Far back, through creeks and inlets making,
>   Comes silent, flooding in, the main,
>
> And not by eastern windows only,
>   When daylight comes, comes in the light,
> In front, the sun climbs slow, how slowly,
>   But westward, look, the land is bright.

Dante Gabriel Rossetti (1828–1882)
Christina Rossetti (1830–1894)
Algernon Charles Swinburne (1837–1909)
Edward Lear (1812–1888)
Lewis Carroll (Charles Lutwidge Dodgson)
  (1832–1898)
Sir William Schwenck Gilbert (1836–1911)   P.P.

This chapter yokes together the Pre-Raphaelite poets of the middle of the Victorian Age, and three masters of light verse who were their contemporaries, Edward Lear, Lewis Carroll and W. S. Gilbert. English poetry, especially Victorian poetry, is particularly rich in light verse. The Pre-Raphaelite poets and Tennyson are the serious groundbase on which the light verse masters built their fantasies. Both Lear and Carroll parodied (consciously and unconsciously) Tennyson, and Gilbert put Rossetti on the stage in the person of Bunthorne, the aesthetic poet, in *Patience*.

The Pre-Raphaelites were probably more successful as painters than as poets, but while only a few of them practised both arts, the creed which all subscribed to insisted on the close relationship of all the arts. By the time William Morris adopted their principles, their ideals included socialism, and amounted to a revolutionary attitude to the place of art in society. Thus Morris wrote poetry and prose tracts, designed wallpaper and furnishings, reformed printing and book production, and encouraged artists of all sorts to break out of the prevailing commercialism. From its earliest formulation under Ruskin to the decadence of the ideal in the nineties, the Pre-Raphaelite Movement was a reaction to the harshness and ugliness of Victorian life, and a conscious return to the medieval concept of craftsmanship.

The painters Holman Hunt, Millais, Ford Madox Brown and Rossetti took the title Pre-Raphaelite to describe their enthusiasm for the clarity and realism of Italian painting in the centuries before Raphael. It was a complete misreading of artists who were not naïve in the way the Pre-Raphaelites thought – as a quick look at the masters of four centuries from Giotto to Pisanello, and then on to Botticelli and Carpaccio, will show. But it revolutionised English painting, bringing in a pictorial freshness and celebration of colour which, in its turn, played a part in the next great European style, Art Nouveau. Pre-Raphaelite pictures are not much like their ostensible models, since their pursuit of simplicity and clarity took them into the picturesque and sentimental. Theirs is a highly literary way of painting and it had its direct literary counterpart in the poems of Dante Gabriel Rossetti, his sister Christina, William Morris and, most importantly, Algernon Charles Swinburne. Rossetti's life was a laudanum-heightened trip into mysticism. His poetry, however, retained something of a painter's sharpness of outline. His most famous poem, 'The Blessed Damozel', is to a real medieval vision what a Pre-Raphaelite painting is to an Italian Primitive. There's too much gold; or tinsel, rather. But Rossetti's craftsmanship survived his exoticism, and just as his life contained much courage and endurance as well as self-consciousness and neurosis, so his best poems have the drama as well as the morbidity of the Middle Ages. And he could be direct and powerful. 'Jenny', for instance, is a surprisingly realistic picture of sensuality, and the sonnets from 'The House of Life' have a honeyed stillness which doesn't cloy.

But Rossetti's most remarkable poem is one he never finished, called 'The Orchard Pit'. It's an harmonious yet mysterious vision of death, here hailed as another of the beautiful and uncanny women who haunted Rossetti's life. Although unfinished, it seems to lack nothing, but to exist within a perfection of its own.

> Piled deep below the screening apple-branch
>   They lie with bitter apples in their hands:
> And some are only ancient bones that blanch,
> And some had ships that last year's wind did launch,
>   And some were yesterday the lords of lands.

In the soft dell, among the apple-trees,
　　High up above the hidden pit she stands,
And there for ever sings, who gave to these,
That lie below, her magic hour of ease,
　　And those her apples holden in their hands.

This in my dreams is shown me; and her hair
　　Crosses my lips and draws my burning breath;
Her song spreads golden wings upon the air,
Life's eyes are gleaming from her forehead fair,
　　And from her breasts the ravishing eyes of Death.

Men say to me that sleep hath many dreams,
　　Yet I knew never but this dream alone:
There, from a dried-up channel, once the stream's,
The glen slopes up; even such in sleep it seems
　　As to my waking sight the place well known.

My love I call her, and she loves me well:
　　But I love her as in the maelstrom's cup
The whirled stone loves the leaf inseparable
That clings to it round all the circling swell,
　　And that the same last eddy swallows up.

Rossetti's sister, Christina, was a devout believer, and shared
her brother's longing to transcend everyday reality, but within
a Christian framework. Her taste and skill are very uneven, and
there is a rather squashy side to her imagination, as evinced by
poems such as 'Goblin Market'. But she was very resourceful in
her choice of styles and she avoided the over-gilding which
affected so many Medievalists at the time. Her love of the country-
side was strong – like most mystics, she saw in the natural
world the hand of its supernatural maker, and she continually
sought ways of drawing a spell over the fallen universe around
her. Her poem 'Amor Mundi' is interesting as an allegory
against worldly love (all love is due to God), but also for its
anticipation of similar warning ballads written years later by
W. H. Auden.

'Oh where are you going with your lovelocks flowing,
　　On the west wind blowing along this valley track?'
'The downhill path is easy, come with me an' it please ye,
　　We shall escape the uphill by never turning back.'

So they two went together in glowing August weather,
   The honey-breathing heather lay to their left and right;
And dear she was to doat on, her swift feet seemed to float
   on
   The air like soft twin pigeons too sportive to alight.

'Oh, what is that in heaven where grey cloudflakes are
   seven,
   Where blackest clouds hang riven just at the rainy skirt?'
'Oh, that's a meteor sent us, a message dumb, portentous,
   An undecipher'd solemn signal of help or hurt.'

'Oh, what is that glides quickly where velvet flowers grow
   thickly,
   Their scent comes rich and sickly?' 'A scaled and hooded
   worm.'
'Oh, what's that in the hollow, so pale I quake to follow?'
   'Oh, that's a thin dead body which waits the eternal
   term.'

'Turn again, O my sweetest, – turn again, false and fleetest:
   This beaten way thou beatest I fear is hell's own track.'
'Nay, too steep for hill-mounting; nay, too late for cost
   counting:
   This downhill path is easy, but there's no turning back,'

Algernon Charles Swinburne was almost ten years younger than Rossetti, but he was accepted by the Pre-Raphaelite Brotherhood as an equal immediately on coming down from Oxford. He was the archetypal poet-rebel, overestimated in his day and subsequently underestimated, but now seen to be one of the most important and original poets of the nineteenth century. He was extremely precocious, establishing a flamboyant virtuosity from the start. His verse-drama *Atalanta in Calydon*, published in 1865, when he was twenty-eight, made him famous overnight. It was a remarkable work and struck a new note in English verse, for all that it was soaked in the classical past. Two things especially were new – the languorous paganism and the elevation of sensuous sound over all other considerations. The story of Swinburne's life from his early success up to his long retirement in Putney is the classic one of the bohemian artist wrestling to control the very demonism which gives power

274

to his art. He continued to publish defiant and highly successful poems during these years, celebrating sensuality and violence, while living out the self-destructive pattern expected of the *poète maudit*, as Baudelaire had done before him. He went on brandy jags and was beaten by professional ladies in establishments in St John's Wood. His poems of pain and bondage, such as 'Dolores', were the outrageous hits of the hour. But there was another side to Swinburne – his love of liberty, which made the Italian patriot Mazzini his life-long idol, and his unswerving hatred of Christianity. Having written in his 'Hymn to Proserpine', 'thou hast conquered, O pale Galilean', he never recanted, even after he became the respectable poet of Putney, limited to one bottle of light ale a day. Christ remained 'the Galilean Serpent' to him till the day he died.

While we still marvel at his resourcefulness and envy him his memorable lines, there's a rhythmic monotony in his versifying which makes all but his best poems rather wearing. His poetry also shows an obsessional recurrence of theme. To reveal him at his most original, if not most characteristic, here is one of his lesser-known poems, with the purely technical title, 'Hendecasyllabics' – i.e. each line contains eleven syllables. As so often with Swinburne, there isn't really a subject at all – it's a mood-piece, in a Victorian version of the saga style of Anglo-Saxon poetry, though the metrical pattern is more probably derived from one of the rare Greek forms he loved to adapt to English. The calculation of the sound is impeccable – Swinburne had a superfine ear for spoken poetry.

> In the month of the long decline of roses
> I, beholding the summer dead before me,
> Set my face to the sea and journeyed silent,
> Gazing eagerly where above the sea-mark
> Flame as fierce as the fervid eyes of lions
> Half divided the eyelids of the sunset;
> Till I heard as it were a noise of waters
> Moving tremulous under feet of angels
> Multitudinous, out of all the heavens;
> Knew the fluttering wind, the fluttered foliage,
> Shaken fitfully, full of sound and shadow;
> And saw, trodden upon by noiseless angels,

Long mysterious reaches fed with moonlight,
Sweet sad straits in a soft subsiding channel,
Blown about by the lips of winds I knew not,
Winds not borne in the north nor any quarter,
Winds not warm with the south nor any sunshine;
Heard between them a voice of exultation,
'Lo, the summer is dead, the sun is faded,
Even like as a leaf the year is withered,
All the fruits of the day from all her branches
Gathered, neither is any left to gather.
All the flowers are dead, the tender blossoms,
All are taken away; the season wasted,
Like an ember among the fallen ashes.
Now with light of the winter days, with moonlight,
Light of snow, and the bitter light of hoarfrost,
We bring flowers that fade not after autumn,
Pale white chaplets and crowns of latter seasons,
Fair false leaves (but the summer leaves were falser),
Woven under the eyes of stars and planets
When low light was upon the windy reaches
Where the flower of foam was blown, a lily
Dropt the sonorous fruitless furrows
And green fields of the sea that make no pasture;
Since the winter begins, the sweeping winter,
All whose flowers are tears, and round his temples
Iron blossom of frost is bound for ever.'

Death, both as a spectre at the feast and as a benediction, was Swinburne's chief theme. So it has been for countless poets, of course, but Swinburne garnished his death-wish more fulsomely and more inventively than any other Victorian, besides Tennyson.

A comparison of Swinburne's and Tennyson's poetry is very interesting. Ostensibly, Swinburne is the more intelligent writer: in practice, he has a much narrower range than Tennyson. He was also more paradoxical – his metres, which are the smoothest and most hypnotic ever invented, are symbols of confidence. His subject is graveyard dissolution. Yet the two work together surprisingly well. The young men of the 1860s and 70s who chanted his lines celebrating pain and excess to annoy their Oxford tutors were not wrong. They saw where Swinburne's unique gift lay – in his power to make the darker shades of feeling supremely melodious. Poetry is closer to any musically shaped cry of pain or pleasure than it is to philosophy. Swinburne knew this intuitively, and gave his contemporaries the best examples of sheer sound they ever encountered – as in his famous poem, 'The Garden of Proserpine', here represented by a short selection of its stanzas.

> Here, where the world is quiet;
>   Here, where all trouble seems
> Dead winds' and spent waves' riot
>   In doubtful dreams of dreams;
> I watch the green field growing
> For reaping folk and sowing,
> For harvest-time and mowing,
>   A sleepy world of streams.
>
> I am tired of tears and laughter,
>   And men that laugh and weep;
> Of what may come hereafter
>   For men that sow to reap:
> I am weary of days and hours,
> Blown buds of barren flowers,
> Desires and dreams and powers
>   And everything but sleep.
>
> Pale, beyond porch and portal,
>   Crowned with calm leaves, she stands
> Who gathers all things mortal
>   With cold immortal hands;
> Her languid lips are sweeter
> Than love's who fears to greet her
> To men that mix and meet her
>   From many times and lands.
>
> From too much love of living,
>   From hope and fear set free,
> We thank with brief thanksgiving
>   Whatever gods may be
> That no life lives for ever;
> That dead men rise up never;

That even the weariest river
  Winds somewhere safe to sea.

Then star nor sun shall waken,
  Nor any change of light:
Nor sound of waters shaken,
  Nor any sound or sight;
Nor wintry leaves nor vernal,
Nor days nor things diurnal;
Only the sleep eternal
  In an eternal night.

The trio of light verse writers who follow, like Swinburne, are all excellent craftsmen. The first, Edward Lear, was a landscape painter in watercolours. Like many humorists he was a melancholy man, a life-long bachelor with a notably eccentric imagination. The best-known of his *Nonsense Poems*, as he christened them, are subliminal parodies of serious Victorian poetry, chiefly Tennyson's. Reading 'The Dong with the Luminous Nose', we are immediately reminded, rhythms, cadences and all, of the Tennyson of 'Mariana', 'Maud' and 'The Lotos-Eaters'. Lear was the promoter of the limerick and his comic muse has never gone out of circulation. One of his most moving poems is his sad self-portrait in verse called, 'By Way of Preface'. Again the ghost of Tennyson is present in the lyrical joking.

How pleasant to know Mr Lear!
  Who has written such volumes of stuff!
Some think him ill-tempered and queer,
  But a few think him pleasant enough.

His mind is concrete and fastidious,
  His nose is remarkably big;
His visage is more or less hideous,
  His beard it resembles a wig.

He has ears, and two eyes, and ten fingers,
  Leastways if you reckon two thumbs;
Long ago he was one of the singers,
  But now he is one of the dumbs.

He sits in a beautiful parlour,
    With hundreds of books on the wall;
He drinks a great deal of Marsala,
    But never gets tipsy at all.

He has many friends, laymen and clerical,
    Old Foss is the name of his cat:
His body is perfectly spherical,
    He weareth a runcible hat.

When he walks in a waterproof white,
    The children run after him so!
Calling out, 'He's come out in his night-
    Gown, that crazy old Englishman, oh!'

He weeps by the side of the ocean,
    He weeps on the top of the hill;
He purchases pancakes and lotion,
    And chocolate shrimps from the mill.

He reads but he cannot speak Spanish,
    He cannot abide ginger-beer:
Ere the days of his pilgrimage vanish,
    How pleasant to know Mr Lear!

Lewis Carroll is too well-known to need much introduction. Another Victorian who led a double-life (Oxford don lecturing in mathematics, and supreme inventor of upside-down verse), Carroll spiced *Alice in Wonderland* and *Through the Looking-Glass* with superb nonsense poems which combine the lyricism of the age with an absurd logic and mastery of subconscious imagery. For many readers, they are the high points of the stories. Carroll's use of songs and rhymes in his prose works is reminiscent of Shakespeare's in his plays. One of the Alice songs will reveal his quality better than an extract from his most effective long poem, 'The Hunting of the Snark', since that is cumulative in effect. These are the verses which the White Rabbit reads in evidence during the trial at the end of *Alice*. As the King of Hearts remarks, it's 'the most important piece of evidence we've heard yet', and is fair comment on the surrealist world of the Law Courts.

They told me you had been to her,
    And mentioned me to him:

She gave me a good character,
    But said I could not swim.

He sent them word I had not gone,
    (We know it to be true):
If she should push the matter on,
    What would become of you?

I gave her one, they gave him two,
    You gave us three or more;
They all returned from him to you,
    Though they were mine before.

If I or she should chance to be
    Involved in this affair,
He trusts to you to set them free,
    Exactly as we were.

My notion was that you had been
    (Before she had this fit)
An obstacle that came between
    Him, and ourselves, and it.

Don't let him know she liked them best,
    For this must ever be
A secret, kept from all the rest,
    Between yourself and me.

The name of Sir William Schwenck Gilbert is soldered forever to that of his musical collaborator, Sir Arthur Sullivan. He must be the only librettist whose name features under listings of composers, in the hybrid, 'Gilbert and Sullivan'. Gilbert's mastery of comic verse is more down-to-earth and mechanical than Lear's or Carroll's – he has little of their lyricism or fantasy. But it's doubtful that another poet of the Victorian Age got so much of the life of his times into his poetry.

His technical resource is astonishing – he can handle any kind of stanza and metre. His huge popularity has kept him underestimated by literary historians, as also has his philistinism. People prefer their poets to be 'poetical', rather than good craftsmen with words. Gilbert is the laureate of *status quo*, the critic of society who attacked only its non-conformists, with the honourable exceptions of the legal profession and the

280

peerage, whom he disliked. But this is no bar to his being a great poet. Here is one of his most audacious set-pieces – the Lord Chancellor's Nightmare song from *Iolanthe*.

When you're lying awake with a dismal headache, and repose
    is taboo'd by anxiety,
I conceive you may use any language you choose to indulge
    in, without impropriety;
For your brain is on fire – the bedclothes conspire of usual
    slumber to plunder you:
First your counterpane goes, and uncovers your toes, and
    your sheet slips demurely from under you;
Then the blanketing tickles – you feel like mixed pickles – so
    terribly sharp is the pricking,
And you're hot, and you're cross, and you tumble and toss
    till there's nothing 'twixt you and the ticking.
Then the bedclothes all creep to the ground in a heap, and
    you pick 'em all up in a tangle;
Next your pillow resigns and politely declines to remain at its
    usual angle!
Well, you get some repose in the form of a doze, with hot
    eyeballs, and head ever aching,
But your slumbering teems with such horrible dreams that
    you'd very much better be waking;
For you dream you are crossing the Channel, and tossing
    about in a steamer from Harwich –
Which is something between a large bathing machine and a
    very small second-class carriage –
And you're giving a treat (penny ice and cold meat) to a
    party of friends and relations –
They're a ravenous horde – and they all came on board at
    Sloane Square and South Kensington Stations.
And bound on that journey you find your attorney (who
    started that morning from Devon);
He's a bit undersized, and you don't feel surprised when he
    tells you he's only eleven.
Well, you're driving like mad with this singular lad (by-the-
    bye the ship's now a four-wheeler),
And you're playing round games, and he calls you bad names
    when you tell him that 'ties pay the dealer'.

But this you can't stand, so you throw up your hand, and
　　you find you're as cold as an icicle,
In your shirt and your socks (the black silk with gold clocks),
　　crossing Salisbury Plain on a bicycle:
And he and the crew are on bicycles too – which they've
　　somehow or other invested in –
And he's telling the tars, all the particulars of a company he's
　　interested in –
It's a scheme of devices to get at low prices, all goods from
　　cough mixtures to cables
(Which tickled the sailors) by treating retailers, as though
　　they were all vegetables –
You get a good spadesman to plant a small tradesman (first
　　take off his boots with a boot-tree),
And his legs will take root, and his fingers will shoot, and
　　they'll blossom and bud like a fruit-tree –
From the green-grocer tree to get grapes and green pea,
　　cauliflower, pineapple, and cranberries,
While the pastrycook plant, cherry brandy will grant, apple
　　puffs, and three-corners, and banberries –
The shares are a penny, and ever so many are taken by
　　Rothschild and Baring,
And just as a few are allotted to you, you awake with a shudder
　　despairing –
You're a regular wreck, with a crick in your neck, and no
　　wonder you snore, for your head's on the floor, and you've
　　needles and pins from your soles to your shins, and your
　　flesh is a-creep for your left leg's asleep, and you've cramp
　　in your toes, and a fly on your nose, and some fluff in your
　　lung, and a feverish tongue, and a thirst that's intense, and
　　a general sense that you haven't been sleeping in clover;
But the darkness has passed, and it's daylight at last, and the
　　night has been long – ditto – my song – and thank goodness
　　they're both of them over!

Gerard Manley Hopkins (1844–1889)
Coventry Patmore (1823–1896)
George Meredith (1828–1909)   A.T.

—————————◆—————————

In 1866, while he was still an undergraduate at Oxford and
a few months before he became a Roman Catholic convert,
Gerard Manley Hopkins wrote a poem which was almost his
last before a gap, a seven-year silence. Written when he was
twenty-one, this poem is the first faint sign, in some of its
language, of what was to come after the seven years of deliberate
drought while Hopkins embraced the discipline of the Society
of Jesus and put on 'The Habit of Perfection':

> Elected Silence, sing to me
> And beat upon my whorlèd ear,
> Pipe me to pastures still and be
> The music that I care to hear.
>
> Shape nothing, lips; be lovely-dumb:
> It is the shut, the curfew sent
> From there where all surrenders come
> Which only makes you eloquent.
>
> Be shellèd, eyes, with double dark
> And find the uncreated light:
> This ruck and reel which you remark
> Coils, keeps, and teases simple sight.
>
> Palate, the hutch of tasty lust,
> Desire not to be rinsed with wine:
> The can must be so sweet, the crust
> So fresh that come in fasts divine!
>
> Nostrils, your careless breath that spend
> Upon the stir and keep of pride,
> What relish shall the censers send
> Along the sanctuary side!

283

O feel-of-primrose hands, O feet
That want the yield of plushy sward,
But you shall walk the golden street
And you unhouse and house the Lord.

And, Poverty, be thou the bride
And now the marriage feast begun,
And lily-coloured clothes provide
Your spouse not laboured-at nor spun.

This is an odd blend of delicate but rather boneless Pre-Raphael-ite stuff (the sort of thing that the young Hopkins admired in Christina Rossetti) and the much more linguistically energetic Hopkins of the later work. There's a strongly sensuous verbal relish, in such lines as

Be shellèd, eyes, with double dark,
And find the uncreated light:
This ruck and reel which your remark
Coils, keeps, and teases simple light.

Palate, the hutch of tasty lust,
Desire not to be rinsed with wine:
The can must be so sweet, the crust
So fresh that come in fasts divine!

But the words are set in very decorous and placid metres. With the long poem that broke his seven-year silence, 'The Wreck of the Deutschland', Hopkins revolutionised the *movement* of his poetry as well. The story of how he came to write it is well-known. In 1875 a ship called the *Deutschland*, carrying five nuns exiled by German law, was wrecked in the mouth of the Thames, and the nuns were drowned. Hopkins was moved by the event, and when he said so to his rector the response was that he wished someone would write a poem about it. 'The Wreck of the Deutsch-land' was the result – a massive and forbidding masterpiece that lies at the entrance to Hopkins's work. Here are a few stanzas from the middle of the second section:

She drove in the dark to leeward,
She struck – not a reef or a rock
But the combs of a smother of sand: night drew her
Dead to the Kentish Knock;

284

And she beat the bank down with her bows and the ride of
her keel:
The breakers rolled on her beam with ruinous shock;
And canvas and compass, the whorl and the wheel
Idle for ever to waft her or wind her with, these she
endured.

Hope had grown grey hairs,
Hope had mourning on,
Trenched with tears, carved with cares,
Hope was twelve hours gone;
And frightful a nightfall folded rueful a day
Nor rescue, only rocket and lightship, shone,
And lives at last were washing away:
To the shrouds they took, – they shook in the hurling and
horrible airs.

One stirred from the rigging to save
The wild woman-kind below,
With a rope's end round the man, handy and brave –
He was pitched to his death at a blow,
For all his dreadnought breast and braids of thew:
They could tell him for hours, dandled the to and fro
Through the cobbled foam-fleece, what could he do
With the burl of the fountains of air, buck and the flood of
the wave?

They fought with God's cold –
And they could not and fell to the deck
(Crushed them) or water (and drowned them) or rolled
With the sea-romp over the wreck.
Night roared, with the heart-break hearing a heart-broke
rabble,
The woman's wailing, the crying of child without check –
Till a lioness arose breasting the babble,
A prophetess towered in the tumult, a virginal tongue told.

Hopkins's treatment of language was quite Shakespearean in
its audacity, and indeed Hopkins was profoundly influenced by
the energy and grammatical disregard of some of Shakespeare's
poetry. Yet throughout the short, intense period of writing his
mature poems – only about a dozen years – he managed some

pieces which, though they're just as linguistically distinct as the rest, are more relaxed than 'The Wreck of the Deutschland'. An example of this is 'Spring and Fall' – a poem addressed 'to a young child':

> Márgarét, are you gríeving
> Over Goldengrove unleaving?
> Leáves, like the things of man, you
> With your fresh thoughts care for, can you?
> Áh! ás the heart grows older
> It will come to such sights colder
> By and by, nor spare a sigh
> Though worlds of wanwood leafmeal lie;
> And yet you wíll weep and know why.
> Now no matter, child, the name:
> Sórrow's spríngs áre the same.
> Nor mouth had, no nor mind, expressed
> What heart heard of, ghost guessed:
> It ís the blight man was born for,
> It is Margaret you mourn for.

But the form which Hopkins used most often was the sonnet, or variations of the sonnet (such as the poem 'Pied Beauty', which, though it has only eleven lines, has a sonnet's balance and shape). The sonnet was a favourite Victorian form, its immediate ancestors being Wordsworth, Keats and Shelley; there are numerous Victorian anthologies of sonnets, and Palgrave in his *Golden Treasury* (published in 1861) did much to fix approval on the form. But Hopkins treats it in a new way, packing it far more tightly and vigorously than ever before, and restoring to it the energy one finds in Shakespeare and Donne. In the year 1877 – one of his two most productive years – he wrote half a dozen or so poems of celebration and ecstasy which are unique in English poetry: 'Spring', 'God's Grandeur', 'The Starlight Night', 'The Sea and the Skylark', 'Hurrahing in Harvest', 'Pied Beauty' and 'The Windhover'. I want you to see several of these, and they can flow one into another without explanation or linking. First, 'Pied Beauty':

> Glory be to God for dappled things –
> For skies of couple-colour as a brinded cow;

For rose-moles all in stipple upon trout that swim;
Fresh fire-coal chestnut-falls; finches' wings;
Landscape plotted and pieced – fold, fallow, and plough;
And áll trádes, their gear and tackle and trim.

All things counter, original, spare, strange;
Whatever is fickle, freckled (who knows how?)
With swift, slow; sweet, sour; adazzle, dim;
He fathers-forth whose beauty is past change:
                    Praise him.

'Spring'

Nothing is so beautiful as spring –
When weeds, in wheels, shoot long and lovely and lush;
Thrush's eggs look little low heavens, and thrush
Through the echoing timber does so rinse and wring
The ear, it strikes like lightnings to hear him sing;
The glassy peartree leaves and blooms, they brush
The descending blue; that blue is all in a rush
With richness; the racing lambs too have fair their fling.

What is all this juice and all this joy?
A strain of the earth's sweet being in the beginning
In Eden garden. – Have, get, before it cloy,
Before it cloud, Christ, lord, and sour with sinning,
Innocent mind and Mayday in girl and boy,
Most, O maid's child, thy choice and worthy the winning.

'Hurrahing in Harvest'

Summer ends now; now, barbarous in beauty, the stooks
    arise
Around; up above, what wind-walks! what lovely behaviour
Of silk-sack clouds! has wilder, wilful-wavier
Meal-drift moulded ever and melted across skies?

I walk, I lift up, I lift up heart, eyes,
Down all that glory in the heavens to glean our Saviour;
And, éyes, heárt, what looks, what lips yet gave you a
Rapturous love's greeting of realer, of rounder replies?

And the azurous hung hills are his world-wielding shoulder
Majestic – as a stallion stalwart, very-violet-sweet! –

These things, these things were here and but the beholder
Wanting; which two when they once meet,
The heart rears wings bold and bolder
And hurls for him, O half hurls earth for him off under his
    feet.

'God's Grandeur'

The world is charged with the grandeur of God.
It will flame out, like shining from shook foil;
It gathers to a greatness, like the ooze of oil
Crushed. Why do men then now not reck his rod?
Generations have trod, have trod, have trod;
And all is seared with trade; bleared, smeared with toil;
And wears man's smudge and shares man's smell; the soil
Is bare now, nor can foot feel, being shod.

And for all this, nature is never spent;
There lives the dearest freshness deep down things;
And though the last lights off the black West went
Oh, morning, at the brown brink eastward, springs –
Because the Holy Ghost over the bent
World broods with warm breast and with ah! bright wings.

And finally, from these poems celebrating the force and beauty
of God revealed in nature, 'The Windhover':

I caught this morning morning's minion, king-
    dom of daylight's dauphin, dapple-dawn-drawn Falcon,
    in his riding
Of the rolling level underneath him steady air, and striding
High there, how he rung upon the rein of a wimpling wing
In his ecstasy! then off, off forth on swing,
    As a skate's heel sweeps smooth on a bow-bend: the hurl
        and gliding
Rebuffed the big wind. My heart in hiding
Stirred for a bird, – the achieve of, the mastery of the thing!

Brute beauty and valour and act, oh, air, pride, plume, here
    Buckle! AND the fire that breaks from thee then, a billion
Times told lovelier, more dangerous, O my chevalier!

No wonder of it: shéer plód makes plough down sillion
Shine, and blue-bleak embers, ah my dear,
  Fall, gall themselves, and gash gold-vermilion.

Seven or eight years later, Hopkins experienced another intensive creative period, but spiritually of a very different sort. Now the spirit is not one of celebration but of desolation, of inadequacy, almost of despair. Again the form was the sonnet, in 'Carrion Comfort', 'No worst, there is none,' 'I wake and feel the feel of dark', 'Patience, hard thing!' and 'My own heart let me have more pity on'. Here are two of them.

I wake and feel the fell of dark, not day.
What hours, O what black hoûrs we have spent
This night! what sights you, heart, saw; ways you went!
And more must, in yet longer light's delay.
  With witness I speak this. But where I say
Hours I mean years, mean life. And my lament
Is cries countless, cries like dead letters sent
To dearest him that lives alas! away.

I am gall, I am heartburn. God's most deep decree
Bitter would have me taste: my taste was me;
Bones built in me, flesh filled, blood brimmed the curse.
  Selfyeast of spirit a dull dough sours. I see
The lost are like this, and their scourge to be
As I am mine, their sweating selves; but worse.

No worst, there is none. Pitched past pitch of grief,
More pangs will, schooled at forepangs, wilder wring.
Comforter, where, where is your comforting?
Mary, mother of us, where is your relief?
My cries heave, herds-long; huddle in a main, a chief
Woe, world-sorrow; on an age-old anvil wince and sing –
Then lull, then leave off. Fury had shrieked 'No ling-
  ering! Let me be fell: force I must be brief!'

  O the mind, mind has mountains; cliffs of fall
Frightful, sheer, no-man-fathomed. Hold them cheap
May who ne'er hung there. Nor does long our small
Durance deal with that steep or deep. Here! creep,

Wretch, under a comfort serves in a whirlwind: all
Life death does end and each day dies with sleep.

And finally from Hopkins, a sonnet he wrote in the last year of
his life, which he sent to his friend Robert Bridges with the
words, 'Observe, it must be read *adagio molto* and with great
stress.' Without any relaxation of Hopkins's characteristic force
and compression, it reminds me towards the end of the poet he
perhaps admired most and with whom he felt the closest fellow-
ship – George Herbert:

> Thou art indeed just, Lord, if I contend
> With thee; but, sir, so what I plead is just.
> Why do sinners' ways prosper? and why must
> Disappointment all I endeavour end?
> Wert thou my enemy, O thou my friend,
> How wouldst thou worse, I wonder, than thou dost
> Defeat, thwart me? Oh, the sots and thralls of lust
> Do in spare hours more thrive than I that spend,
> Sir, life upon thy cause. See, banks and brakes
> Now, leavèd how thick! lacèd they are again
> With fretty chervil, look, and fresh wind shakes
> Them; birds build – but not I build; no, but strain,
> Time's eunuch, and not breed one work that wakes.
> Mine, O thou lord of life, send my roots rain.

A great deal of devotional or religious poetry was written and
published in England during the second half of the nineteenth
century: Hopkins, in his subject-matter, was not a rare clerical
freak. But most of these products are justly forgotten, being
religiose rather than religious. There are a few survivors, two of
them, oddly enough, being friends and correspondents of
Hopkins: one or two short poems by R. W. Dixon, the most
sympathetic of his readers (and one ought to remember that
hardly any of Hopkins's poems were published in his lifetime, and
none of the important ones); and a few by Coventry Patmore, a
convert to Catholicism who had some success in his own life-
time, but whose major efforts ('The Angel in the House' and 'To
the Unknown Eros') I don't much like. But there's one poem
from this second sequence which I do find oddly moving,
sentimental though it certainly is. Both as a domestically circum-

stantial piece, and in what one might call its troubled smugness, 'The Toys' is a long way from Hopkins, though Hopkins admired Patmore, and wrote to him in a letter: 'Your poems are a good deed done for the Catholic Church and another for England, for the British Empire.'

My little Son, who look'd from thoughtful eyes
And moved and spoke in quiet grown-up wise,
Having my law the seventh time disobey'd,
I struck him, and dismiss'd
With hard words and unkiss'd,
His Mother, who was patient, being dead.
Then, fearing lest his grief should hinder sleep,
I visited his bed,
But found him slumbering deep,
With darken'd eyelids, and their lashes yet
From his late sobbing wet.
And I, with moan,
Kissing away his tears, left others of my own;
For, on a table drawn beside his head,
He had put, within his reach,
A box of counters and a red-vein'd stone,
A piece of glass abraded by the beach
And six or seven shells,
A bottle with bluebells
And two French copper coins, ranged there with careful art,
To comfort his sad heart.
So when that night I pray'd
To God, I wept, and said:
Ah, when at last we lie with trancéd breath,
Not vexing Thee in death,
And Thou rememberest of what toys
We made our joys,
How weakly understood,
Thy great commanded good,
Then, fatherly not less
Than I whom Thou hast moulded from the clay,
Thou'lt leave Thy wrath, and say,
'I will be sorry for their childishness.'

But the poet of the period who, technically, most resembles

Hopkins, though different in every other way, is George Meredith: I'm thinking of Meredith's sequence of sixteen-line poems, *Modern Love*, which has in parts the congested, dramatic, struggling and almost suffocated quality of those so-called 'terrible' sonnets of Hopkins such as 'I wake and feel the fell of dark'. Meredith made a disastrous marriage: *Modern Love* is an emotional record of that marriage recorded in many moods. Here is the thirty-fourth in the sequence of fifty, in which horror smoulders under the nervous, jerky tone:

> Madam would speak with me. So, now it comes:
> The Deluge or else Fire! She's well: she thanks
> My husbandship. Our chain on silence clanks.
> Time leers between above his twiddling thumbs.
> Am I quite well? Most excellent in health!
> The journals, too, I diligently peruse.
> Vesuvius is expected to give news:
> Niagara is no noisier. By stealth
> Our eyes dart scrutinising snakes. She's glad
> I'm happy, says her quivering under-lip.
> 'And are not you?' 'How can I be?' 'Take ship!
> For happiness is somewhere to be had.'
> 'Nowhere for me!' Her voice is barely heard.
> I am not melted, and make no pretence.
> With commonplace I freeze her, tongue and sense.
> Niagara or Vesuvius is deferred.

Ernest Dowson (1867–1900)
Arthur Symons (1865–1945)
William Ernest Henley (1849–1903)
Rudyard Kipling (1865–1936)

P.P.

————◆————

By the time we get to the nineties, we find English poetry already showing signs of Modernity. This isn't in the style – in fact, the very self-conscious and technically precise writing of the poets of the last decade of the Victorian Age are further from our present-day poetical modes than many much older styles. The modernity is in the self-consciousness, the awareness that the poet can sell himself on his life better than by his verses – at least as far as the public is concerned. Following the Pre-Raphaelites, the seriousness of William Morris's Aesthetic principles was vulgarised and watered down by Oscar Wilde and made into a good vehicle for self-advertising. The Aesthetic Movement, as Wilde presented it, was not so very different from Bernard Shaw's parallel teasing of the British public for its philistinism and lack of political sense. Shaw never pretended to any poetical ability (though he was a good critic of Shakespeare's verse) and Wilde was the first of a long line of men who have preferred 'being a poet' to writing poetry. Even among the truly dedicated poets of the nineties, there was a strong element of posing. In the best of them, Ernest Dowson and Arthur Symons, the personal doom and morbidity were genuine, however dandified and imitated from the French. After the heyday of the Victorian giants, Tennyson, Browning and Arnold, English poetry became very derivative from France. Baudelaire, Rimbaud, Corbière and Laforgue were the men who created the dominant tone of the new poetry which Pound and Eliot introduced into England. The great Victorians (with the exception of Browning) have had no progeny: for the first time since Boileau in the seventeenth century, English verse came under the influence of French models. Baudelaire had rebelled against the suburbanism which threatened to destroy poetry – his phrase for it was '*l'ésprit Belge*'. Rimbaud, one of the greatest poets of all time, was an inspired forecaster of the desolation of spirit which was growing up in the monstrous cities already dominating English and American life. None of the English nineties poets had the power to sustain visions of this size, but they too were in rebellion against the stifling conventionality of English life, and reacted against the horrors of poverty and suffering which lay beneath the Victorian confidence.

With the exception of W. E. Henley, they did this not by reportage but by rejecting optimism and embracing a special sort of world-weariness and death-fixation. Since they nearly all died young (some from characteristically morbid diseases such as tuberculosis, or by suicide), they backed up their writings by their lives. Perhaps the most gifted of these minor masters was Ernest Dowson. He is comparable, if not equal, to the illustrator, Aubrey Beardsley, in that every one of his poems is beautifully calculated and technically perfect. Dowson was by no means the passive doomed figure that the poems present – he had a strong and sardonic humour – but for most of his life he was in poor health and a hopeless love affair with a young girl primed the deliberately morbid love poems he wrote. Dowson was fond of giving his poems long Latin titles, such as the one called *Non sum qualis eram bonae sub regno cynarae*, usually known as 'Cynara'. The atmosphere of decadence, of love as a disease and the poet's theatrical infidelity, reach back beyond their immediate model, Baudelaire, to similar attitudes adopted by the Earl of Rochester in Restoration times. Dowson is especially accomplished in his rhythms, which are far more experimental than his language or his attitudes.

> Last night, ah, yesternight, betwixt her lips and mine
> There fell thy shadow, Cynara! thy breath was shed
> Upon my soul between the kisses and the wine;
> And I was desolate and sick of an old passion,
>   Yea, I was desolate and bowed my head:
> I have been faithful to thee, Cynara! in my fashion.
>
> All night upon mine heart I felt her warm heart beat,
> Night-long within mine arms in love and sleep she lay;

Surely the kisses of her bought red mouth were sweet;
But I was desolate and sick of an old passion,
    When I awoke and found the dawn was gray:
I have been faithful to thee, Cynara! in my fashion.

I have forgot much, Cynara! gone with the wind,
Flung roses, roses riotously with the throng,
Dancing, to put thy pale, lost lilies out of mind;
But I was desolate and sick of an old passion,
    Yea, all the time, because the dance was long:
I have been faithful to thee, Cynara! in my fashion.

I cried for madder music and for stronger wine,
But when the feast is finished and the lamps expire,
Then falls thy shadow, Cynara! the night is thine;
And I am desolate and sick of an old passion,
    Yea, hungry for the lips of my desire:
I have been faithful to thee, Cynara! in my fashion.

The desire to shock respectable society made the nineties writers very interested in religion. They needed traditional religious imagery to establish their own sense of doom, and many also were converted to the Church towards the ends of their lives. It's interesting how Catholic and incense-laden the poetry and prose of the time is. Another one of Dowson's best poems is 'Extreme Unction', which comes closer than any other work of his to offering a positive vision. Of necessity it is the Church's vision. Yet, even here, the sense of sin and the hopeless fate of physical love get a richer response from the poet than piety does.

Upon the eyes, the lips, the feet,
    On all the passages of sense,
The atoning oil is spread with sweet
    Renewal of lost innocence.

The feet, that lately ran so fast
    To meet desire, are soothly sealed;
The eyes, that were so often cast
    On vanity, are touched and healed.

From troublous sights and sounds set free;
    In such a twilight hour of breath,

Shall one retrace his life, or see,
    Through shadows, the true face of death?

Vials of mercy! Sacring oils!
    I know not where nor when I come,
Nor through what wanderings and toils,
    To crave of you Viaticum.

Yet, when the walls of flesh grow weak,
    In such an hour, it well may be,
Through mist and darkness, light will break,
    And each anointed sense will see.

Dowson was a miniaturist, and to succeed, had to be both exquisite in craftsmanship and capable of writing memorable lines. One of his shortest poems is also one of his most proverbial – its eight lines have passed into the language, so that they are known by many people who have never heard of Dowson. It sums up perfectly his sweetly morbid talent, both classical and decadent at the same time.

'Vitae summa brevis spem nos vetat incohare longam'

They are not long, the weeping and the laughter,
    Love and desire and hate:
I think they have no portion in us after
    We pass the gate.

They are not long, the days of wine and roses:
    Out of a misty dream
Our path emerges for a while, then closes
    Within a dream.

Arthur Symons was the chronicler and chief apologist for the nineties Decadents, partly because he survived into the new century. Symons introduced the French Symbolists to England, and was a moving figure behind many nineties manifestations – Dowson's poetry, *The Yellow Book* and its raffish backer, Leonard Smithers, for example – and he took his role of advocate for the new art seriously. This has led to his own work being under-estimated; he is always quoted as the chief authority on the period, but his poems, which are both more symbolical and yet more realistic than Dowson's, are little read. He is an impression-ist – his typical love poems are much closer to Continental erotic models, and have little of that classical feeling which is still present in Dowson. Like the French novelist Huysmans, and the hero of his novel *A Rebours*, Symons is interested in the sensuality of objects, places and scents as well as of people, as his poem 'White Heliotrope' shows.

> The feverish room and that white bed,
> The tumbled skirts upon a chair,
> The novel flung half-open, where
> Hat, hair-pins, puff, and paints, are spread;
>
> The mirror that has sucked your face
> Into its secret deep of deeps,
> And there mysteriously keeps
> Forgotten memories of grace;
>
> And you, half-dressed and half-awake,
> Your slant eyes strangely watching me,
> And I, who watch you drowsily,
> With eyes that, having slept not, ache;
>
> This (need one dread? nay, dare one hope?)
> Will rise, a ghost of memory, if
> Ever again my handkerchief
> Is scented with White Heliotrope.

The impressionistic surface of his writing is revealed in his poem dedicated to that most muted of English painters, Sickert. It's called, after one of Sickert's own paintings, 'At Dieppe: Grey and Green'.

> The grey-green stretch of sandy grass,
> Indefinitely desolate;
> A sea of lead, a sky of slate;
> Already autumn in the air, alas!
>
> One stark monotony of stone,
> The long hotel, acutely white,
> Against the after-sunset light
> Withers grey-green, and takes the grass's tone.
>
> Listless and endless it outlies,
> And means, to you and me, no more
> Than any pebble on the shore,
> Or this indifferent moment as it dies.

Symons's breakdown is prefigured in much of his poetry. In a poem called 'Nerves', he turns from the usual dilemmas of love – obsessional jealousy, the sense of time passing and beauty fading – to a more modern sense of apprehension, the nervous system of the lover being already at a point of derangement. The self-regarding modern neurotic is anticipated in this poem dated 1897 – the feelings described by Symons could be put into an interior monologue by any American novelist's hero or heroine without a trace of anachronism. In temperament, if not style, Symons is one of the most modern of the Victorians. He lived on till 1945 but his mind collapsed and all his best work belongs to the nineties.

> The modern malady of love is nerves.
> Love, once a simple madness, now observes
> The stages of his passionate disease,
> And is twice sorrowful because he sees,
> Inch by inch entering, the fatal knife.
> O health of simple minds, give me your life,
> And let me, for one midnight, cease to hear
> The clock for ever ticking in my ear,
> The clock that tells the minutes in my brain.
> It is not love, nor love's despair, this pain
> That shoots a witless, keener pang across
> The simple agony of love and loss.
> Nerves, nerves! O folly of a child who dreams
> Of heaven, and, waking in the darkness, screams.

Realism of the kind which the Georgians introduced in the first decade of the twentieth century is also to be found in late Victorian verse. The nineties was the age of the ruthless metropolis, with its appalling fogs, insanitary and crowded life among the teeming slums, as well as the glittering West End good-time girls and their customers. W. E. Henley, who is best known for his brave words about 'his unconquerable soul' and his head being 'bloody but unbowed!', wrote many vignettes and studies of London suburban life, in two collections, *London Types* and *London Voluntaries*. These are surprisingly effective pictures of contemporary people and places, and are written with a humour and lightness which is less grinding than that hymn to genteel poverty by John Davidson, 'Thirty Bob a Week'. In one poem

Henley's cheeky Cockney style manages to attain a grim power of personification. It's the sort of poem which raises a minor poet to greatness for a moment in his career. This is 'Madam Life's a Piece in Bloom'. The opening stanza gave Joe Orton the title of his first play.

> Madam Life's a piece in bloom
>> Death goes dogging everywhere:
> She's the tenant of the room,
>> He's the ruffian on the stair.

> You shall see her as a friend,
>> You shall bilk him once or twice;
> But he'll trap you in the end,
>> And he'll stick you for her price.

> With his kneebones at your chest,
>> And his knuckles in your throat,
> You would reason – plead – protest!
>> Clutching at her petticoat;

> But she's heard it all before,
>> Well she knows you've had your fun,
> Gingerly she gains the door,
>> And your little job is done.

One great poet came into prominence, and indeed wrote most of his best poetry, in the nineties, who is utterly unlike the others. This is Rudyard Kipling. He gets $21\frac{1}{2}$ columns in the *Oxford Book of Quotations*, more than any other author born since Tennyson. He has suffered from the familiar assumption that poetry requires a special state of mind rather than a verbal technique, and Kipling's mind, though complex, is not 'poetic' in that special sense. He was England's unofficial Poet Laureate, guiding, scolding and occasionally praising the Island Race at the time of its crisis, as Empire turned to Commonwealth and the quick decline away from world dominance began. In some respects, Kipling was a very untypical Englishman. Born of a family with Pre-Raphaelite connections, related to both Burne-Jones and Stanley Baldwin, he was raised partly in Imperial India about which country nobody has ever written better, then became an immigrant in America, and finally a recluse in Sussex, where he brewed his own special broth of English history, which bears little relation to what the textbooks say. Kipling fell in love with England and tried to get the country to live up to his high opinion of it. The English doggedly went on pleasing themselves rather than him. His exasperation with his countrymen's refusal of their Imperial responsibility is equalled, however, by his great sympathy for the men on the spot in the cruel conditions at the ends of Empire.

Kipling left India for good by the time he was thirty, yet his picture of it is the most inclusive we have. Not only did he seem to understand Indian life intuitively (his stories are far from being patronising exercises in pointing up the power of the Raj) but he also understood the Civil Servants who ruled the country and the unfortunate mercenaries who made up the army of occupation. Underneath the swinging metres of Kipling's most famous collection of poems, *Barrack Room Ballads*, there's a human feeling and central understanding which amounts to genius. Kipling had the sort of knowingness which is born into a great writer. The *Barrack Room Ballads* are enormously popular still, in a world utterly different from the one Kipling wrote about. They are far from being official – their approach is often satirical and they leave a surprising number of virtues un-mentioned. But they're recognised instantly as telling the truth by all men who have been soldiers. One of the most famous is 'Danny Deever'. The precision of Kipling's scene-painting makes this ballad as riveting today, in the climate of *Catch-22*, as it was at Queen Victoria's Jubilee.

'What are the bugles blowin' for?' said Files-on-Parade.
'To turn you out, to turn you out,' the Colour-Sergeant said.
'What makes you look so white, so white?' said Files-on-
    Parade.
'I'm dreadin' what I've got to watch,' the Colour-Sergeant
    said.
    For they're hangin' Danny Deever, you can hear the Dead
      March play,
    The Regiment's in 'ollow square – they're hangin' him
      today;
    They've taken of his buttons off an' cut his stripes away,
    An' they're hangin' Danny Deever in the mornin'.

'What makes the rear-rank breathe so 'ard?' said Files-on-
    Parade.
'It's bitter cold, it's bitter cold,' the Colour-Sergeant said.
'What makes that front-rank man fall down?' said Files-on-
    Parade.
'A touch o' sun, a touch o' sun,' the Colour-Sergeant said.
    They're hangin' Danny Deever, they are marchin' of 'im
        round,
    They 'ave 'alted Danny Deever by 'is coffin on the ground;
    An' 'e'll swing in 'arf a minute for a sneakin' shootin'
        hound –
    O they're hangin' Danny Deever in the mornin'!

''Is cot was right-'and cot to mine,' said Files-on-Parade.
''E's sleepin' out an' far tonight,' the Colour-Sergeant said.
'I've drunk 'is beer a score o' times,' said Files-on-Parade.
''E's drinkin' bitter beer alone,' the Colour-Sergeant said.
    They are hangin' Danny Deever, you must mark 'im to 'is
        place,
    For 'e shot a comrade sleepin' – you must look 'im in the
        face;
    Nine 'undred of 'is county an' the Regiment's disgrace,
    While they're hangin' Danny Deever in the mornin'.

'What's that so black agin the sun?' said Files-on-Parade.
'It's Danny fightin' 'ard for life,' the Colour-Sergeant said.
'What's that that whimpers over'ead?' said Files-on-Parade.
'It's Danny's soul that's passin' now,' the Colour-Sergeant
    said.
    For they're done with Danny Deever, you can 'ear the
        quickstep play,
    The Regiment's in column, an' they're marchin' us away;
    Ho! the young recruits are shakin', an' they'll want their
        beer today,
    After hangin' Danny Deever in the mornin'!

Throughout his long career, Kipling experimented with the
right language for the changing concerns of his poetry. When
he came to recreate the history of England in *Puck of Pook's Hill*
and other works, he found a special anachronistic language for
the poems he included, and he was capable of hymn-like

solemnity and Swinburnian melodiousness as well as of realistic patois. The definitive edition of his poems runs to over 800 pages, and there's enormous variety within its covers. It's true, perhaps, that he never matured as a writer, and that some of his later poems tend to be colourless and dry by comparison with the energy of his work in the nineties. Also, that he could rarely resist good thumping rhythms and unsubtle refrains. Here is a very different kind of poem from the previous one to illustrate both his resource with language and his wide-ranging imagination. It's Kipling's ventriloquistic recreation of an old Saxon ritual, one of the more successful of his forays into the deep past of England. The language is cool, the words chosen for their mystery and authority. It's called 'The Runes on Weland's Sword', and proves convincingly that Kipling was not a simple-minded jingo with a mission to bring the world under British rule, but a far-reaching artist, at home in both verse and prose, whose imagination was more truly at ease in the real world which lies beyond the frontiers of literature than any of his contemporaries.

> A smith makes me
> To betray my Man
> In my first fight.
>
> To gather Gold
> At the world's end
> I am sent.
>
> The Gold I gather
> Comes into England
> Out of deep water.
>
> Like a shining Fish
> Then it descends
> Into deep Water.
>
> It is not given
> For goods or gear,
> But for The Thing.
>
> The Gold I gather
> A king covets
> For an ill use.

The Gold I gather
Is drawn up
Out of deep water.

Like a shining Fish
Then it descends
Into deep Water.

It is not given
For goods or gear,
But for The Thing.

Thomas Hardy (1840–1928)
Alfred Edward Housman (1859–1936)
William Butler Yeats (1865–1939)
Edward Thomas (1878–1917)   A.T.

———————————◆———————————

This final section packs in a number of poets whose only unity
is that they were writing towards the end of the nineteenth
century and at the beginning of the twentieth. If one were to
pick, quite arbitrarily, a year when something called 'modern'
poetry began in English, I suppose it might be 1914: the year
not only of the outbreak of the First World War, but also the
year in which Conrad Aiken brought with him from America to
England the unpublished manuscript of a poem by a friend of
his, to try to place it in a magazine: this was 'The Love Song of
J. Alfred Prufrock', by the young T. S. Eliot.

But at the turn of the century, when Eliot was twelve years
old and reading Shelley, an old tradition was still apparently
tenacious. Broadly, it was a Romantic tradition. It also ran
alongside a strong and popular tradition of prose fiction; and
one of the most controversial novelists was Thomas Hardy, who
between the mid-1870s and the end of the century was writing
his great sequence of Wessex novels. Yet to me Hardy is far
more importantly a poet. Some of his best poems, without
actually being narrative, are those of a story-writer. One of my
favourites, and one that's very seldom anthologised, is 'The
Harbour Bridge':

> From here, the quay, one looks above to mark
> The bridge across the harbour, hanging dark
> Against the day's-end sky, fair-green in glow
> Over and under the middle archway's bow:
> It draws its skeleton where the sun has set,
> Yea, clear from cutwater to parapet;

On which mild glow, too, lines of rope and spar
    Trace themselves black as char.

Down here in shade we hear the painters shift
Against the bollards with a drowsy lift,
As moved by the incoming stealthy tide.
High up across the bridge the burghers glide
As cut black-paper portraits hastening on
In conversation none knows what upon:
Their sharp-edged lips move quickly word by word
    To speech that is not heard.

There trails the dreamful girl, who leans and stops,
There presses the practical woman to the shops,
There is a sailor, meeting his wife with a start,
And we, drawn nearer, judge they are keeping apart.
Both pause. She says: 'I've looked for you. I thought
We'd make it up.' Then no words can be caught.
At last: 'Won't you come home?' She moves still nigher:
    ''Tis comfortable, with a fire.'

'No,' he says gloomily. 'And, anyhow,
I can't give up the other woman now:
You should have talked like that in former days,
When I was last home.' They go different ways.
And the west dims, and yellow lamplights shine:
And soon above, like lamps more opaline,
White stars ghost forth, that care not for men's wives,
    Or any other lives.

The titles of some of Hardy's books of poems suggest his
habitual subject matter: *Satires of Circumstance, Human Shows,
Moments of Vision* – not 'moments of vision' in any religious
sense but with a disenchanted feeling of seeing things as they
really are. Here's a short poem which beautifully catches a
moment of chilling revelation. It's called 'In Church':

'And now to God the Father,' he ends,
And his voice thrills up to the topmost tiles:
Each listener chokes as he bows and bends,
And emotion pervades the crowded aisles.

Then the preacher glides to the vestry-door,
And shuts it, and thinks he is seen no more.

The door swings softly ajar meanwhile,
And a pupil of his in the Bible class,
Who adores him as one without gloss or guile,
Sees her idol stand with a satisfied smile
And re-enact at the vestry-glass
Each pulpit gesture in deft dumb-show
That had moved the congregation so.

What I haven't yet shown is Hardy's marvellously original and
strange lyricism. Philip Larkin has said that almost every Hardy
poem 'has a little tune of its own . . . Immediately you begin a
Hardy poem your own inner response begins to rock in time with
the poem's rhythm.' This isn't done in any obvious ballad-like
or Kiplingesque way, but with an extraordinary mixture of
awkwardness and grace, as in 'After a Journey':

Hereto I come to view a voiceless ghost;
    Whither, O whither will its whim now draw me?
Up the cliff, down, till I'm lonely, lost,
    And the unseen waters' ejaculations awe me.
Where you will next be there's no knowing,
    Facing round about me everywhere,
        With your nut-coloured hair,
And gray eyes, and rose-flush coming and going.

Yes: I have re-entered your olden haunts at last;
    Through the years, through the dead scenes I have
        tracked you;
What have you now found to say of our past –
    Scanned across the dark space wherein I have lacked you?
Summer gave us sweets, but autumn wrought division?
    Things were not lastly as firstly well
        With us twain, you tell?
But all's closed now, despite Time's derision.

I see what you are doing: you are leading me on
    To the spots we knew when we haunted here together,
The waterfall, above which the mist-bow shone
    At the then fair hour in the then fair weather,

And the cave just under, with a voice still so hollow
   That it seems to call out to me from forty years ago,
     When you were all aglow,
And not the thin ghost that I now frailly follow!

Ignorant of what there is flitting here to see,
   The waked birds preen and the seals flop lazily;
Soon you will have, Dear, to vanish from me,
   For the stars close their shutters and the dawn whitens
     hazily.
Trust me, I mind not, though Life lours,
   The bringing me here; nay, bring me here again!
     I am just the same as when
Our days were a joy, and our paths through flowers.

And from the same period, and in the same mood, but with
different and I think even subtler fingering, 'At Castle Boterel':

   As I drive to the junction of lane and highway,
     And the drizzle bedrenches the waggonette,
   I look behind at the fading byway,
     And see on its slope, now glistening wet,
       Distinctly yet

   Myself and a girlish form benighted
     In dry March weather. We climb the road
   Beside a chaise. We had just alighted
     To ease the sturdy pony's load
       When he sighed and slowed.

   What we did as we climbed, and what we talked of
     Matters not much, nor to what it led, –
   Something that life will not be balked of
     Without rude reason till hope is dead,
       And feeling fled.

   It filled but a minute. But was there ever
     A time of such quality, since or before,
   In that hill's story? To one mind never,
     Though it has been climbed, foot-swift, foot-sore,
       By thousands more.

   Primaeval rocks form the road's steep border,
     And much have they faced there, first and last,

Of the transitory in Earth's long order;
    But what they record in colour and cast
      Is – that we two passed.

And to me, though Time's unflinching rigour,
    In mindless rote, has ruled from sight
The substance now, one phantom figure
    Remains on the slope, as when that night
      Saw us alight.

I look and see it there, shrinking, shrinking,
    I look back at it amid the rain
For the very last time; for my sand is sinking,
    And I shall traverse old love's domain
      Never again.

A. E. Housman's poems are altogether narrower in range than Hardy's, indeed the product of a much narrower sensibility; but what they share with Hardy is a strange and individual cadence, as recognisable as Hardy's but utterly different. What they also share is a sense of distancing (the worlds of the poems seem slightly archaic, even within the terms of the period in which they were writing, and this is stressed by the slight archaism of the language); and they share a pessimistic stoicism of tone, which is given particular force in Housman by the plainness of the verse forms with their regular tread. Economy is mated with resonance:

    In valleys green and still
      Where lovers wander maying
    They hear from over hill
      A music playing.

    Behind the drum and fife,
      Past hawthornwood and hollow,
    Through earth and out of life
      The soldiers follow.

    The soldier's is the trade:
      In any wind or weather
    He steals the heart of maid
      And man together.

The lover and his lass
    Beneath the hawthorn lying
Have heard the soldiers pass,
    And both are sighing.

And down the distance they
    With dying note and swelling
Walk the resounding way
    To the still dwelling.

As strongly as in Hardy, there is in Housman the sense of time passing, of the wheel coming back on itself, of the endless repetition and disappointment of history, as in 'On Wenlock Edge':

On Wenlock Edge the wood's in trouble;
    His forest fleece the Wrekin heaves;
The gale, it plies the saplings double,
    And thick on Severn snow the leaves.

'Twould blow like this through holt and hanger
    When Uricon the city stood:
'Tis the old wind in the old anger,
    But then it threshed another wood.

Then, 'twas before my time, the Roman
    At yonder heaving hill would stare:
The blood that warms an English yeoman,
    The thoughts that hurt him, they were there.

There, like the wind through woods in riot,
    Through him the gale of life blew high;
The tree of man was never quiet:
    Then 'twas the Roman, now 'tis I.

The gale, it plies the saplings double,
    It blows so hard, 'twill soon be gone:
To-day the Roman and his trouble
    Are ashes under Uricon.

What there's very little sense of in Housman is a man speaking directly, autobiographically, circumstantially about his experiences: there's a classic filter through which the muddled stuff of life is passed and purified – or avoided. Housman's strongly emotional period was so brief in its span, and so awful for him to contemplate, that very rarely does he face the trouble head-on. But he does so in this painfully tight-lipped poem:

> Because I liked you better
>   Than suits a man to say,
> It irked you, and I promised
>   To throw the thought away.
>
> To put the world between us
>   We parted, stiff and dry;
> 'Good-bye,' said you, 'forget me.'
>   'I will, no fear,' said I.
>
> If here, where clover whitens
>   The dead man's knoll, you pass,
> And no tall flower to meet you
>   Starts in the trefoiled grass,
>
> Halt by the headstone naming
>   The heart no longer stirred,
> And say the lad that loved you
>   Was one that kept his word.

Some of Housman's poems are crammed into very few lines indeed: 'Into my heart an air that kills', 'Eight o'clock', 'Epitaph on an Army of Mercenaries', 'Crossing alone the nighted ferry', and over thirty others, have eight lines or less. After the amplitude and prolixity of so much nineteenth-century verse, it's a relief. Here's one of Housman's briefest and most tight-lipped poems:

> Crossing alone the nighted ferry,
>   With the one coin for fee,
> Whom, on the wharf of Lethe waiting,
>   Count you to find? Not me.
>
> The brisk fond lackey to fetch and carry,
>   The true, sick-hearted slave,
> Expect him not in the just city
>   And free land of the grave.

With Yeats, of course, the main problem in this book is that his best work was written after the closing date we've fixed of round about 1914. He published his first book in 1889, and it's true that some of his best-known poems (such as 'The Lake Isle of Innisfree') date from the 1890s. But it wasn't in fact until 1914 itself, and the publication of a book called *Responsibilities*, that we can begin to see the direction in which he was going to go. I'd thought of picking one poem from his 1899 volume, one from *The Green Helmet* of 1910, and one from *Responsibilities*, to show a progression. But that would make only a critical-historical point and would in no way represent him properly. So I decided to go for a major poem of his poetic maturity and ignore chronology. Here, from the 1920s, is Yeats's poem 'Among School Children'.

I walk through the long schoolroom questioning;
A kind old nun in a white hood replies;
The children learn to cipher and to sing,
To study reading-books and histories,
To cut and sew, be neat in everything
In the best modern way – the children's eyes
In momentary wonder stare upon
A sixty-year-old smiling public man.

I dream of a Ledaean body, bent
Above a sinking fire, a tale that she
Told of a harsh reproof, or trivial event
That changed some childish day to tragedy –
Told, and it seemed that our two natures blent
Into a sphere from youthful sympathy,
Or else, to alter Plato's parable,
Into the yolk and white of the one shell.

And thinking of that fit of grief or rage
I look upon one child or t'other there
And wonder if she stood so at that age –
For even daughters of the swan can share
Something of every paddler's heritage –
And had that colour upon cheek or hair,
And thereupon my heart is driven wild:
She stands before me as a living child.

Her present image floats into the mind –
Did Quattrocento finger fashion it

Hollow of cheek as though it drank the wind
And took a mess of shadows for its meat?
And I though never of Ledaean kind
Had pretty plumage once – enough of that,
Better to smile on all that smile, and show
There is a comfortable kind of old scarecrow.

What youthful mother, a shape upon her lap
Honey of generation had betrayed,
And that must sleep, shriek, struggle to escape
As recollection or the drug decide,
Would think her son, did she but see that shape
With sixty or more winters on its head,
A compensation for the pang of his birth,
Or the uncertainty of his setting forth?

Plato thought nature but a spume that plays
Upon a ghostly paradigm of things;
Solider Aristotle played the taws
Upon the bottom of a king of kings;
World-famous golden-thighed Pythagoras
Fingered upon a fiddle-stick or strings
What a star sang and careless Muses heard:
Old clothes upon old sticks to scare a bird.

Both nuns and mothers worship images,
But those the candles light are not as those
That animate a mother's reveries,
But keep a marble or a bronze repose.
And yet they too break hearts – O Presences,
That passion, piety or affection knows,
And that all heavenly glory symbolise –
O self-born mockers of man's enterprise;

Labour is blossoming or dancing where
The body is not bruised to pleasure soul,
Nor beauty born out of its own despair,
Nor blear-eyed wisdom out of midnight oil.
O chestnut-leaf, great-rooted blossomer,
Are you the leaf, the blossom or the bole?
O body swayed to music, O brightening glance,
How can we know the dancer from the dance?

I'm not going to attempt to deal with the poets of the First World War: I can't tuck in Owen and Sassoon and Rosenberg as afterthoughts. Their best poems are about the war and of the war. But there was one poet who didn't begin to write until the war had begun, who was killed in it, and yet who wrote little about it. Edward Thomas's poems stand at a turning-point: they have nothing to do with the modern movement, with Eliot and Pound who were writing at this time, yet they are quite centrally part of an English tradition that continues today, and that I like to think Chaucer would have recognised too. This final poem has a voice – strong, sensitive, subtle, related closely to the turns and cadences of our speech – that proceeds rationally and yet which is aware of the irrational and the mysterious as well. 'Old Man':

> Old Man, or Lad's-love, – in the name there's nothing
> To one that knows not Lad's-love, or Old Man,
> The hoar-green feathery herb, almost a tree,
> Growing with rosemary and lavender.
> Even to one that knows it well, the names
> Half decorate, half perplex, the thing it is:
> At least, what that is clings not to the names
> In spite of time. And yet I like the names.
>
> The herb itself I like not, but for certain
> I love it, as some day the child will love it
> Who plucks a feather from the door-side bush
> Whenever she goes in or out of the house.
> Often she waits there, snipping the tips and shrivelling
> The shreds at last on to the path, perhaps
> Thinking, perhaps of nothing, till she sniffs
> Her finger and runs off. The bush is still
> But half as tall as she, though it is as old;
> So well she clips it. Not a word she says;
> And I can only wonder how much hereafter
> She will remember, with that bitter scent,
> Of garden rows, and ancient damson trees
> Topping a hedge, a bent path to a door,
> A low thick bush beside the door, and me
> Forbidding her to pick.
> > As for myself,

Where first I met the bitter scent is lost.
I, too, often shrivel the grey shreds,
Sniff them and think and sniff again and try
Once more to think what it is I am remembering,
Always in vain. I cannot like the scent,
Yet I would rather give up others more sweet,
With no meaning, than this bitter one.
I have mislaid the key. I sniff the spray
And think of nothing; I see and I hear nothing;
Yet seem, too, to be listening, lying in wait
For what I should, yet never can, remember:
No garden appears, no path, no hoar-green bush
Of Lad's-love, or Old Man, no child beside,
Neither father nor mother, nor any playmate;
Only an avenue, dark, nameless, without end.

Index

First lines of untitled poems are indicated by an asterisk

316

318